LATE CEN-
DREAM

MOVEMENTS IN THE US INDIE
MUSIC UNDERGROUND

**black dog
publishing**
london uk

CONTENTS

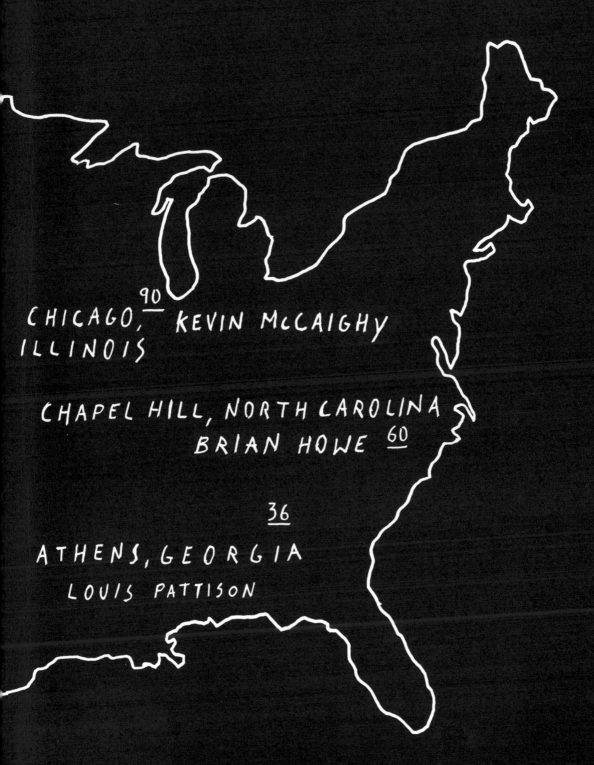

CHICAGO, $\underline{90}$ KEVIN McCAIGHY
ILLINOIS

CHAPEL HILL, NORTH CAROLINA
BRIAN HOWE $\underline{60}$

$\underline{36}$

ATHENS, GEORGIA
LOUIS PATTISON

INTRODUCTION

"You are me and I am you/Looking back it's just reflections/
It's just something else to do/... Sound on sound"
Big Boys—"Sound on Sound", 1983.

In a world where music is often a decentralised art form disseminated via the Internet, it's sometimes easy to forget that the nascent eras of underground punk and indie rock revolved around close-knit social ties, the evolution of grassroots networking, handshake record deals and a determination to get in the van and drive. Variously born of ennui, teenage enthusiasm, disdain for mainstream pop culture and the cultural adversity of middle America (at a time when wearing a punk t-shirt could, and *would*, get the shit beaten out of you) and, more than anything, a straight passion for music, the scenes discussed in this book are stylistically varied but essentially similar in their initiatives and conceptions. People jam, bands start, get signed and dropped, and a few groups come out the other side intact. Making it 'big' was rarely an aim, or even a valid possibility; the pitfalls of the industry are written heavily into these narratives. It's worth pointing out that many of the groups and artists in this book exist today in reunited or post-hiatus forms. Most don't exist at all anymore. What lives on, and is reflected so effectively in these texts, is the lasting artistic legacy carved out by those involved.

Late Century Dream's six key texts (supplemented by extended interviews where appropriate) each revolve around a relatively un-discussed key city and/or hub of artists: Pavel Godfrey supplies a definitive alternative take on grunge-era Seattle, largely circumnavigating the populist Sub Pop hegemony to look at seminal fringe groups like The Accused, Gruntruck, Skin Yard, Vexed, The Gits, 7 Year Bitch and Engine Kid; Jimmy Martin focuses on the early cop-baiting punk rock, weirdo skronk and post-psychedelic rock which came out of the Texan cities of Austin and Houston (and beyond), by way of The Dicks, Big Boys, Butthole Surfers and Pain Teens (et al); Louis Pattison provides a varied oral account of the art school-derived post-punk scene in Athens, Georgia responsible for The B-52's, REM and Pylon; Brian Howe recounts a personal immersion in the proto-indie and college rock hotbed of Chapel Hill, North Carolina that sprung up around bands like Superchunk, Archers of Loaf and Polvo, as well as Merge Records and venues such as Cat's Cradle; Noel Gardner looks in depth at Phoenix, Arizona's rich history of left-field alternative and punk rock from The Consumers and The Feederz through JFA, Meat Puppets, Sun City Girls, Killer Pussy and Mighty Sphincter via the chaotic hubs of the Hate House and Mad Garden; and Kevin McCaighy breaks from the trend with a geographically decentralised primer on Chicago's Drag City Records.

A comprehensive account of the underground US indie scene at the tail end of the twenty-first century would have been a monolithic undertaking, but in compiling *Late Century Dream* we hope to have provided a fresh, lasting insight into those featured.

"Why so serious?/Life is the art that you make"
Superchunk—"Art Class (Song for Yayoi Kusama)", 2001.

Thomas Howells

AUSTIN & HOUSTON, TEXAS

"MURDER DOESN'T BOTHER
TO WHISPER /
IN THIS FUCKING TOWN
IT ROARS."

AK-47 "THE BADGE MEANS YOU SUCK"

JIMMY MARTIN

The phrase "Don't Mess With Texas" started out as the slogan for an anti-litter campaign, predominantly aimed at 18–35 year old men, and supposedly credited with shaming its target demographic into reducing litter on Texas' highways roughly three-quarters in the late 80s. Yet beyond that, this humble advertising strategy has unintentionally become synonymous with a certain kind of bullish regional pride, a stubborn disinclination to compromise. It's an impulse that was paradoxically followed through by an alternative music scene that largely concerned another group of young men, and flourished in splendid isolation in the South. Away from the media spotlight and music business hurly-burly of the East and West Coasts, Texan punk, hardcore and alternative bands were free to follow their own path. Whether rebelling against the oppressive conservatism of their surroundings, or merely through being inspired by each other to greater heights of outrage and originality, Texan bands were a truly rare breed.

For many, the roots of Texan punk rock came as a result of Malcolm McLaren's decision to book most of the Sex Pistols' debut US tour in 1978 in the Deep South, the implication being that it was better to spark off friction by playing where the band weren't wanted first, and to provoke mischief and controversy. Such a move proved the Sex Pistols' undoing and, with Sid Vicious' drug problems having escalated amidst John Lydon's dissatisfaction for the whole shebang, the Pistols In Texas were reportedly a sorry affair. Nonetheless, a certain number of youthful punters had never seen the like.

Jeffrey "King" Coffey, later of Butthole Surfers, was living in Forth Worth near Dallas at the time. "I was 15 when the Sex Pistols came to town", he relates, "and all the hype was, they can't play, all they do is they vomit on people and try to offend everyone. Which I found to be really intriguing! It was like, I already like this band, but it was really hard to even find a copy of the record, because there was only a couple of mainstream chain stores and there was a real animosity towards punk rock or new wave or whatever, but I tracked it down. And round about the same time this teenage punk band, about the same age as me but on the other side of town started out called The Hugh Beaumount Experience, and they were able to put out the first punk rock 45s, out of the Dallas, Fort Worth nexus, and I think it shows how clueless they were because their idea of punk rock was really mine, which was the Sex Pistols; we didn't know any other punk rock records or bands at all, in fact the singer sang with an English accent because that's what punk rock was to him."

"It's comical now that we were just aping our heroes, pretty much, but as we began to play though, and we got a little bit more sophistomocated, we began to see bands playing in Dallas, and in Texas and we got a sense of what American punk rock might sound like, and certainly Texas punk rock", he elaborates. "That's what kind of got us on the path. But you have to keep in mind that this was all before the dawn of the Internet, so we were in a little enclosed room, our own bit of the desert. And Texas is so far spread out—it's four hours to Austin from Dallas, it's about five hours to Houston, and then again all the major cities are about three to five hours away. You don't even count El Paso, that's in a whole different time zone! In The Hugh Beaumount Experience's case we were all minors anyway; we didn't have a car, and it was hard to get to Dallas, but I think that kind of sense of isolation played itself out all throughout Texas. The only bands you really got to see were your hometown bands because nobody really came through. We were really left to our own devices."

Tim Kerr, then with the benefits of living in the comparative bohemian oasis of Austin, was a few years older than Coffey, and these two factors lead to a different perspective on punk rock's high-profile arrival in Texas. "I was going to college at the University of Texas and working at a record store when punk hit here", he notes. "I remember hearing that the Sex Pistols would be playing in San Antonio but at the time I was more into The Clash, XTC, and Wire as far as that sort of music, so was not that interested in going. As far as a scene here at that point it was small and consisted for the most part of art and film students and people that were into glam with assorted 'characters' thrown in the mix. It was a small bunch and they centred around a club at the end of the main drag called Raul's. Punk and new wave were all the same thing at this point, and that music and the people listening to it—and, more so, *celebrating* it—might as well have come from Mars to the rest of Texas and the world".

A disproportionate amount of Texas' musical identity indeed derives itself from Austin, which developed a reputation as a place where outsiders and those of an artistic temperament could find like-minded individuals apart from the more conservative tendencies of the rest of the state.

"Austin absolutely is a liberal mecca", opines Craig Clouse, a veteran of a number of loud and obnoxious troupes (including $hit and $hine, Hammerhead and Crown Roast) who has yo-yoed back and forth from Texas to London since the late 80s. "[That's] most likely because of the University of Texas here. That and we have a local natural spring-fed swimming pool right in the middle of the city that has attracted a lot of hippie types for years! Plus the fact that it's just a very pleasant town. Lots of trees and lovely weather most of the year. Thousands of great places to see bands, drink, eat, whatever. It's a fucking great place; nowhere like it in America. It's very live-and-let-live, and I think that's been a pretty crucial aspect of why bands develop here. It certainly changed my life. It's all very 'can-do'."

"I'm not sure how much punk bands were reacting against the surroundings here in Austin", he adds. "I mean, life was probably pretty sweet for a lot of punk bands here compared to most US cities. Rent was cheap, bands could practice at home and mostly neighbours were cool about it. Encouraging, even. It was relatively easy to get shows. People were having fun. Lots of drinking, girls, drugs, everything. Bands from Houston and Dallas had a lot more to get angry about. Houston was a fucking rough town back then and still is. Dallas had a notorious violent skinhead scene back then. Austin has always been a totally different scene."

For Coffey, a youthful iconoclast intent on self-expression, it was clear very early on what the obvious course of action would be.

"I was maybe 17, 18, and I had a cool dad who let me get away with murder. I said 'Dad, I'm going to take off for Austin for the weekend'; as long as I did my homework I could get away with it. I was with some friends and we stayed in Austin, and I saw Butthole Surfers play a farewell gig, 'cos they were just about to go to California, to 'make it famous'", he laughs. "I was just blown away—they were a punk rock band but they really weren't playing punk rock, and what really blew me away about them was they were playing... you know that band Bloodrock? They were from Forth Worth, and they had a hit in the area with a song called 'D.O.A.', one of the goofiest but most amazing songs ever, and they were doing it totally straightahead. I mean, with complete sincerity, they weren't trying to speed it up or trying to be funny or anything, they were just doing their best to do it spooky. I mean it was scary but I was sort of laughing too-it was like 'They're playing BLOODROCK!' It blew my mind."

This, of course, would turn out to be rather a fateful meeting for King. Yet this wasn't all. "So anyway, they certainly impressed me, and then the next night at the same venue was The Dicks. And Oh My Fucking God, to this day it's one of my favourite shows I've ever seen. One, just because of the crowd, because Austin, I think because of the university here, the University of Texas had a big punk rock scene, unlike Dallas or even Houston, so when Dicks played there were like 300 punks there, which for me was like four million punks. They played a song, "Fake Bands", and everyone was like flying off the stage, and all this maelstrom of arms, legs... it was something else. The fact that this was our music, from the distinct vision of Gary Floyd, who was such a great soul singer, and such a great lyricist, and he brought his own sense of Texas blues and soul to punk rock, that was really eye-opening to me. What Butthole Surfers were doing, that was really eye-opening to me too, plus bands like Big Boys, all these awesome bands who were just fantastic. So I came back to Forth Worth and I told the rest of the guys, really after high school, 'We have to move to Austin, that's the place to be, it's a real fun city, it really welcomes all the rejects of Texas!' So as soon as we all came out of high school, we went to Austin, and there you go!"

One of the members of the selfsame Big Boys was Tim Kerr, who had seen their genesis arrive from strange origins. "When we first started, the scene was no rules, do what you want", he emphasises. "Funk and soul were a big part of our lives and our skating soundtrack, so of course that was going to be brought in to the mix. You also had a guitar player—me—coming from an open-tuned acoustic vocabulary with no history playing electric or rock and no interest really in that world other than old blues. Chris [Gates] at that time was in high school and played Ted Nugent, Aerosmith, Rush type guitar that he pretty much ended up going back to later in Junkyard. We flipped a coin to see who was going to play bass with the idea of trying to play once at Raul's. If that flip had gone the other way, it would have been a completely different band!"

Big Boys, along with The Dicks, were to be perhaps the two most prominent punk rock bands in Austin; although both were markedly different, they were as intense as each other, and were the bands that no-one wanted to follow on stage. Big Boys already had a degree of notoriety as local skaters when they played their first gig in late 1978, yet forged a truly innovative sound that blended infectious funk, full-pelt hardcore punk and a borderline combative theatrical extravagance, courtesy of 18-stone, gay and frequently drag-clad frontman Randy "Biscuit" Turner. The Dicks were led by Gary Floyd, also an out gay man and drag queen, and possessed of a vulpine howl of a voice that took the Texas blues traditions of Johnny Winter into unheard-of territory, as well as a Marxist ire that fuelled

Above left
Flyer for The Dicks, The Stains and Big Boys at
The Island, 1980.

Above right
Big Boys, Minor Threat, The Dicks and Marching
Plague at The Ritz.

Opposite top
Big Boys at The Island, Houston 1980.
By Ben DeSoto.

Opposite bottom
Big Boys at Fitzgerald's, Houston 1984.
By Ben DeSoto.

anti-anthems like the vicious "Dicks Hate the Police" (later to find even greater notoriety when covered by noted punk rock record collectors Mudhoney as "Hate The Police") and "Kill From The Heart".

Hatred of the police, in fact, was something of a common theme in Texan punk. One landmark early Texan punk single was AK-47's 1980 seven-inch "The Badge Means You Suck", its title a corruption of the Houston police slogan "The Badge Means We Care", which caused a considerable stir in the region. This was a remarkable record in a number of ways—not only was it a punk rock record made by a band who were eventually unmasked as disenchanted hippies (perhaps discernible by its suspiciously psychedelically inclined and slightly virtuoso guitar solo) but it took caustic agit-prop to new heights: amidst a diatribe more eloquent than the majority of first wave punk, seven victims of the legendarily racist and confrontational Houston police department are named both on the sleeve and in the lyrics, and the wearers of the badge in question even attempted to sue to the alleged tune of a million dollars only for the lawsuit to be foiled by the anonymity of the band's members.

Yet although Austin was devoid of the brutality of a city like Houston, its nascent punk rockers still had a strange relationship with the area's musical history. To its credit, the city had birthed The 13th Floor Elevators, whose unflinching devotion to psychedelic mind expansion both earned them the almost ceaseless attention of the local constabulary and temporarily cost at least one member of the band his sanity, yet made them cult heroes for an entire generation of enlightened wasters.

"We certainly took a certain comfort that we had those pioneers who came before us, and there's a certain regional pride in The 13th Floor Elevators", reckons

Big Boys at The Island, Houston 1980.

By Ben DeSoto.

The Dicks, "Hate the Police", 1980.

AK-47, "The Badge Means You Suck", 1980.

King Coffey. "Even though Texas has a chip on its shoulder about being backward, it's that we've contributed a lot to the innovative and the forward thinking aspects of music. I certainly cherished the 13th Floor Elevators records, when I was getting into punk rock; punk rock for me meant opening the doors to anything and everything that was obscure or not fully loved and I was 'Wow! This is from Texas. This all makes sense.' It makes sense in the heat, it makes sense in the way it's delivered and also the soul tip and the blues tip. You had those roots to pull from if you're from Texas."

For Tim Kerr, on the other hand, the antithesis of the Big Boys' attack was the 'cosmic cowboy' tradition that the city had become famous for—the likes of Willie Nelson, Waylon Jennings, and lesser known but equally revered troubadours like Michael Murphey had reached mythical status by forging a kind of countercultural outlaw country music that rebelled against the more saccharine mainstream country scene. For the punks of the time, however, the anti-establishment aspect of this style was a moot point.

"I will tell you that the first time The Clash ever played here they had Joe Ely open. It was five dollars at the Armadillo World Head Quarters, which was Austin's version of the Fillmore. If you were into The Clash at that time and lived in Austin, the last thing you wanted to see was another singer songwriter who you associated with cosmic cowboys. For The Clash, being from England, something like Joe Ely was really unique and, I guess, a renegade novelty in their eyes. You could see them on the side of the stage confused and astonished that his hometown wasn't welcoming him. You might hear Joe Ely at that time on the radio here; you would *not* hear The Clash. On a side note it was like that well into the early 90s here in Austin as far as mainstream radio and even today when someone talks about 'Texas Music', they are not talking Butthole Surfers, Archie Bell or even Ornette Coleman. It's blues and cosmic cowboy type singer songwriters."

On the other hand, Dave Dictor—who was to sing in one of the most confrontational of all Texan punk bands, The Stains, who subsequently morphed into Millions Of Dead Cops—moved to Austin specifically because he wanted to live in the same town as Willie Nelson. And even for King Coffey, the cosmic country tradition wasn't quite so divisive: "The country scene was based in Nashville and it was slick, commercial three-minute songs, and then you had people like Willie Nelson and Waylon Jennings basically smoking dope and hanging out with hippies in the scene in Austin and creating their own form of punk rock in the realm of country music. In Austin at the time, everything was like 'Willie Nelson this, Willie Nelson that', and there was a local punk rock reaction to what was happening then. But even that was a pretty cool scene in terms of everything else that was happening in the nation. Cosmic country itself was a backlash against mainstream country."

As the punk scene progressed, divisions and factions began to open up amidst its ranks, particularly between those who saw themselves as hardcore musicians and those they identified as having 'new wave' sensibilities—the implication being that the latter party had their eye on a kind of compromise for mainstream success that was anathema to the more devoted punk rockers. One of The Dicks' most incendiary ditties, "Fake Bands", tackled this matter in no uncertain terms, yet not everyone was sure that this taking of sides was a positive thing for the Texan scene at large.

"You know, with the rise of hardcore—and that's more what I gravitated to—there was very much a mentality of us against them", clarifies King Coffey. "That's what Gary Floyd was getting at, when he's mocking all the new wave people, and

Above
Biscuit of Big Boys at Fitzgerald's,
Houston c. 1984. By Ben DeSoto.

Opposite top and bottom
Crowd shots from a Mydolls, Butthole Surfers
and Stickmen With Rayguns show at The Island,
January 1982. By Ben DeSoto.

Overleaf
Crowd shot from a Buttholes show at the
Longhorn Ballroom, Dallas 14 November 1966.

I kinda regret that phase that punk rock went through, but at the time we were laying down the gauntlet I guess. Which was a shame because really early on you couldn't afford to be so picky about it. The difference between new wave and punk rock was minimal, and it was all included and it was all good. Just a year before, every hardcore person loved The B-52's, but then hardcore got to be so exclusionary that people were selling off their B-52's records, which was a shame."

Henry Owings is one of the men behind *Chunklet* magazine, a particularly acerbic organ that deals with the American punk underground. "Please don't think I'm name-dropping, but I talk to David Yow from The Jesus Lizard and Scratch Acid all the time", he elucidates. "I know what a big Dicks fan he is, and I mean he's thanked on the first Big Boys record, so he was there, he was an active part of the scene. So when I asked him point blank, 'Was there even a competition between The Big Boys and The Dicks?', and he was like 'Man, The Dicks had 'em by a mile'. I personally am a much bigger Big Boys fan than a Dicks fan, but that really resonated with me: the Dicks records are good, but I think the Big Boys are kind of transcendent, I think they poked their head outside of the—God, this is going to sound really cheesy—the punk rock *milieu*, instead of thinking inside the bubble. They were like the MC5. There are so many rules to punk rock and then it was like, 'Why should there be *any* rules?'"

"For me and my friends, new wave became the term that you associated with bands that were jumping on this new thing to get a mainstream record and be on MTV", notes Tim Kerr. "At the same time, there was a movement [hardcore] going on around the US that was realising that you needed to do this on your own with the help of your friends. To put on your own shows so that everyone could come

Above
Butthole Surfers at The Island, 1982.
By Ben DeSoto.

Opposite top to bottom
Butthole Surfers records:
Physic... Powerless... Another man's sac, 1984.
Rembrandt Pussyhorse, 1986.
Locust Abortion Technician, 1987.
Hairway to Steven, 1988.

Overleaf
Butthole Surfers at the Longhorn Ballroom,
Dallas 14 November 1986.

and hopefully become a part [of it]. As far as tribalism, that was going on before, during and after but if you don't subscribe, you're not part of their world and don't have to play by their rules."

"I think what started this all was the same thing that started beatnik, hippy, mod, Dada, whatever", he adds. "When a group of friends take it on themselves to make their own creative celebration because they are not happy with the choices they are given to work with, it's inevitable and unfortunate that that DIY spirit will be given a name and uniform and a set of rules by others that contradict the original freedom and spirit the originators came with."

As was widely documented, hardcore essentially started to eat itself around about the year 1986, overly regimented by its own scene politics and, increasingly, the preserve of angry, militant and ego-driven zealots rather than a mode for self-expression. For many, it was at just this stage that things started to become interesting for America's underground DIY music network. It was also during this period that Scratch Acid, another influential Austin band, made a series of scabrous records for the local label Rabid Cat that took a Birthday Party/Pere Ubu-derived art-damage approach and welded it to a demented Cramps assault. Memorably heralded by no less than Kurt Cobain as a major influence, the band would eventually contribute the notorious loose-cannon frontman David Yow and bassist David Wm. Sims to The Jesus Lizard, a group who would have notable success in the 90s.

"I really got into noisy antisocial music during the whole early noise rock thing, just as hardcore was ending", notes Craig Clouse. "I found noise rock to be much more interesting than punk; no attitude, no particular look, no particular rules about the music being made. Punk was all about attitude and fashion and

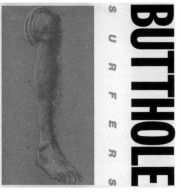

pseudo politics and misguided aggression, which I started to find very formulated and tedious. Noise rock took the best of punk music and turned it a much more creative open art form, and you could be a total nerdy dork and it was OK! You didn't have to wear Doc Martens and a wifebeater."

"I fast forward a bit and that's why Butthole Surfers meant a lot to me, because I realised real quickly that these guys were doing their own thing, and were more open-minded", adds Coffey. "It was a lot more acid, you know, 'big mind' kind of stuff that the Buttholes were doing—we were playing hardcore shows with hardcore bands after I joined, but we were also mocking the hardcore bands as well, like how Cro-Magnon, how limited, how stupid the whole thing had become. We realised that punk rock was painting itself into a corner when it could, and can be so much more."

Butthole Surfers, the San Antonio-based band who Coffey joined, proved to be a landmark band for Texan music in general, not to mention a band whose debauched mania blazed a widely-documented global trail. The experience of attending a Butthole Surfers show has indeed become the stuff of legend, as Craig Clouse notes: "Imagine tripping really hard in a massive dark room with hundreds of other people, and on a big screen behind the band was a very graphic video of a circumcision while the most fucked up, loud, total bad trip music is pounding through your head. I think that's the basic vibe that was going down!"

Butthole Surfers, by the end of the 1980s, had become no less than the ultimate force of transgressive absurdity in the indie underground—along with a number of EP releases, four increasingly intimidating platters of splatter emerged from the band after King Coffey had joined in 1983–1984's *Psychic, Powerless... Another Man's Sac*, 1985's *Rembrandt Pussyhorse*, 1987's magisterial work of malignance *Locust Abortion Technician* and 1988's equally demented *Hairway To Steven*, and elevated them to a global concern, living their parade of debauchery as enthusiastically offstage as on.

Yet King Coffey, scarcely believably, wasn't entirely satisfied with this, and had other ambitions besides. As the 80s turned into the 90s, he set about establishing a record label, Trance Syndicate.

"It was always something I wanted to do", he affirms. "I always bought into the whole DIY aspect hook line and sinker as a kid, so for me personally when I got into punk rock I wanted to be in a band. I didn't really know how to play, so I got some drums together and learnt the basics just so I could be in a band. The next possible thing to get together was the fanzine so I started doing the fanzine."

This was *Throbbing Cattle*, which King freely admits contained "NO punk rock at all! Basically, I put it together in my typing class at high school, and I would review my typing teacher, and I would review TV shows like soap operas. By and large we wanted to move beyond music and mostly play around with cattle images."

"The next two goals were a lot harder: starting a club and starting a record label. I tried the club for about a week, and I realised that you need money and you need to know what you're doing; it was way over my head with permits and stuff." He reflects, "I always wanted to do the label but again you need money, and I didn't know what distribution was, and it wasn't until 1990, I'd say, that I finally had some understanding of how record labels worked, I finally had some money saved up from my time in the Buttholes, and I saw a need to put out some Texas music."

"With Butthole Surfers, we were so dedicated to touring that we were prepared to tour without a record, but that's really putting the cart before the horse, so it's really hard for bands to put a record out without leaving Texas. I was seeing really good bands—I mean, my god, if Stickmen With Rayguns had been from California

or the East Coast or whatever, they would've been huge, but because they had no records out and they were playing for the same 20 people in Dallas or whatever, there was nowhere for them, in terms of their career, and understandably they got discouraged and broke up. So I started seeing this more and more with bands that I liked. It was kind of an unofficial ambition of mine to do it, and round about that time I was friendly with Touch and Go, and they agreed to do a production and distribution deal, which was amazing. So I got to have all the fun part really."

Among the first and most prominent bands that Coffey signed were Pain Teens, who were from Houston—the project of Bliss Blood and Scott Ayers—and had a head start on many of their contemporaries, having already released a number of cassettes on their own label Anomie. They forged a unique style that blended dystopian psychedelia, raw sexuality and intimidating industrial noise; a strange marriage of beauty and brutality that doesn't bear close comparison to any other band before or since.

"My parents moved to Houston at the beginning of my last year of high school", relates Bliss. "Needless to say I was pretty miserable. I didn't have a car, so I was basically trapped in suburbia. I didn't meet Scott until I was in college. Houston was pretty awful back then. The mood of the place definitely contributed to concept of the band, this horrible limbo that there was no escape from."

Yet things were to improve. "A few years later we had great friends who enjoyed the same things we did. We were into really dark books, industrial and noise music, and sick old films that were coming out on video at the time. But there were times when there were no venues for underground music. Nothing. Houston was hot and sticky during the day in the summer time. It was basically an uninhabited swamp until air conditioning was invented, home to not much but the oil drilling industry. I tried to only go out at night if possible, and there were some cool places where you could hang out in the evenings. There were a few cool influential people when I was first getting into the scene. Ronnie Bond from the Marxist punk band Really Red, who ran a cool record shop called Real Records, he always turned us on to cool music."

"Really Red were a great band, *Teaching You The Fear* is one of the best records period", concurs Tim Kerr. "Ronnie is sort of responsible for us getting the word out to 'Go Start Your Own Band'. I remember we were in his record store before a Houston show, and I remember Ronnie asking a kid that had come up to the counter when his band was going to play. The kid looked confused and left. I asked Ronnie what band the kid was in and Ronnie said 'Oh, he doesn't have one yet'. That really stuck with me!"

A wildly disparate brew of influences went into the Pain Teens' music; everything from the industrial skullduggery of SPK to the microtonal avant-garde work of Harry Partch, from the classic rock thud of Grand Funk to the theatrical extravagance of Nina Hagen. "They were a band who were certainly unique and are still unique now, in terms of the noise/art thing. [They had] a feminist perspective, a lot of industrial elements; they had so many different things happening in their music", enthuses King Coffey. "Bliss is such a unique presence, in how she sings, not just her presence onstage. And Scott is such an amazing guitar player. Even to this day I have trouble thinking of a similar band who do industrial collages with cool rock energy and a sexual feel and approach to it."

Pain Teens soon made a name for themselves in Houston. "I have to say that when we started releasing tapes, it seemed like something started to change", remembers Bliss. "My friend Dorothy released singles by Sugar Shack and The Mike Gunn, Dead Horse started releasing cassettes, then an LP, other people started

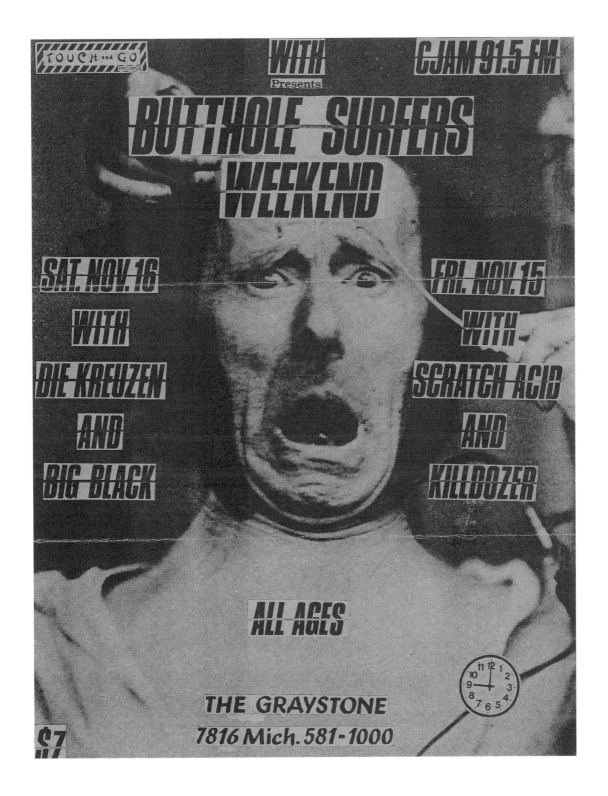

Butthole Surfers weekend at The Graystone,

Detroit 1985

Really Red at Parade, Houston c.1980.

By Ben DeSoto.

Ronnie Bond (Really Red) and Klaus Flouride
(Dead Kennedys) at The Island, 1982.
By Ben DeSoto.

making records. There was suddenly the beginning of a real music scene. Our friend JR Delgado opened a club called the Axiom in downtown Houston and then there was a place for shows. This was right around the time we started playing out, so we were available when a suitable band came to town to be the opening act. We were basically the opening act for any band that was noise-oriented who played at the Axiom, including Sink Manhattan, The Honeymoon Killers, Swans, Cop Shoot Cop, White Zombie, Psychic TV, Foetus, etc.. But mostly it was local shows with Ed Hall, Crust, Evil Mothers, Angkor Wat, Bayou Pigs, Miracle Room, Cherubs, Sugar Shack, The Mike Gunn and Turmoil in the Toybox."

Meanwhile in Austin, Craig Clouse was discovering a parallel new era of vibrant nastiness. Legend has tended to insist that Emo's was the most important venue for alternative music in the city, yet to the connoisseur at the time, it would appear this was not the case. "Yeah, Emo's came along during the whole Nirvana thing", he reflects. "There were far more important venues than Emo's in Austin. A lot of people, me included, did not trust Emo's when it appeared. First of all they had this big sign out front of the club that said 'alternative lounging' which I thought was the stupidest shit ever. Back then hipster types were called 'alternatives'. God, that's so embarrassing. Emo's sort of centralised and cashed in on a scene that was developed through smaller venues that didn't have a stupid 'cooler-than-thou' attitude like that club was famous for."

Indeed, one bunch of local party animals even saw fit to name their band Fuckemos in defiance of the place. Yet there were plenty thrills to be had elsewhere. "In the late 80s and early 90s, the Cannibal Club was *the* place to see

Above left
Scott Ayres and Bliss Blood of Pain Teens, 1993

Above right
Pain Teens, 1993.

bands", he enthuses, warming to the theme. "God, I saw everybody from Melvins to Pussy Galore there. Another massively, *massively* important venue was the Cavity Club. The Cavity was just a few doors down from Emo's and was where the real shit went down. Emo's was for posers. I saw GG Allin at Cavity—one of his most famous shows. Absolute total dangerous mayhem. Shit eating, violent fighting, tear gas, riot police. GG ended up being arrested that night. He was then sent to Michigan where he had to serve time for some previous wrong doings there! I saw Crash Worship at the Cavity; they were lighting fires and fireworks inside the packed venue. It was total madness; people were actually fucking on stage! That was a definite early inspiration for $hit and $hine. Just the whole repetitive, loud tribal thing, not the fucking on stage!"

Meanwhile, Trance Syndicate were putting out other great records by the likes of Cherubs, whose 1994 album *Heroin Man* was a prime cut of sludgy noise rock bedlam in the sadistic style of Melvins and Unsane, yet unfortunately coincided with their untimely demise. Crust and Ed Hall, meanwhile, seemingly followed slightly more in line with the disorienting and queasy aesthetic of Butthole Surfers themselves; Crust, fronted by the unforgettable figure of The Rev. Art Bank Lobby, put out the first ever Trance release, 1990's *The Sacred Art Of Crust* EP, and were prone to disturbing onlookers with sleeves of aggressive bloodshot eyes (1991's eponymous debut) and songs called "Chlamydia Is Not A Flower" (from 1994's *Crusty Love*) alike. Ed Hall, meanwhile—famed for being sued by their own fans and performing covered in blacklight paint—took hypnotic, repetitive, Flipper-esque riffage and overloaded squalling guitar noise and hectoring vocals on opuses of wrongness like 1992's *Gloryhole* and 1993's *Motherscratcher*.

Other labels in Texas flourished in the 90s by releasing records in a more garage rock'n'roll oriented direction. No Lie Records, also from Houston, put out the *Texas Speed Trials* series of compilations, which brought the likes of The Satans, The Inhalants, The Cryin' Out Louds and The Motards to wider attention, yet they also released many records by Jack O'Fire and The Lord High Fixers, both of whom featured Tim Kerr in their ranks.

Yet of the bands that gestated in Texas as the 1990s continued, the strange twin effect of the locale meant that a uniqueness of delivery was combined, at least initially, with a complete inability to build up an audience. One band who started out in Austin and eventually found success on a global scale was And You Will Know Us By The Trail Of Dead, who quickly came to the attention of King Coffey and released their self-titled debut on Trance Syndicate. "I first saw them at

Bliss Blood in Cleveland, 1993.

a small drag queen ball... I don't know what it is about punk rock and drag queens around here. It maybe held about 50 people, and it was one of those things where the line between the band and the audience was just so blurred because it was this explosion of sound that enveloped everyone in the crowd in the room. I was a fan right then and there, and I was kind of stalking them for months, going 'Can we please do a record?' They were one of these bands who were so amazing locally and were just getting ignored."

Yet as Henry Owings reckons, bands like Trail Of Dead—not to mention At The Drive-In, who were developing both a fiercely innovative sound and an incendiary live show over in El Paso—were far from an overnight sensation on the touring circuit. "I put on a few shows with them: to me it's very strange, like this revisionist history where once they break up everyone's into them. And it's like 'Dude I can swear to you; no-one was there!' The final show they did in Atlanta was, I think, on the first Queens Of The Stone Age tour, and there might have been 20 people there. And that was At The Drive-In's final American tour! I think that I put on a couple of Trail Of Dead shows in '98, '99 maybe. The first time they played in town it was at a place called Dotty's and there were maybe eight people there. The second time they were opening up for Superchunk, and there was maybe 50 people, but every one of the people who was that show was like 'Holy shit, this band is amazing'."

"I think, and I mean this with all due respect", he ponders, "that a lot of times the English music press hype machine creates some disparities. It's like I remember when Trail Of Dead blew up in England, and then Rocket From The Crypt.... It's very peculiar, so that's kind of what—at least from my perspective—jump-started Trail Of Dead. But I saw At The Drive-In quite a bit, but Good God, what a bizarre part of the state. In El Paso, there is *nothing* to do, so you can totally see where At The Drive-In came from: 'Oh yeah, they're bored shitless!' They have nothing to do. I would probably say you could drive four or five hours in any direction and get *nowhere*."

Despite putting out a good many of the seminal Texan records of the 90s, the pressures of running Trance Syndicate became too much for King Coffey as the new century dawned. "I think I was getting burnt out in a way", he muses. "We did it for nine years, and I think partly it was frustrating that it wasn't getting any more attention—we were putting out records, and were working our ass off, and we were usually just breaking even. Plus, there was the unfortunate legal row Butthole Surfers had with Touch and Go which kind of sucked a lot of the fun out of it. That was a drag, and I really felt like a bystander on that one, but I kind of got sucked into it. We all had to be very adult about it, but it became hard to be an adult. It was like, 'this is no longer fun'."

"I think it's one of the reasons that I quit doing the label was I became tired of seeing music as a commodity", he reckons. "Every time I'd see a local band I'd begin thinking 'OK, is this a band that can sell records, how would we present them, what would they be like to work with'; I couldn't help but begin this weird A&R strategy on this poor band who're just trying to play a show, so I found that to be a relief, to not have to do this.... To just appreciate music as a fan. Plus these days I'm playing with people just for the sheer fun of playing drums, without any goal or putting out a record on my own label. So it's all good."

Indeed, one such recently-formed group is Same Sac, an avant-sludge project that also involves Craig Clouse. Although Austin is now a fulcrum of no little attention as the result of the annual South By Southwest (SXSW) festival, these punk scene veterans understandably have mixed feelings about the music business hoopla this entails, not to mention the annual Austin Psych Fest.

"SXSW is a love/hate thing for most people in Austin", thunders Craig. "Yeah, it's a world class nauseating schmoozefest! Its fucking beyond horrible! But that's because it's become so blatantly corporate. The non-corporate side of SXSW is still always so much fun. It's a huge party for a week and loads of really great bands all come to Austin, so it's really amazing. Of course all the best stuff during SXSW is the non-official stuff. It's cool if you just ignore all the shit because you're guaranteed to run into old friends and every year there are so many great bands playing free, low-key, fun shows in places like record shops or pizza parlors or just about anywhere really!"

Thus, though Texan music may have moved on some distance from the nascent days of punk rock and hardcore, the thrills of the underground—and of freaks finding solace in a creative community—will always remain, as the rather sage-like Tim Kerr will testify:

"If you think about it, it's pretty obvious that the first and second generation of kids involved in it had never had anything like that before, so they knew they had to work to keep the community going…. By the third generation, those kids had come up through all-ages shows happening every weekend, so it was not 'special' anymore. The scene had gotten bigger so it was inevitable that it was less a community and more just groups of friends. Because the community feeling had gone you could now have the couple of trouble makers fuck up shows whenever they felt like it, because for the most part all that was going to happen was they might get thrown out for the night. This set the stage for the uniformity of shows and the rules that come with that. as opposed to coming to be a *part* of something. College radio and Nirvana breaking through sealed the deal."

"I think one of the main differences between then and now as far as alternative music goes, is that then people came to be part of what was going on here. There was no thought of, 'My goal is to come to Austin and be discovered and my career will get bigger', because at that time, there was no 'career' in doing this other than being part of a crazy creative community. Once again though, there are pockets of creativity going on. You just have to look a bit harder, dig deeper. There will ALWAYS be that person/group that will pick up that DIY flag and start up something else."

An interview with Bliss Blood
(Pain Teens)

Can you tell me a little about how Pain Teens started out? What were the main things that initially inspired you personally and in terms of starting the band?
The aesthetic of the band had already been sort of set by Scott Ayers' home recordings. Dark, weird, creepy, druggy. The first appearance by the Pain Teens on a local compilation tape called *The Dog That Wouldn't Die* featured a "band portrait"—a xerox of photo taken from an old automobile fatalities book from the 1950s, of human hair squished thru a shattered glass windshield as seen in side view. It was basically Scott's solo project at that point, but I was intrigued and wanted to get involved.

I was not an instrumentalist, but a singer and writer. I was then into horror fiction, an aesthetic which carried on through the years and got darker and darker. One of my early contributions turning Scott on to HP Lovecraft's writing (Innsmouth, Brown Jenkin, etc.) and English ghost stories by MR James ("Count Magnus") which helped mostly to use as song titles for weird improvised pieces that sat there like a throbbing mound of goo once they were recorded.

Scott was prolific, cranking out soundscapes, so I started trying to identify and name them or write lyrics that could transform them into "songs". We also did improv jams, recording two tracks and then rewinding the reel-to-reel tape and recording two new improv tracks without listening to the first two. Those came out very interesting. We also used old psychology books for lyrics ("Puzzling Diagnoses"), the strangest stuff we could dig up. We made "vocals" from old horror movies ("Brown Jenkin"), vocals from creepy talk shows ("Geraldo 666", "Hippy Cult Leader", "The Shoemaker", "Shock Treatment", "Sexual Anorexia", "Symptoms"), vocals from radio talk shows or evangelists ("You Got To Waste It", "Secret of Good Luck", "The Poured Out Blood", "Secret is Sickness"), even Reagan's state of the union address ("Freedom is on the March").

We were into the cut-up concept of William S Burroughs, but in a more edited, less random form. Making the people say what we wanted them to. Once I played a track ("A Continuing Nightmare") on a late-night college radio show with a voiceover taken from a major network news digest program, a horror story about a woman being abducted, the narrator's voice was recognisable as this mainstream commentator, and someone called the radio station to complain about "sexist" content. It was fun pushing the envelope in "apathy city"; I used to call Houston "a hotbed of apathy", seeing what would shock people. Once a friend suggested we should call the local Christian radio station to complain on the air about what a sick, bad influence the Pain Teens were on Christian teenagers, but I didn't want to deal with the fallout from that!

We started getting into reading true crime books, and then stories about murderers and the psychology of violence made its way into our lyrics around the time of "Stimulation Festival". I did an interview once with someone in the Czech Republic who told me that our song "Shallow Hole" was very popular there at the time—the psychology of violence that they were living through daily in their culture. When I wrote it, it was just sort of a meditation on what makes a person do those things, but they were actually experiencing it. That was really profound. Films like *Kwaidan* and Roman Polanski's *Repulsion* were fascinating to me and we tried to create a similar feeling through our music.

Given that you were born in Nebraska, how did you end up in Texas in the first place? What's your relationship with the place like in general (as in what would you say were the good and bad things about living there in the period you did)?
My parents moved to Houston at the beginning of my last year of high school. Needless to say I was pretty miserable. I didn't have a car and couldn't drive, so I was basically trapped in suburbia, an hour from downtown Houston, doomed to hang around the house and read books or watch TV. There was more culture in Houston, like repertory film houses so I got to check out cool movies like *A Clockwork Orange* in the theatre, but mostly it was suburban nightmare.

I didn't meet Scott until I was in college at the University of Houston, when I finally started driving. We had Anthropology class together. Houston was pretty awful back then. The mood of the place definitely contributed to the concept of the band, this horrible limbo that there was no escape from.

A few years later we had great friends who enjoyed the same things we did. That was the best part about living there, finding other kindred spirits that had fun poking around in the dark side of our culture. We had a friend who was the projectionist at the local art museum cinema, so we got to see a lot of great foreign and underground films. All of our close friends were into really dark books, industrial and noise music, and sick old films that were coming out on video at the time. We knew most everyone in the music and art community, painters, filmmakers, musicians, writers, so that part of Houston was great.

Actually living there, driving everywhere on the freeways, was a grind. I was happiest when I moved to an apartment three blocks from my job, at the Sound Exchange record store, so I could walk to work instead of a 45-minute drive each way. I lived there two years and it made such a difference to have a more chilled out lifestyle.

How much of that would you say specifically came from being based in Houston? Was there much about the culture, climate and whatever passed for a local scene there that you drew from? Did you have much in common with the other bands around Texas during that period, or find any of them inspiring?
Don't get me wrong, the local scene was great. We knew all of the creative people. But there were times when there were no venues for underground music. Nothing. Houston was hot and sticky during the day in the summer time. It was basically an uninhabited swamp until air conditioning was invented, home to not much but the oil drilling industry.

I tried to only go out at night if possible, and there were some cool places where you could hang out in the evenings. There were a few cool influential people when I was first getting into the scene. Ronnie Bond from the Marxist punk band Really Red, who ran a cool record shop called Real Records, he always turned us on to cool music. I really missed out on the punk scene because I lived so far away and had no way of getting downtown to check it out. I had a friend who was really into 60s music who turned me on to a lot of old 60s bands, which we listened to along with punk rock, and saw the parallels between the Stooges, and punk. My friends in college had pretty cutting edge taste compared to the rest of the people around, in Huntsville and Houston.

Scott played in several bands, Naked Amerika and the Anarchitex, as well as an early college group called Alien Labor, that were sort of political satire oriented punk, with some experimental stuff going on too. Culturcide was probably the biggest influence on us. Scott had been a big fan, took a recorder to their live shows and made his own bootleg tapes. He was in Naked Amerika with Dan Workman, the guitarist, and we were friends with Perry Webb, the other original band member, vocalist, theorist behind the band. They were funny, social satire, and really creative sonically. He was into stuff like Julian Jaynes' "Bicameral Mind" theories, etc., and friends with other industrial groups like Graeme Revelle and SPK. And I'm sure he knew many more.

There were other local bands like Grindin' Teeth (a country/noise band, which was pretty out there—they opened a couple of times for Sonic Youth… and so did we, once). Punk bands like the Party Owls, Sik Mentality, Keel Haul, were all over the place in Houston, nobody really had any records out. There weren't very many places where bands outside the mainstream music scene could play. Culturcide had a single and an LP. The Mydolls had an album, and Really Red, but not many other local releases.

I have to say that when we started releasing tapes, it seemed like something started to change. My friend Dorothy released singles by Sugar Shack and The Mike Gunn, Dead Horse started releasing cassettes, then an LP, other people started making records. There was suddenly the beginning of a real music scene. Our friend JR Delgado, the bass player from Party Owls and Sugar Shack, opened a club called the Axiom in downtown Houston and now there was a place for shows. This was right around the time we started playing out, so we were available when a suitable band came to town to be the opening act. We were basically the opening act for any band that was noise-oriented who played at the Axiom, including Sink Manhattan, The Honeymoon Killers, Swans, Cop Shoot Cop, White Zombie (!), Psychic TV, Foetus, etc.. But mostly it was local shows with Ed Hall, Crust, Evil Mothers, Angkor Wat, Bayou Pigs, Miracle Room, Cherubs, Sugar Shack, the Mike Gunn, Turmoil in the Toybox, etc..

I was into Einsturzende Neubaten, Throbbing Gristle, Cabaret Voltaire, and goth stuff like The Birthday Party and Bauhaus, and Siouxsie, Nina Hagen, Diamanda, and punk bands like the Minutemen and Black Flag. Scott was playing around with Burroughs-style cut-up vocals, and we would get lyrics from old warped psychology books, etc.. Scott was also into Hendrix, Grand Funk, Zeppelin, and turned me on to Black Sabbath and stuff like that which I hadn't really been interested in prior. We both liked stuff like Alice Cooper, and I started getting into bands like the Melvins, Killdozer, Big Black, Scratch Acid, and world music, Harry Partch and weird percussion music and old 1920s blues, reefer songs, jazz. As far as other Texas bands from outside of Houston, we mostly liked Butthole Surfers. We met them a couple of times but never got to open for them. We got to be friends with Ed Hall and Crust after we got signed to Trance.

Do you remember much about your initial meeting with King Coffey and ending up on Trance Syndicate? It seems they understood where you were coming from in general. What difference did it make to be on a bigger label after going it alone?
We went backstage in Houston once and met Butthole Surfers after they played. We were pretty starstruck. I mostly talked to Gibby and some chick named Kathleen who was their go-go dancer. Scott was pumping Paul Leary about his guitar effects rack. I think I talked to Teresa, but King was really shy and I don't remember speaking to him at all. After we played in Austin with Crust the first time, we got a letter from him proposing to sign us to his label, which of course we jumped at in a heartbeat. Trance was manufactured by Touch and Go, so we benefited from the promotional network already in place thru T and G. But things back then were a little different. There was a service called Rockpool that sent music to college radio stations, you gave them 50 copies of your LP and they distributed them to radio stations and wrote a review in their accompanying

magazine. We got a postcard from John Peel at the BBC lauding our second LP *Case Histories* which he received from Rockpool. He came to see us in London in 1991 after *Born In Blood* was released on Trance and we did a short tour with Cop Shoot Cop from New York. It was great to have that network of promotion so people actually had heard of us when we went to a new city. And were excited to hear us. And we got interviewed by magazines, *Maximum Rocknroll*, *Option*, *Your Flesh*, etc.. and were treated with some respect. Most of the big stars in the music scene at the time were either from the East or West Coast, UK, or the Chicago area because of Touch and Go.

What were your best touring experiences during this period? Are there any shows you did back then that have been particularly memorable?

We did our first tour of the West Coast, El Paso, Phoenix, San Diego, Los Angeles, San Jose, and two shows in San Francisco in 1990, I think. We met Kazuyuki (KK) Null in Los Angeles and he toured with us. After the first show in LA when he was about three times louder than we were, opening for us, playing nothing but "the subtleties of feedback" we realised we would have to make him the headliner or he would drive out the entire roomful of people every show. So he became the star of the tour. One show, I think in San Jose, a woman actually came out of the audience and unplugged his guitar effects on the stage! He was aghast that someone could be so rude. She was aghast that someone could be so loud.

The later tours were really good, we usually circled the perimeter of the US, going West first, through Arizona, up California, playing in Portland, Seattle, cutting over to Minneapolis, Detroit, Chicago, Ohio (we always had the best shows at the Euclid Tavern in Cleveland), Lexington, Richmond. Most of the places we played the first couple of tours it seemed like we were pretty much an unknown quantity. We played in Olympia, Washington with Bikini Kill and made them be the headliners because we knew everyone would leave after they played, then we all dropped acid and the mothership took off from the stage during our set.

The third tour was with The Boredoms from Osaka, Japan and Brutal Truth from New York. That was a lot of fun, because we weren't all by ourselves. The Boredoms were a trip. Seeing ghosts in the cabins in the Redwood Forest. I don't doubt that they actually saw them! That was a real freak show, the weirdest band in Japan, us, and a death metal band from New York City. The crowds were a pretty mixed bunch, headbangers, intellectual noise freaks, college radio people. Hanging out with Brutal Truth was funny. After the first extended three-day drive, Danny Lilker, the bassist came and sat in our van and asked us "are you crustin' yet?" Erm, no. The only other woman out of 16 people was Yoshimi, the Boredoms' drummer. But they really didn't speak much English so it was hard work communicating. They put on a great show every night, that was their *Wow 2* hardcore rock era, which I have to say is my favourite Boredoms record. Brutal Truth were the loudest thing we had ever heard. At least until Fudge Tunnel. We got a real education in the metal scene. We were crossover enough to pull our weight. But playing after the Boredoms every night was really hard, they basically used up all the crowds' energy. The only time we got to play before them was in New York, and we ruled at that show. It was our best show of the tour. In Minneapolis, my best friend from high school showed up backstage, whom I hadn't seen since 1979.

The last tour was with Fudge Tunnel, an Earache band who had recently signed to Sony/Columbia and Season to Risk from Kansas, who were also on Columbia. That time we started with New Orleans, went east to Atlanta, Columbia, SC, DC, headlined in New York City at the Limelight, then met up with Fudge Tunnel in Providence and to Boston, Montreal, Toronto, Detroit, Minneapolis, then to Seattle, Portland, SF, LA. The craziest incident was taking two days to get allowed to enter Canada because the tour manager for Season to Risk had the word "Skinhead" tattooed across the front of his neck in Old English script.

He had to go into a room and strip so they could photograph all his tattoos in case he committed a crime or something. We had to spend the night in a hotel because the customs people wouldn't let us in the first day.

Frankly, though, what I really enjoyed was the songwriting and recording, the creative part of the band. Going on tour was always a brutal grind, terrible food, long drives, hung over bandmates, no one to talk to. It got old. I liked playing shows around Texas. Performing was fun but the other 23 hours of the day were often less than exciting. And having "rock" songs to play with the band led to us limit what we recorded to things we could play onstage with them.

It seemed like you were a pretty hard-working band in the early days, and put out a load of cassettes on Anomie before you ever did anything that had a wider release. How did you find the practicalities of putting your own records and being self-sufficient back then?
We just wanted to release our music for people to hear it. Lots of people were selling home made tapes in Houston back then. We were surprised by the success of our first tape (I worked in a record store and we had friends who were DJs on local radio stations who gave us some airplay) so we just kept releasing stuff on tape as we recorded it and then used the "hits" as filler on our first three real album releases, including *Born In Blood* on Trance. With *Stimulation Festival* we were concentrating on creating our album releases and had excess material, though Scott still had some. We didn't especially want to be record moguls, but there was no other way to get your music out there. Our stuff was so odd that no label was really interested, when we sent cassettes to magazines or fanzines, we usually got some snide dismissive review. Suddenly, when we were on Trance, we were respected as artists.

There was a fairly dramatic shift stylistically towards *Beast of Dreams* when you put that one out in 1995 (as I may have mentioned, that one's a bit of a personal fave of mine). It sounds a lot more kind of David Lynch/Angelo Badalamenti to me although I could be wide of the mark there. What were the influences that led to that, and how d'you feel that record went down at the time? Was there anything about that record's making that precipitated your splitting up?
We decided to stop touring in 1993 and went back to what we were doing originally, which was just a recording project. That was why, for me, going back to just pure creative recording for *Beast of Dreams* was more fulfilling artistically and I was happier with the final product. It was the album I had the most input on, too. Before Scott made up all of the music, made all the decisions, but on *Beast of Dreams* I finally had some say on the sound of the whole album. I had gotten interested in jazz and Scott had borrowed a bunch of interesting world music instruments from a friend, sitar, marimba, and I bought a violin, he got a saxophone, so we were experimenting with incorporating instruments like that. I thought my lyrics were the sexiest and most magical ever, I was drawing from the *Kama Sutra* in "Coral Kiss", frankly erotic on "Swimming" and "Voluptus" and Greek Rembetika music on "Manouche", and covering Artie Shaw's "Moonray" in a really beautiful setting, and another famous jazz standard "Invitation" on what was probably one of the weirdest and most minimalist pieces Scott ever did, just Eno-esque bell tones spaced randomly over 14 tracks. It was pretty sophisticated in the context that we were coming out of, too much I guess. It also had really cool tunes like "The Sweet Sickness" and "Frigid Idol" which I thought were great, so cool and atmospheric. I really love that whole album, I think it's the most cohesive and consistently interesting collection of songs we released. We weren't worried about being "rock" like on the earlier albums, where we always had a few tunes that were ready for our rock band. It would have been interesting to continue along those lines, but our personal relationship was pretty much at an end by that point, and so I moved to New York.

I was really hurt when *College Music Journal* wrote off the whole album as "New Agey" and equated songs like "Manouche" to Led Zeppelin's "Kashmir". It was totally misunderstood and not promoted by Trance because we weren't playing live or touring any more. Then a month or so after it was released, I moved to New York. And then, in 1997 or so, Butthole Surfers sued Touch and Go to get their back catalogue away from them, and when they won, all the Trance records were discontinued.

Apparently you played some shows recently with Pain Teens, or was it just the one show in Austin? How did this come about? And how did it go? D'you think you'll do any more in the future?
We did two shows last November, in Houston and Austin. The Houston show was organised by our friend from back in the day, JR Delgado, who paid to fly me down to do an Axiom (the club he ran back in the late 80s) reunion weekend. We did the Houston show on Friday night, and a show at Emo's East in Austin on Saturday with former labelmates Crust and Ed Hall re-uniting to play with us. Both shows were sold out. The Emo's show had 1,700 people there, Houston about 800. Then we went back to Austin in February to open for Neurosis. I won't play again unless we get paid more, which probably won't happen.

ATHENS, GEORGIA

"LET'S PUT OUR HEADS TOGETHER/
AND START A NEW COUNTRY UP."

REM "CUYAHOGA"

LOUIS PATTISON

P unk was a seed, but what that seed grew into had a lot to do with where it landed. As 1978 dawned, on the American West Coast a new generation of faster, angrier hardcore punk groups—the likes of Black Flag and Dead Kennedys—were filling up the van for the first time. Over on the East Coast, Blondie and Television were transmuting CBGBs scuzz into louche, stylish new wave. But in Athens, a sleepy liberal enclave in the southeastern state of Georgia, punk fell on unusual soil. In April of that year, a band of jiving Athens oddballs in thrift store cast-offs—boys with oxford shirts tucked into slacks, girls in prom dresses sporting beehive haircuts—made their debut with a bizarre and wonderful single titled "Rock Lobster".

For all their subsequent commercial success, The B-52's would later be eclipsed by that of another Athens group to emerge from the flux of post-punk. With their chiming, Byrdsian guitars, cryptic, mumbled vocals and espousing of liberal and political concerns, REM would become regarded as the founding fathers of 80s alternative rock. But while very much an Athens band, Athens would not be defined by them. Indeed, there was no common template shared by REM, Pylon, and lesser-known Athens groups like Oh-OK, Love Tractor and the Bar-B-Que Killers—save perhaps a residual artiness, an eccentricity, an aversion to boredom whatever the cost.

Vanessa Briscoe Hay moved from Atlanta to Athens in 1978 to attend the University of Georgia. In February 1979, she joined the band Pylon, who played their debut show in Athens three weeks later. Pylon released two albums, 1980's *Gyrate* and 1983's *Chomp* and toured with groups including The B-52's, Mission of Burma, Gang of Four, and U2. They split in 1983, but interest in the band was rekindled when REM covered their song "Crazy" on 1987's *Dead Letter Office*, Bill Berry dubbing them "the best rock'n'roll band in America". They reformed in 1989 and again in 2004. The Pylon discography was recently reissued on DFA.

Paul Butchart moved to Athens in 1977 to attend the University of Georgia. His band The Side Effects played their first show in April 1980 supporting the still-to-be-named REM at St Mary's Episcopal Church. The Side Effects would disband two years later, but Butchart remains a key part of the Athens, Georgia musical community, leading musical walking tours organised through the Athens Welcome Centre.

Bertis Downs met Peter Buck and Bill Berry of REM while still a student at the University of Georgia Law School, and started working with the band in earnest after his graduation in 1981. First advising the band on legal counsel and contracts, he later became the band's manager, advisor, and unofficial "fifth member". He still lives in Athens, and continues to administer the band following their split.

Maureen McLaughlin first visited New York in 1976, where she worked with the Patti Smith Group and became Athens' insider on the city's burgeoning post-punk scene. After facilitating The B-52's' first show at Max's Kansas City, she became the group's first manager. She is currently a board member of non-profit organisation Art Rocks Athens, who are currently organising a major retrospective exhibition focusing on the art and music that came out of the University of Georgia's Lamar Dodd School of Art between 1975 and 1985.

Robert Croker was a painting instructor at the Lamar Dodd School of Art in the late 70s, teaching and partying with many of Athens' art-inclined groups.

Bill Cody was the producer of *Athens, Georgia: Inside/Out*, a 1987 documentary film that captured interview and live footage of bands including REM, The B-52's, Pylon, Flat Duo Jets and Love Tractor, as well as the famous local folk artist Howard Finster, who collaborated with Michael Stipe on the cover art of REM's 1984 album *Reckoning*.

———————————————————

Paul Butchart: Athens' location has made it the cultural centre of this part of North Georgia since the city's founding. People have been coming from small towns all around for over 200 years to attend concerts, see plays and engage in other social activities. Ether parties were popular in the mid 1800s. In the late 1800s there were dance battles with bands comprised of the employees of the various manufacturing and other local businesses. A black vaudeville theatre was built at the turn of the century. There were gospel music publishing companies in the 1920s, local string bands playing live on the radio in the 40s, and James Brown and Jackie Wilson playing fraternity parties in the early 60s, with local blue-eyed soul bands opening for them. By the 70s, a few national acts came through every once in a while, but the local scene was mostly cover bands. Even Ricky and Keith of The B-52's played in a high school talent competition in 1972.

Vanessa Briscoe Hay: Athens was a slow and sleepy Southern town that was centred around the University of Georgia. The music scene centred around the southern rock/bluegrass element over in Normaltown. The Nitty Gritty Dirt Band's *Will The Circle Be Unbroken* was highly influential, and a lot of local musicians were interested in reclaiming their Appalachian roots. The southern rock scene had blown through along with trappings of hippiedom. Bands like the Allman Brothers, Atlanta Rhythm Section. Lynyrd Skynyrd and the Dixie Dregs were all in their heyday. Long-haired boys hung around outside the dorms playing frisbee to these tunes and getting high. They really sort of frightened me at first, because I was a small-town girl.

Bertis Downs: Athens has a very formidable athletic culture, especially around the sport of football. Football is a really big thing, especially in the fall. When there's a dominant culture like that, you're always going to find a counterculture, especially in an artistic town. There was a definite art influence to a lot of those early Athens bands.

Vanessa: I found my niche and fellow earthlings over at the UGA art department. We were in the process of discovering music on seven-inch vinyl by bands like Television, Au Pairs, Pere Ubu, Blondie, Talking Heads, Elvis Costello, Wire, Vibrators, Cabaret Voltaire, Devo and loads more at our local record shop. Most of us were already aware of David Bowie, The Velvet Underground and Roxy Music. A dance party scene sprang up populated by gays, art students, art professors and fun-loving folks where the records were spun, kegs tapped and sweaty, blissful dancing took place at various peoples houses. Androgynous dressing and behaviour and an element of create-your-own-style with whatever you had was the way to go.

Bertis: I was still at law school when I first met Peter Buck. He was an employee at the record store, Wuxtry, and I was a frequent customer. Peter had an encyclopaedic knowledge of Neil Young, I had been getting into Neil Young, and he knew the priority records to get on a limited student budget. I knew Bill Berry from the concert committee at the university union. They'd put on shows at coffee shops and the occasional big shows of the day would take place at Stegeman Coliseum, a big basketball arena that held about 9,000 people. But there was no music infrastructure. There really weren't places to play, so The B-52's and later REM would play at these unusual places. Print shops, rehearsal places, old churches. It was a frontier.

───────────────

But few frontiersmen looked like The B-52's. Their name was a reference to the beehive hairstyle worn by members Cindy Wilson and Kate Pierson, last chic in the 1960s. There was a big splash of Warhol to their style, but their sound had none of the icy pretension of the New York new wave: "Rock Lobster" coasts along on what guitarist Ricky Wilson called "the stupidest riff of all time", the hook to a manic cut of high-camp, pop-Dada surf-pop that found frontman Fred Schneider playing new wave frogman diving amidst an underwater menagerie: "Here comes a sting-ray/There goes a manta-ray/In walked a jelly fish/There goes a dog-fish/Chased by a cat-fish!" Released April 1978 on Atlanta's DB Records, "Rock Lobster" would go on to sell 20,000 copies, and in Athens, The B-52's became hometown heroes.

Vanessa: I saw The B-52's the third time that they played. It was at The Last Resort, a coffee house that catered to folk and jazz music lovers. That night was wild wild wild! All of our friends from art school and a lot of our friends who we knew from parties, art professors, cross-dressers, etc. were all there. It wasn't like anything I'd ever seen before. It was colourful, funny—people were dancing their jeans off. There was an inflatable love doll being tossed around and instead of being shocking, it was hilarious! When Fred and Kate and Cindy sang "Rock Lobster", we all went down, down, down to the floor. When they broke into "Dance This Mess Around" we did all 16 dances. Their style was not serious black-garbed, leather-wearing stuff. It was a style you could make up raiding mom's closet if she was into Jackie O or find at the thrift store. They gave a focus to the Athens, Georgia scene. They were our 'tacky little dance band' from Georgia and we were very proud of them.

The B-52's, s/t debut, 1979

Above and Opposite
The B-52's playing Heatwave, near Toronto,
23 August 1980.

Bertis: There was a punk aesthetic there, I think, in terms of the ethic, or to use a cliché, keeping it real. But the bands that came out of Athens didn't *sound* punk.

Paul: I remember first seeing them in Atlanta in 1978 and thinking how weird, but how compelling. Their sound was like no other band. There was nothing one could compare them to in my previous high school musical world.

Maureen McLaughlin: I was working as a jury consultant for Howard Hughes' family on the Mormon Will Trial cases in Houston and Las Vegas when The B-52's started sending me postcards, asking if I would get them a gig in New York City. An Atlanta band, The Fans, had earlier asked my to use my contacts on their behalf, and once I got them an initial booking at Max's Kansas City, they had gone on to gain a respectable following among New York audiences and music critics.

   The Bs wanted me to book them as well, even though I told them that they needed to have more than six songs before they went to New York. Either the Thanksgiving weekend of 1977 or very soon after, I contacted Deer France, and booked the Bs at Max's. Their first foray into the New York music scene was dismal. "They get a Monday night", Deer France said. "Everybody starts on Monday night." The Bs were the opening act for Teenage Jesus And The Jerks. I missed the sound check, because I was on a plane from Raleigh, North Carolina where I had been helping to select a jury for some close friends who had been caught smuggling a ton or so of marijuana. After the defence team finished picking the jury, I ran to the airport and caught a plane, and by 6pm I was lugging my suitcase and a briefcase

packed with files up two flights of extremely steep and narrow steps to the B's dressing room. In court clothes. And high heels. I quickly changed into a yellow silk kimono, hot pink tights and Chinese slippers while the band went into hysterics about Lydia Lunch and crew next door. Teenage Jesus And The Jerks were not very friendly, to be sure, but I am certain that to the Jerks we looked like we had just pulled into town from Hicksville, USA. No black, no leather, and no safety pins to be seen anywhere in sight, just bright colours, big hair, and a lot of hairspray. What must they have thought? The time came for the Bs to go on, and I ushered them downstairs. They put on a pretty rocking show for the eight or ten people in the audience. The Bs played their six songs so fast, they had to play most—if not all—of them twice. A couple of months later, I called Deer again, and this time the band got a Tuesday night. Based on the first performance, I was not expecting much of anything to happen. That night, though, the joint was jumping. I was so stunned, I can only remember two things. One was that Lou Reed was sitting in the back of the room in a raised area with tables, eating a steak—downstairs, Max's was a steakhouse. My only other memory was that Judy Wilmot's boyfriend came up and told me that Ivan Kral from Patti's band had personally called every music critic, rock star, novel writer, journalist, and photographer in the place. Later on, I realised that Judy's boyfriend was Lester Bangs, the same writer whose articles I had been clipping from *Tiger Beat*, *Creem* and *Rolling Stone*.

Paul: The B-52's had this "life is a party" attitude, but also this aesthetic that one did not have to be a musician' to create music; anyone could pick up a guitar or other instrument and create their own sound. But they only played six shows in Athens before signing to Warner Brothers and moving to New York. There was absolutely no scene in Athens for them to fit into at the time.

––––––––––––––––

The B-52's went national, then international. Their self-titled debut album, recorded with Chris Blackwell at Compass Point studio in the Bahamas and released in July 1979, hit 59 on the Billboard Top 200. And while their sudden ascent to fame plucked them out of the Athens party underground, their gleeful anyone-can-do-it style proved a valuable example to a bunch of younger bands. The greatest of these was Pylon. A four-piece comprised of guitarist Randy Bewley, bassist Michael Lachowski, vocalist Vanessa Briscoe Hay and drummer Curtis Crowe, Pylon were very much an art-school band, having sprung from the creative flux around the University of Georgia's Lamar Dodd School of Art. Their music was as funky and infectiously danceable as that of The B-52's, but more austere of presentation, as comparable to Mission of Burma or sometime tourmates Gang of Four as to their campy forbears. Their 1980 debut *Gyrate* surges forth on an almost constant driving rhythm, Bewley's guitar jagged and precise, Briscoe Hay spitting enigmatic, epigrammatic phrases that scatter across the songs like sharp tacks.

Vanessa: Michael Lachowski was a photographic design major at UGA art school and I met him while we both took an independent study class. Through Michael, I met his roommate, Randy Bewley. Sometime in the fall of 1977, Michael and Randy had begun practicing in Michael's studio downtown. At first Randy was the drummer and Michael played bass. They weren't getting very far, so Randy switched to guitar and they taped everything they did. They spent hours playing the same riffs over and over. Upstairs, Curtis Crowe was hanging out loft with his friend Bill Tabor listening to this for what seemed like aeons to him. One evening Curtis couldn't take it anymore, he went downstairs and rapped on the door and asked them if they needed a drummer. They auditioned some of their male art pals and were ready to give up on a vocalist. They decided to use pre-recorded "vocals" from vinyl records like "Teach Your Bird To Talk". Randy suggested they audition me. On Valentines Day, 1978, I auditioned. There was a music stand set up with the lyrics neatly typed on it. I gave it some effort, but hadn't any idea what they thought. The next day, Randy told me I was in. Two weeks later, Pylon played our first party above Chapter Three Records, and then not long after that at Curtis' studio, The 40 Watt Club, with the Tone Tones.

Paul: The 40 Watt Club morphed out of a do-it-ourselves party space in a loft downtown, with free beer and good times and no eye on legitimacy to becoming what it would become—an actual business, charging for beer, hosting bands from NYC and beyond. The sorts of bands who played the 40 Watt were very much of the 'new wave' of music being created at the time, which made it unique amongst all the other offerings in town.

Vanessa: Curtis lived in the top floor, which was a huge open room that probably held around 100 people, lit by a single 40 watt bulb. He dubbed it his 40 Watt Club when he threw his first party and the name stuck. The Side Effects opened the club and the floor was reinforced with extra beams propped up for safety to prevent the floor from crashing in because of the heavy dancing. This spot is a Starbucks now.

Above left and right
Pylon records:
Gyrate, 1980.
Chomp, 1983.

Bertis Downs: Pylon were a great band. Very original. The REM guys spoke of them with some reverence.

Vanessa: I think having the four of us created a unique sound together. We wrote all of our own parts and jammed until it gelled. Randy had his own tunings. Michael had a certain idea of how he wanted his bass to sound. Curtis was an incredible drummer who hit the hell out of his drums. I let the music suggest to me what I was going to do. One of our idols was James Brown—not that we sounded like him, but we would warm up before shows listening to "Cold Sweat".

Paul: The house party scene required the music to be up-tempo, rhythmic, and not so loud as to drive everyone out of the room. The best way to keep your audience at the time was keep them dancing and not talking to each other. There were not any clubs at the time that were willing to book unheard-of bands, so the attitude was to just play for one's friends and have a good time doing it.

Vanessa: I was a painting major at the time. We loved the European sensibility of iconic images created from the industrial totally against the romantic aesthetic. For Pylon, we wanted a pleasing, consistent and formal look to our product. All of our imagery, posters were created or overseen by Michael Lachowski and we used only one font, Microgramma Bold Extended—this, before the idea of branding really took off. We were influenced by our professors and also art and photography which moved us at the time, by artists like Hilla and Bernd Becher, Alice Neel, Andy Warhol. One of our professors, Robert Croker was very interested in chance and played John Cage and other wild stuff during painting class.

Robert Croker: I tried to sneak in a little music education by keying sounds to the sense of whatever exercise we were doing that day, or week, or whatever. Baroque or Modern Jazz Quartet for light, airy line drawings. Beethoven or Shostakovich for studies of weight and balance, Bach's "Die Kunst der Fuge" for sustained

contemplation, Gid Tanner & His Skillet-lickers just for the helluvit. This was not 'mood music' (another trope: "Drawing is not a passive activity... it's a dance with an external form"—unless it's a bayonet fight). Truth is, I didn't really care much for rock'n'roll—too mechanical and rhythmically predictable for sustained application, but... holy cow, what energy! So, sometimes when I just needed to juice it up a bit—gabba gabba hey.

Vanessa: Lots of late night discussions took place after art critique wherever the cheapest pitcher of beer could be found. Robert's 24 Hour Party was one of the seminal parties of the time.

Robert: I used to throw a party—which I called a "mixer", just to be quaint—each school term. UGA is on a quarter system, so this means four a year. I'd start by inviting everybody I know. Sometimes I'd make hand-drawn invitations and maps and post them around the art department. Then everybody I know invites everybody they know, and they, in turn, invite everybody they know (some restrictions may apply). Then, on the day of, I bribe, with some combination of beer and food, a few impecunious (hence easily-bribed) undergraduates to come out and help me square the place away and a couple more to drive the Dodge around to a beer distributor and the seafood joint for oysters, while someone else goes with me in my Volkswagen to help me figure out which one's the eggplant and which one's the zucchini, and another person takes charge of the music and maybe the bottle-rockets, depending. As people start to show up we mill around for a little while until somebody taps the keg or thinks up something else to do, like fill the wading pool or set up a DJ station, and I wander idly about, loose off a few bottle-rockets just to get things stirred up, and watch for the cops. The electronic musicians set up in the studio, the DJ in the living room, and the acoustic contingent forms up on the lawn. Then whatever happens, happens until evening falls, when throwing spaghetti at the kitchen wall becomes an artform, and I maybe take a little time out from my host duties to do my patented public reading from *The Miller's Tale* or the *Disgusting British Candy Drill* from *Gravity's Rainbow*. Later, I'd go out in the yard, sit in the swing, take a few deep breaths. The house is literally rocking. This is not a chemically-induced hallucination: the walls are actually shaking, the roof pulsating.... There. Are. People. On. The. Roof. How in blue-eyed, ever-lovin' cotton-pickin' hayull did they get there, forget why? What are they doing!? How, for the luvva mike, will they get down? Well, there are more people inside the house than the laws of physics would seem to admit; maybe Werner Heisenberg could explain it. I'll hafta ask next time I see him. I could swear he was here a few minutes ago he and Oley were discussing the existential implications of the Split-T Formation.

Into this artsy, often inebriated space, dozens of bands took their first faltering steps: scratchy but dynamic post-punk duo The Method Actors, whose PiL-meets-Wire sound won them some acclaim in the UK music press; the instrumental art-rock group Love Tractor, featuring UGA students Kit Swartz and Mark Cline; coy, wide-eyed indie-popsters Oh-OK, featuring one Lynda Stipe on bass; rambunctious party band The Side Effects. In an interview with the *Washington Post*, Pylon's Michael Lachowski denied there was anything as fixed as a shared sound, but conceded the bands shared "an Athens aspect... the common element here is getting out on the dancefloor and drinking beer. And they all have a sort of raw, naïve sound."

Paul: The Side Effects were the first time I had ever done anything related to music at all in my entire life. Our first show occurred six months after sitting behind a drum kit without a clue about what to do. Never had a lesson in my life. We'd rehearsed and learned how to play in the suburbs of Athens on our roommate's equipment when they would be out of the house. We were influenced by the other bands in town—especially The B-52's, Pylon, and The Method Actors—but our biggest influences were the Gang of Four and the Ventures.

Vanessa: We played parties the first couple of months or so. There was really nowhere to play in Athens at the time. The first two times we performed, the audience just stood there and stared at us. I don't know if we were horrible or what, but the third show we played was at a party out in the country, the brick house out in Oglethorpe County. The B-52's came and checked us out, and it all gelled. Everyone started dancing, the rooms in this old enormous house became speakers with the wind rushing in and out. People were dancing in the house, running around and out in the yard they were dancing too. Kate and Fred came up to us afterwards and said "you have got to play in New York".

Paul: I first met Peter Buck through his job at Wuxtry Records, but I knew his brother a little better because we worked together at a local restaurant in town called O'Malley's. I met Mike Stipe, as I first knew him, when we worked together at another restaurant in town about a year later. There was no thought of a band at that time. A few months later, I mentioned to Peter about how Kit Swartz and I had been learning to play together, and he said we should try to get together with him and Michael. Alas, we never did.

Vanessa: I met Michael Stipe at a party before he formed the band. He asked if there was room for another Athens band, and I said that there were room for a lot of bands! He was and is a very nice, beautiful man. I liked him right away.

Paul: The first time I heard REM was the night before both bands' debuts, when we had a soundcheck and rehearsal at St. Mary's Episcopal Church.

Bertis: It was the birthday party of Bill's girlfriend, Katherine O'Brien. 5 April 1980.

Paul: We loaded our equipment through a back door into the sanctuary of the church, set up our equipment in the dark and dusty chamber, and ran through our set. We were quite nervous, since they had just finished performing some of their songs for us. They were much more professional, quite tight.

Bertis: They hadn't hit on a name yet. They'd been considering a list of names and couldn't find one they really liked.

Paul: Come our set, the whole place was packed. There were people hanging in the windows next to the stage, being careful not to fall through the holes in the floor. We were scared to death! For some reason the idea of playing before an audience gave us some weird boost of energy and we brought the crowd to a dancing frenzy. At the end, everyone was screaming for an encore, so we play our first two songs over again.

Oh-OK, 1983 (maybe 1982). By Laura Levine.

Metropolis presents

LOVE TRACTOR
PELL MELL
RED MASQUE

advance $5

Sat. April 28

at the Crown

Tickets at:
Cellophane Squ./Acme records/Bombshelter/Roxy
Rubato / Dreamland / Urban renewal

1616 4th ave.

Above left
Love Tractor, Pell Mell and Red Masque
at The Crown.

Above right
The Method Actors.

Vanessa: REM made an immediate impact on the audience. A group of girls called the Di-Fi-U's, an alternate sorority of sorts, screamed and ran towards the stage to dance. I had never seen anyone do that before.

Paul: During their set they were asking the audience to vote on band names—'Twisted Kites', 'Third Wave' and 'Negro Wives'. A few days later, when I was cleaning out the van we had driven to go to NYC I found a pair of tightie whities in the refrigerator. I was eternally perplexed as to their origin. Years later upon mentioning this story to Peter Buck, he laid claim to the underwear, saying that he had had an intimate encounter in the back of the van on the night of their very first show.

Bertis: Two weeks later, on 19 April, that's the first time I saw them. By then they were REM, because they wanted to put posters up, and they had these little handbills to give out. The venue, or non-venue, was the Koffee Klub—the back of a print shop on Oconee Street. I think it's a club now, the Caledonia. Later, we recorded the video to "Turn You Inside-Out" in that room, but eight years earlier it was the site of their first proper performance. They played at 1.45 am. I remember they had amazing songs. I knew they were playing some covers, and I had to ask my friend, Russell Carter—who ended up working with us, and managed Matthew Sweet and The Indigo Girls—what they were playing. Russell was a little older, knew his music, everything back to The Beatles. So I'd lean over and go in his ear, is that a cover? And Russell would be like, "I don't know it, so it must be one of theirs". Basically they were doing these classics—The Troggs, The Monkees—but I thought their stuff was just as good. Michael was barely 20 at the time, they were essentially college students—but it seemed to me they had a very fully-formed songwriting ability even then. And they had a pretty good sense of performance; there was no stage, no lights, but they looked kind of captivating. A lot of those songs they ended up not even releasing—I think "Gardening At Night" was one from that era. They only played half an hour, and then the cops came and shut the place down: operating a discotheque without a license. After that they started playing proper clubs—Tyrones and the 40 Watt became their home.

———————————————

Despite The B-52's' stratospheric success and the growing popularity of REM, in the early 1980s the Athens scene seemed largely immune to dreams of rock'n'roll stardom. Few bands viewed their music as anything like a career option, but the flipside to this was that groups could mature and evolve at their own pace, largely divorced from commercial imperatives and the eddying currents of fashion.

Vanessa: Our music was only intended to be a project that had only one goal—to play New York City and be written up by New York Rocker. We played our first out-of-town date in Philadelphia at the Hot Club and Gang of Four were also supposed to perform. We performed and a local band played and the promoter told everyone at the club that the Gang of Four had broken down in the Lincoln Tunnel, but were on their way. The crowd thinned. People were giving up. Finally, they blew into the club and played one of the best shows I've ever seen by anyone, anywhere. Two days later, we were opening for them at Hurrah and it was packed. I don't remember much about the first show, except after we played. All these young guys were reaching up to shake Randy's hand and Gang of Four were very complimentary, especially about our song "Danger". We didn't get written up by the *New York Rocker* that first time, but Glenn O'Brien wrote a nice piece in his column about us in *Interview*. He said we "ate dub for breakfast". We had no idea what that meant, so we turned it into a song lyric.

Paul: I liked all the local music. Each band at first strived to have their own unique sound. Oh-OK were great and completely innocent and original, as was Love Tractor. My favourite band, I would have to say, was Limbo District—one of the most original bands in town since The B-52's. After REM's popularity grew, bands in town seemed to start to sound a bit more jangly. Matthew Sweet moved to Athens with the exclusive purpose of being part of the scene. He was amongst the many 'real musicians' who came to town to try to surf on the focus Athens was getting with the rise of REM. My favourite bands have always been bands that completely originated in Athens.

Vanessa: Pylon toured sporadically every couple of months. We would go out for around three or four weeks, but we were not into being a career band. I guess it was some sort of adventure and way to see the country and a little bit of the world. I actually was able to survive on the money I brought home from touring for a few years as I had very low overheads. Cheap rent and a bicycle.

Pylon on the cover of *NY Rocker*, March 1981.

Overleaf
Bill Berry, Michael Stipe and Peter Buck of REM,
1984. By Paul Wright.

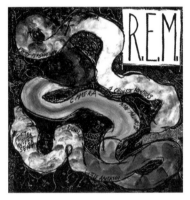

Above top and bottom
REM records:
Murmur, 1983.
Reckoning, 1984.

Previous left
REM playing live, 1984. By Paul Wright.

Previous right
Michael Stipe, 1984. By Paul Wright.

Bertis: The "Radio Free Europe" single first came out on a local label in 1981. It was later re-recorded and came out on REM's debut album *Murmur* in 1983. And they played it on *Letterman* later that year. We definitely had the leisure of time to develop. They wanted to write more and more good songs, and by they time they went into the studio, they had dozens. They didn't play New York until a year and a half into your career—you'd hop in the van and go to New York quite frequently, if you were a band in those days. But they just didn't. They grew up slowly.

Paul: It took a while for major labels to come sniffing around Athens, but the release of *Murmur* changed that. Most attention prior to that was among the underground magazine scene and locally. DB Records out of Atlanta began to release many of the local bands from Athens. Soon came IRS, Capitol, and even Capricorn Records who all released music by local bands. Soon national magazines began to wonder what was going on here. One of the first national magazine articles about Athens appeared in *People* in 1983.

Bertis: One thing, if anyone tells you that REM used to play a lot of fraternity parties—not true. They never played one. There seems to be a myth that REM played mostly covers, and mostly played fraternity parties. That's bollocks. They enjoyed doing covers, did a few early on, but once they started doing their own songs they would do maybe one or two covers a night, out of 25 songs. They had a lot of fraternity people coming to the shows. They had a broad appeal. But they were never on that frathouse cover band circuit, and that somehow gets mentioned as fact. That's absolutely not fact.

Vanessa: When REM became really famous, we had already broken up. We spoke to some label people who said, we were about to sign you when you broke up. We weren't very interested in any of that at first. We really never approached anyone, and were never directly approached by anyone.

Perhaps the finest document of the early Athens, Georgia scene is *Athens, GA: Inside/Out*. Released in 1987 but filmed a couple of years earlier, it's a whimsical but characterful documentary which mixes up performances and interviews with the likes of REM, Pylon and The B-52's with footage aiming to articulate something of Athens' essential, eccentric spirit: a meeting with the banjo-playing Baptist minister and outsider artist Howard Finster, William Orten Carlton of used record store Ort's Oldies waxing lyrical about "the zen of Athens", the staff of REM's favourite takeaway joint, Walter's BBQ. Peter Buck is interviewed in his pyjamas on his front porch, while Michael Lachowski of the then-defunct Pylon sounds quite content about the group's decision to turn their back on rock'n'roll: "All of us now are working odd jobs to get by, I manage a bike shop... everyone's just gone back to, just, living. I like it here a lot, it just depends what kind of balance I want between career and quality of life. If I want quality of life, I'll stay here for a long time." The film really belongs to REM, though, their performance of "Swan Swan H" at the Lucy Cobb Chapel a glimpse of the band rapidly approaching the height of their powers.

Bill Cody: The groundwork for the film *Athens, GA: Inside/Out* started shortly after I stopped working for the film director John Milius in 1985. We were big fans of Errol Morris and we wanted to make Vernon, FL with music. The concept being that if you show a bunch of people from a town you will understand what it is like to be there. I always loved REM and had heard about Athens. There is also the fact that the city was small and easy to get around for making a film. I enjoyed all the bands in one way or another. I mean, the Bar-B-Que Killers were an influence on the riot grrrl scene in Seattle and Olympia. Of course, the Flat Duo Jets have been a major and admitted influence on the White Stripes and several other bands. But I also liked Time Toy, The Squalls, all the other bands. And I was always a huge fan of Love Tractor. They would be huge today.

Vanessa: There were many people that made that period special. Ricky Wilson of The B-52's was a gentle soul. He passed out cards when in high school that said "Ricky Wilson loves you". How brave he must have been for the time in this place. His impact can't be underestimated. He has influenced so many guitarists and was a true original.

Bill: The thing about the 80s that is hard to understand unless you lived through it is that there was a real sense that something was changing but we weren't sure what it was exactly. The best and most exciting bands of the time never got played on the radio. REM didn't get played on the radio and they were the best band in America. They went on to play big arenas and even stadiums but at the time, they were just trying to get their art out their and find a way to make a living and I think *Athens, GA: Inside/Out* showed that. Which is why I think the film still has resonance, and why all those Elephant 6 people like Jeff Mangum and Kevin Barnes still talk about the film. It shows a group of people who fought their way out of the malaise that was the mid-80s and literally changed the way music was being done. It wasn't just them either. It was the SST bands like Black Flag, Hüsker Dü and the Meat Puppets, the Replacements and Soul Asylum from Minneapolis, people in the Austin scene like the Buttholes or the San Francisco scene, the Dead Kennedys, all those people. It was people finding a way to open a door that people had said was closed. And when those bands showed people that the door was actually open, a lot of people went through it.

Paul: I still give tours of the local musical history in Athens. Groups can be booked through The Athens Welcome Centre, and they will often refer individuals to me for smaller groups. Popular sites include the Steeple and the trestle from the back cover of *Murmur*, but there's a wealth of anecdotes and stories that crop up as you explore the rich musical history of Athens, Georgia.

The story of *Athens, Georgia: Inside/Out* as told by producer Bill Cody

The groundwork started shortly after I stopped working for the film director John Milius in 1985. Tony [Gayton, director] was from the South—if you can call Florida the South—and I am from Seattle, WA, but we were both living in LA at the time. The idea behind the film was actually rather simple. We were big fans of Errol Morris and we wanted to make *Vernon, FL* with music. The concept being that if you show a bunch of people from a town you will understand what it is like to be there. Too often people think that having a set point of view and only interviewing a certain kind of person, i.e. the musicians, the artists, will let you know what it is like to live someplace. I think that is, how do the English say—bollocks.

I always loved REM and had heard about Athens. There is also the fact that the city was small and easy to get around for making a film. We also love the south for a lot of reasons. The people there are very special. I don't think it is a surprise to anyone who has spent time there that so much of the best art from America is somehow connected to the southern region of the country.

REM became the band they were because they didn't have the record industry looking over their shoulders. If you look at the great periods for art in New York City, the time when real giants came out of there, it was the 50s when it was a hell hole and the 70s when the city was broke. Artists churn out different material when they have to turn a huge profit just to survive. I have no beef with commercial art but for a young artist of any type to find their way it really helps when you don't have to worry about everyday survival. Athens in the 80s was a place where you could survive on practically nothing.

The first time Tony and I went to Athens... it got a little weird. The whole town closed up for the most part until we went and talked with the resident filmmaker Jim Hebert. He did these wild art films, and shot one of REM's videos. We talked with him for a whole afternoon and after that everything was OK. I mean, we still had to meet everyone but it was a lot better after that. Then we made tapes of stories and started figuring what we wanted to do with the overall film. We did that over the course of the fall and I think between us we went to Athens three or four times. You have to understand this was old school filmmaking with 16mm cameras. You didn't get to shoot hours of tape. You had to set up shots and film with ten-minute loads. You needed to light everything. Filmmaking was a completely different process back then.

It was also during this time that Jeremy Ayers—the writer of "52 Girls" and "Old Man Kensey"—sent Tony a long letter about the folk art scenes and also about Dexter Romweber and the Flat Duo Jets. It has always been a bit of a bone of controversy that Dex was in the film, because he has mostly lived in North Carolina but he was living there at the time and Jeremy and a lot of other people said we had to have Dex in the film. Once we saw him play it was really a no-brainer. He was at the height of his powers back then and you can see why Jack White readily admits that Dex is his main influence.

We shot for three weeks, plus a day. That's because The B-52's called near the end of filming and said "we hear there's a party going on in Athens and we'd like to join". We couldn't get them all to come but having Kate and Keith there really tied everything together. I'm not sure a lot of people know, but Ricky—who was Keith's partner and Cindy's brother—had just died and they weren't even sure they wanted to continue on at that point. So when they said they wanted to come and be part of the film the entire crew voted to stay a couple of extra days. We actually shot them after the wrap party, which was a very fun event!

Well, I have to give a lot of props to Lisa Wells Fincannon for the idea to film REM in the Lucy Cobb Chapel idea. You have to understand that was big thing to the people who were a part of that scene. They hated the idea that these great old buildings were not being saved. If you saw the end of the film you see a card that says 'Save The Morton Theater' and an address to send money to. One of the things I am proudest of regarding the film is that both the Lucy Cobb Chapel and the Morton Theatre ended up being saved and renovated.

As far as the song… that was REM's idea. I got summoned to Michael's house where they were practicing and they had just written the song. At that point it was called "Swan Song" and they said they wanted to play that and the Everly Brothers song. That, and they wanted to wear suits. We just used two stereo mics into a mixer. Jim Hawkins recorded it— he was the engineer on a lot of the Capricorn stuff in the 70s, like the Allman Brothers and the Marshall Tucker Band. Then we lit smoke cookies to cut the light, put them on the stage and filmed it.

Michael was probably the only one in town who understood what we were doing and he asked if he could do some performance pieces. We never asked Michael to sit down and do an interview. And Pete did his interview impromptu after he did a tour of his house. The only real sit down interview we did was with Mike Mills. If I had one thing I wish I could have changed it would have been getting an interview with Bill. I love Bill Berry and always will. He asked me if he could opt out because he hated being on camera and now I wished I would have pushed him to do one with Mike. There's not a lot of footage with Bill and he's such a talented and funny man.

As far as Michael: he wasn't cryptic at all. He was very fun to be around back then. I mean, Michael is Michael, if you know what I mean, but it was really a matter of what we asked them to do at the time. They were very gracious with their time.

Tony and I always loved all the folk art in the film but not everyone in Athens was so thrilled. That changed over time and I know for a fact that a lot of people who complained about the inclusion of the folk artists are some of the people who went and hung out with both Howard and Rev Ruth later in their lives. I think it pointed up the significance of how art can be made without all the schooling that some people go through—the whole DIY concept that was a big part of all the great 80s music and art scenes.

I spent an hour with Howard Finster when the crew was filming the chapel, and he showed me picture after picture of his art over the years. I also remember my crew having to take breaks because of that tractor enamel he painted with in that little room. My grip, John Glazer, famously said one time, "I don't [know] if they're from God, but I'm very sure he has visions. I'm having a few myself from that tractor enamel."

I enjoyed all the bands in one way or another. I mean, the Bar-B-Que Killers were an influence on the riot grrrl scene in Seattle and Olympia. Of course, the Flat Duo Jets have been a major and admitted influence on the White Stripes and several other bands. But I also liked Time Toy, the Squalls and all the other bands. And I was always a huge fan of Love Tractor. They would be huge today.

I think the thing about the 80s that is hard to understand unless you lived through it is that there was a real sense that something was changing but we weren't sure what it was exactly. The best and most exciting bands of the time never got played on the radio. REM didn't get played on the radio and they were the best band in America. But back then people were just trying to get their art out there and find a way to make a living and I think *Athens, Georgia: Inside/Out* showed that. Which is why I think the film still has resonance. Why all those Elephant 6 people like Jeff Mangum and Kevin Barnes still talk about the film. The film shows a group of people who fought their way out of the malaise that was the mid-80s and literally changed the way that music was being done. It wasn't just them either. It was the SST bands like Black Flag, Hüsker Dü and Meat Puppets, the Replacements and Soul Asylum from Minneapolis, people in the Austin scene like the Buttholes or the San Francisco scene, like the Dead Kennedys. It was people finding a way to open a door that people said was closed. Then when those bands showed people that the door was open a lot of people went through it.

We were lucky that REM was part of the film. They were the band that really led that movement. A lot of people forget that now because they became a big old rock band and played stadiums. But back then they not only helped build that movement, they were the biggest cheerleaders of the other bands that were a part of that scene.

CHAPEL HILL, NORTH CAROLINA

"AND THERE'S A CHANCE
THAT THINGS WILL GET WEIRD/
YEAH THAT'S A POSSIBILITY."
ARCHERS OF LOAF "WEB IN FRONT"

BRIAN HOWE

I got sucked into the Chapel Hill music scene just as the millennium rolled over—the same time, not incidentally, that I turned old enough to drink in nightclubs. Like many young people before the Internet dissolved the twentieth century's commercial boundaries, I had grasped the concept of "indie" late by today's standards. In the 1990s, I grew up on alternative rock, gangster rap, nth-generation punk, and random indie bands for whom I had no cultural context, such as Pavement and Shudder to Think. The CDs in the mall shops were simply either by groups I had heard on the radio and MTV or groups I puzzlingly hadn't.

That changed when I started frequenting independent record stores such as Schoolkids, which quickly led me to indie music venues, in Chapel Hill—a university town of fewer than 50,000 residents at the time—and its smaller neighbour, the artsy mill town of Carrboro. There was the nationally venerated Cat's Cradle, where local bands shared bills with the likes of Nirvana and Pearl Jam in the wild early 90s, and the smaller but vital Local 506. There was The Cave, the smokiest dive around before the indoor cigarette ban, and the blood-red box of Go! Room 4, now dearly departed.

I learned that the metropolitan "Triangle" region of North Carolina, which includes Chapel Hill, the city of Durham and the state capitol of Raleigh, was known for more than college basketball rivalries and a progressive Southern culture at odds with the conservative countryside surrounding it. There was also a music scene connected to similar pockets of activity all over the country, with young bands streamlining and collectivising to skirt a still-formidable major label system. Archers of Loaf, Superchunk and Polvo, three of the bands who had put Chapel Hill on the musical map, instantly joined my favourites.

But Archers had been done for two years. Instead, I saw shows by Sorry About Dresden, a band including Bright Eyes' brother Matt Oberst. They filled the gap Archers left for burly, wounded anthems. Superchunk was off touring the world, playing something more like orchestral pop than their careening early music. Instead, I saw The White Octave (featuring another Nebraskan transplant, Cursive's Steve Pedersen, who'd come to Duke for law school). They filtered Superchunk's poppy sneer through the emo-punk epitomised by labels such as Deep Elm. And Polvo was defunct. Instead, I saw Fin Fang Foom, who still carry on Polvo's style of dark guitar heroism today, and The Comas, whose rickety dream-pop was its polar opposite.

These were all good bands, though none made the lasting national impact of their predecessors. While reporting on the changing musical landscape of the Triangle over the next dozen years and counting, I realised that I had entered at the end of a story; an indie rock creation myth replicated in scenes all over the country. It centred on one sea-change in the music industry: the alternative rock boom of the early 90s, which poked holes in the division between indie and the mainstream. It closed on another: the rise of the commercial Internet, which tore that division down. But where did it begin?

Was it after Nirvana's breakthrough in the early 1990s, when Chapel Hill was briefly but pivotally hyped as "the next Seattle?" Was it in the late 80s, when Superchunk and Merge Records cofounder Mac McCaughan moved to Chapel Hill—a time when bands and labels corresponded by post, their addresses circulating in record sleeves and photocopied 'zines? Or even earlier, when Raleigh and Durham's hardcore scenes produced the legendary Corrosion of Conformity before seeding the first generation of local indie bands?

After interviewing the people who nationally defined a Chapel Hill sound—the ones Cursive's Tim Kasher meant when he jadedly sang "Chapel Hill around the early 90s" in a list of his prefabricated influences on 2001's "Sink to the Beat"—I knew that this story should contrast their relationships to the time when indie became "alternative", and new music industry players, some based on the intimate efficiency of Merge and others with grander ambitions, rifled through town. It should begin at the Cat's Cradle, a venue immortalised by indie kingmakers Sonic Youth on their 1992 song "Chapel Hill", which anchors the network of local stages that makes a music scene possible. And it should branch out through the Triangle, whose interconnected towns have always been greater than the sum of their parts.

─────────────────

"The Cradle", as it's always known in the local parlance, moved to its current location in Carrboro around 1994 after losing a lease in Chapel Hill, where it had kept a roving address since 1969, nurturing important architects of the local independent music tradition long before there was any such thing as indie rock.

The Stones-y rock band Arrogance gained a wide southeastern following in the 1970s by touring and self-releasing albums before foundering on a Warner Brothers subdivision in 1980, foreshadowing the big-label woes of some indie bands a decade later. The Pressure Boys, who played ska with Devo-like pop affectations, cemented the DIY mould in the 80s, making lasting impressions on a teenaged Ash Bowie (who would later form Polvo) and Mac McCaughan by opening Triangle shows for marquee acts such as Duran Duran and Billy Idol.

Current owner Frank Heath bought the Cradle in 1986. "Frank was a linchpin for the whole scene", drawls Archers bassist Matt Gentling, a self-deprecating raconteur whose stories veer around like his band's music. And Bowie—sharp and taciturn as Gentling is relaxed and gregarious—says that he only had two goals when he formed Polvo: to put out a seven-inch single and to play at the Cradle. This was before the ethical term "indie rock" came to displace the more descriptive "college rock".

"We would listen to the college radio stations that are still around here", McCaughan said at the Merge offices a couple years ago. "Coming out of the 70s and classic rock, anything else was alternative for me and my friends. We were into hardcore bands because their shows were all-ages and there was a good scene here for that. At the same time, a WXYC DJ could be playing Let's Active and the dBs,

Frank Heath, owner of Cat's Cradle and Paul
Lowery, manager of Cat's Cradle, 1994.
All Chapel Hill photography by Jason Summers.

Overleaf
New Cat's Cradle between bands, 1994.

and we wanted to hear and see it all." WXYC is the radio station of the University of North Carolina at Chapel Hill, and its grassroots programming was part of a campus movement that gave college rock its name as much as the ages of its practitioners did.

"To me", Bowie explains, drawing a distinction with indie rock, "college rock was more of an 80s thing that REM had a lot do with. It was more poppy." Surprisingly, given his association with alternate guitar tunings, jangle-pop bands from Georgia and North Carolina were Bowie's gateway into underground music, not Swans and Sonic Youth. He especially liked the work of Mitch Easter of Winston-Salem, who helped set the template for college rock with his band Let's Active and as a producer for REM.

"It was just punk rock", Superchunk and Merge Records cofounder Laura Ballance protests, "music that wasn't top 40 or classic rock. Obviously, none of us had made up a name for it. The first thing I remember it being called after punk rock was college rock, and there was another name I can't remember that some people in Chapel Hill used."

She means "young rock", a coinage memorialised in the title of a 1994 VHS documentary by Norwood Cheek. "Eventually, everything became indie rock", she says, "and now that term is completely meaningless. It used to mean 'on an independent label'—you were not major-label material. But some of the bands in Chapel Hill at the time had a more jazz influence, or were just really weird."

Whatever you called this new music, it found support in an archipelago of Triangle stages—far more than can be mentioned here, and many continuing in some form today. There was the Brewery, a focal point for Raleigh's early hardcore

scene, which was demolished, after 28 years, in 2011. Raleigh's Fallout Shelter and Durham's Under the Street were also 80s punk crucibles, where a teenaged McCaughan played with his high-school band Slushpuppies.

For about a decade now, the Local 506 has been a testing ground for both local talent and touring bands who can't fill the Cradle. One address upstairs used to be La Terraza, "a great, low-key place where they'd let anybody play", according to Gentling—including a widely remembered, ferocious early show by Polvo. "That seems different today. With so many bands around, clubs are not as willing to take a chance and let things happen."

At a perennial venue spot at Brewer Lane in Carrboro, there was briefly but influentially The Turning Point, which inspires divergent memories: "A kind of avant-garde teen place behind the Sparkle Carwash", recalls Katharine Whalen of the retro-pop upstarts Squirrel Nut Zippers. "A kind of cheesy place", counters Bowie. "An art-space with barefoot kids running around", remembers McCaughan. From 1998 to 2004, it was Go! Room 4, a nightclub and rehearsal facility that was similar in size to the 506.

There was Rhythm Alley, which could hardly have been more different than the building's current occupant, the Chapel Hill noise and electronic music bastion Nightlight. "That was a great place where you saw more grownup bands", says Whalen, whose tastes always tended antique. "I saw Bo Diddley there and hung out with him when I was 16 or 17."

And there have always been plenty of house shows. Bowie remembers being able to walk through four backyards and arrive at the house of punk heroes Pipe, whose frontman Ron Liberti would go on to give Chapel Hill flyers their iconic look with his bold screen-printing. There was the Zen Frisbee house—locally significant art-rockers who never made a huge impression out of town—and the house that Chunk Johnson of post-rock forerunners Spatula shared with members of the mostly forgotten band 81 Mulberry.

One reason that the Triangle has been able to support so much music is that it contains three major universities, with NC State in Raleigh rounding out Chapel Hill's UNC and Durham's Duke. This creates a constant influx of new young people to get sucked into the music scene, in the audience or onstage. They supplement the ones who move here specifically to play music in an affordable touring hub, a day-trip away from New York and New Jersey, Florida and the Midwest—all places that have contributed waves of musicians to the area's musical culture.

"Mac [McCaughan] got things rolling after his time up in New York", says Gentling, "with his connections there." But the most catalytic connection happened locally. If the Cradle was a lightning rod for local music and touring bands, the spark came when McCaughan and Ballance met.

In 1985, McCaughan left his hometown of Durham for school at Columbia. When he moved to Chapel Hill two years later, the Triangle already had its first indie bands in the modern post-punk sense, such as Angels of Epistemology and Wwax, led by Wayne Taylor, which McCaughan soon joined. He also got Slushpuppies going again with Jonathan Neumann, and they recorded new material with Jerry Kee, who remains one of the most important North Carolina producers this side of Brian Paulson.

Ballance spent her high-school years on the Raleigh hardcore scene before moving to Chapel Hill to attend UNC. She got a job at Pepper's Pizza on Franklin Street, the main commercial drag by UNC's campus, where McCaughan also worked. As recounted in the indispensable Merge oral history *Our Noise*, he set about breaking her up with a guy in a popular Raleigh punk band—McCaughan and Ballance would be a couple until the early 90s—and drafted her as a bassist into short-lived party bands with names such as Quit Shovin'. The odd thing was that Ballance didn't play bass.

"In order to make me feel better about the fact that I didn't know how to play an instrument at all", she says, "Mac and Jonathan [Neumann] both played instruments they weren't used to playing. A lot of my friends were in bands, so it seemed like a fun thing to do even though I was terrified. I don't think I would have kept doing it, except that Mac really put the pressure on. I would have serious panic attacks trying to play in front of people, even at parties."

Another of McCaughan and Ballance's pre-Superchunk bands was Metal Pitcher with Angels of Epistemology's Jeb Bishop, who recorded what would become the first Merge Records seven-inch (following a pair of cassette singles from Bricks and Wwax), "A Careful Workman is the Best Safety Device". Today, the adaptable indie label is based in Durham, and is internationally renowned as the home of bands such as Arcade Fire. But it began out of simple necessity and belief.

Inspired by DIY imprints such as Homestead and Dischord, McCaughan and Taylor pressed the *evil i do not to nod i live* box-set of seven-inch singles from bands in his circle—Angels of Epistemology, Black Girls, Egg, Slushpuppies and Wwax—which made a big stir locally. Around a year later, in 1989, Merge was named and conceived as an ongoing venture. "If we were going to put out records ourselves", McCaughan says, "we had to call the label something. And as long as we're doing that, we should put out our friends' records too. It just kind of piggybacked from there. If you have releases by a few different bands, then distributors and stores start to give you an identity. It's a scene instead of just this band."

Superchunk live at Cat's Cradle, 1994

Superchunk, *No Pocky For Kitty*, 1991.

McCaughan and Ballance formed another band, Chunk, with drummer Chuck Garrison and guitarist Jack McCook. Both were replaced within a couple years by Jim Wilbur and Jon Wurster to cement the contemporary line-up of Superchunk, as they soon came to be called in deference to an existing band. While they released iconic early singles "Slack Motherfucker" and "Cool" on their burgeoning label, they signed with the more established indie Matador for their classic self-titled debut and its follow-up, *No Pocky for Kitty*, where they laid the noisy, melodic template for the Chapel Hill sound.

"When we put out singles", McCaughan says, "we were basically borrowing money from people, sometimes the bands themselves, to get them pressed. CDs and LPs were beyond what we could imagine doing, and Matador was a way to do so. Merge kept growing to the point where by the time our deal with them was up, we had the means and the distribution"—via Chicago label Touch and Go—"to do full-lengths ourselves." Merge's second full-length CD, following a collection of Superchunk singles, was 1992's *Cor-Crane Secret*, the debut album by a mysterious new band called Polvo.

Ash Bowie grew up in the rural town of Reidsville with standard teenage rock tastes—AC/DC, Def Leppard, Journey. Moving to Chapel Hill to attend UNC at the end of the 80s, he befriended Dave Brylawski, a guitarist and WXYC DJ with more sophisticated listening habits. Bowie decided to take up guitar himself and slowly waded into the local music scene, seeing shows by early Merge signees Erectus Monotone and Raleigh's Willard, both including drummers he would later play with in Polvo.

Opposite top
Polvo, 1993.

Opposite bottom
Polvo rehearse at the old gas station, 1994

"Seeing Willard with the light-show and the sound at the big club", he says, "was the first time I saw a local band that felt like a band from somewhere else. They weren't just playing at the cafeteria, and they were really good. It was sort of an epiphany."

Polvo's thorny, spiralling guitar music was quite different from the strident but infectious pop of Superchunk; more aligned with what would later be called math-rock and post-rock. "I hated Polvo the first three times I saw them", Gentling, who counts the band as good friends, admits. "Their stuff was just so out there that it took me awhile to digest. Then something clicked and I fell I love with them. By the time their first record came out, we were all really blown away by them."

Bowie developed a guitar style full of unusual tunings and droning open strings that he claims were inspired by misguided attempts to sound like My Bloody Valentine. "I was aware that because I couldn't play pentatonic scales", he says, "I couldn't play in a blues idiom, and it was easier to play these scales that sounded Eastern in a way I can't explain academically." It was Brylawski who pushed the band further in that direction with his collection of global stringed instruments, which he would later explore more fully alongside Spatula's Chuck Johnson as Idyll Swords.

Polvo put out the "Can I Ride" single on their own Kitchen Puff label—its sole release—because no one else wanted to. "We went through our record collections and just sent it to everybody", Bowie says. "If we'd heard back from anyone, we could easily have fallen prey to any kind of shitty label. When Merge came along, it was really good timing, keeping us from doing anything stupid."

As "Can I Ride" was getting played on college radio stations across the country, Merge, having just made their distribution deal with Touch and Go, asked if Polvo wanted to record a full-length, which was closely preceded by a split seven-inch with Erectus Monotone. Unlike Superchunk's two albums to date, *Cor-Crane Secret* was born into a strange and speedy new world after *Nevermind*. Merge was more than 20 numbers into its catalogue, Chapel Hill was buzzing in the national media, and a new band called Archers of Loaf was gaining steam.

"I love the Archers guys", says Bowie, "but back then I didn't see them that often. They were always on the road." Polvo, in stark contrast, only went out for perhaps a month after each record. "We were sort of in the same era, but we already had our double seven-inch and an album. I saw them as a new band."

The members of Archers all grew up in Asheville, a mountain town a couple hundred miles west of Chapel Hill, before going off to different colleges. All of them had at least been aware of each other in Asheville, but they convened in Chapel Hill by accident after each independently transferred to UNC. Guitarist Eric Johnson recognized singer/guitarist Eric Bachmann on a bus and asked him about playing some music together. Bachmann called Gentling to play bass, who brought in drummer Clay Boyer, who quit after a couple house shows but suggested Mark Price as his replacement, who had been friends with Gentling in Asheville.

Price, whom Gentling tags as Archers' secret-weapon arranger as well as its pummelling timekeeper, cemented the band's long-term line-up at the beginning of 1992. "Mark came to visit me one weekend", Gentling says, "and went home to find out he'd been laid off from his job. So he said 'to hell with it' and moved to Chapel Hill to drum for us."

Beginning their seven-year journey as tireless road warriors, Archers set out on their first tour, with Zen Frisbee and Bicycle Face, a charismatic rockabilly-tinged trio from Greensboro. "They were hilarious guys", Gentling says of Bicycle Face, "so biting and caustic onstage. We were worried we were going to get beat up in Tallahassee because there were all these frat guys—well, about four—and Bicycle Face was talking smack about Jimmy Buffett. We left town that night."

Opposite
Archers of Loaf in an alley, 1994.

These were the kinds of bands that early Archers fit in with better than Superchunk and Polvo. "I didn't feel that we were the black sheep", Gentling says, "but I did feel we were different: this bunch of Asheville guys that didn't quite get it. People were extremely nice to us, but I do think some people were frustrated that we did pretty well and it didn't seem like we were around to build that up. I can understand that; I think it's valid. We didn't get close to Superchunk until we had a couple albums out. Once we were touring a lot, we opened for them a couple times and wound up becoming good buddies."

"The Archers guys moved from Asheville", says Ballance, "and at first my impression was that they wanted to 'make it.' So you're looking at them out of the corner of your eye like, 'What are you doing? You moved here for this?' They signed to Alias, and at some point we realised, 'Oh my God, we should have put out your records. Too bad you signed that contract!' They didn't know what they were getting into." Merge would reissue Archers' catalogue in 2011 and 2012, as if to correct this snag in history.

Founded in 1988, Alias was a California indie that operated differently than Merge, signing bands with whom it had little social connection to more elaborate contracts. (Merge, at least in the small days, would split profits in half with a handshake.) Archers signed a four-record deal with Alias that began with *Icky Mettle*, their raw and furious 1993 debut, and ended with *White Trash Heroes*, their exhausted 1998 finale. For an *INDY Week* article in 2011, Gentling told me half-jokingly that they signed the contract because Alias were the first people to offer them a van.

They were still locked into it—the contract, not the van—when offers from big dogs such as Capitol started coming in. But the problem wasn't that Archers wanted to be on a bigger label. To the contrary—they would have liked more control over their own image and marketing. "I'd be lying if I said I didn't regret signing with Alias", Eric Johnson said in 2011, "though I'm not unappreciative of all they did. I think there were just some fundamental philosophical differences. It seemed like they wanted to make us a 'cute pop band' or something."

Gentling remembers a dinner in Chicago with Alias owner Delight Hanover where Archers discovered that she had licensed their music, to their chagrin, to Urban Outfitters. They also felt pressure to make music videos, which they were ambivalent about. Nowhere is this clearer than in the video for "Web in Front", which conveys an utter indifference to the enterprise and seems designed to be made fun of by Beavis and Butthead.

Alias wasn't the only new label making moves in Chapel Hill, trying to build upon what Merge had done, capitalise on a burgeoning scene, jackpot on the next Nirvana, or some combination. On the left side of the continuum, there was Jettison in Durham, which in the early 90s released music by local psych-poppers Mind Sirens, volatile rockers Picasso Trigger and the indefinable Blue-Green Gods, the band of label owner and local character Todd Goss. "Todd was thin as a beanpole and strong as an ox", remembers Gentling, "just way into pro wrestling, with dreadlocks that obscured most of his face, one eyeball glaring balefully between them. To me, Jettison was emblematic in terms of what was going on here."

Somewhere in the middle was Carrboro's Mammoth Records. Releasing respected local bands such as Dillon Fence and Vanilla Trainwreck alongside the renowned likes of Victoria Williams and Joe Henry, it became synonymous with 90s indie despite partnering with Atlantic Records after just a few years of independence. Jay Faires sold Mammoth to The Walt Disney Company in 1998, after which it released about a dozen more albums before vanishing into Disney's Hollywood

Archers of Loaf live at Cat's Cradle, 1994.

Records. Even early on, the label cultivated a striking air of prestige in a local musical culture often wary of it.

"They had a very nice office", remembers Squirrel Nut Zipper Katharine Whalen. "Steve Balcom, the vice president, was a really nice guy and a tireless champion of music. We pretty much worked with him—[Faires] kind of lived in LA and you'd just see him there. We were getting a damn good deal through Mammoth; everybody was making money. But it seemed like a bad decision, I thought, when Mammoth was bought and we became part of Disney. That seemed to make everything far more stressful and not as personable."

To Bowie, the differences between Mammoth and Merge were stark. "I think Mammoth was sort of the epicentre of one of the overlapping circles of the scene that Polvo wasn't going anywhere near", he says. "Other little circles were like Merge, putting out seven-inches, as opposed to taking a slightly more traditional route toward success, thinking about what to do to get signed [to a major label]. To me, Mammoth was either a stepping-stone to one of those labels, or they just were one. When you looked at the contracts, it was complete corporate bullshit. It was the same deal with this Moist/Baited Breath label that popped up, who offered us one. Mac was just more hip to what was going on, with a DIY component in his approach."

But Polvo wasn't completely immune to the atmosphere of upward mobility. After two albums for Merge, they moved to Touch and Go for 1996's *Exploded Drawing* and the following year's *Shapes*. "Back when we put out Polvo's records", remembers Ballance, "Merge was way smaller and we didn't really have a staff. Superchunk would be on tour a lot of the time. I think Polvo might have felt like they would be second-fiddle to Superchunk. Them jumping to Touch and Go was

Greg Humphreys during a Dillon Fence
rehearsal, 1993.

Overleaf
Picasso Trigger, July 1994

painful for us at the time. We just assumed we were putting out the records, and they never voiced their concerns to us. But it's always like that—friends have a hard time talking about business."

"[Touch and Go] was a bigger label at the time", Bowie explains, "and we were with them in Europe from the beginning, so it just made sense to us. I think it was to get more resources—making more money, getting an advance—though different people in the band had different hopes. I didn't have a strong opinion, but it seemed like there was a feeling that we ought to try something else instead of re-upping with Merge, and I wasn't arguing with it." But Superchunk and Polvo continued to tour together, and any lingering rift was sealed when the band returned to Merge for 2009 reunion album *In Prism*.

Then there was the evanescent but ambitious Moist/Baited Breath label. It released Metal Flake Mother's locally influential 1991 LP, *Beyond the Java Sea*— shortly after which the band broke up—and put on the notorious Big Stardom Record Convention all over Chapel Hill in the summer of 1992, where almost every area band played and out-of-town journalists were invited to crash on couches and floors.

"It did attract a lot of people and press from out of town", Bowie concedes. "All the talk of [Chapel Hill] being the new Seattle was bullshit, but people came down. There was a guy that stayed at my house, an economics writer from *Details* for some reason—this snide New York guy who didn't know much about music taking stock of this provincial scene he saw in this dismissive article. I remember that weekend being a lot of fun, but there was also something weird about it. It felt like a marketing platform for these people we weren't necessarily friends with."

Moist/Baited Breath was the enterprise of Kelley Cox, who had moved here from Kentucky, and Andrew Peterson. Neither had deep local connections, which bred some distrust when they tried to put their imprimatur on Chapel Hill. "They were just trying to start a label and be a player", Bowie says. "They probably had good intentions, but it seemed like they were based more on the Mammoth than the Merge model, with a big-label mindset. I could understand people being excited about a music scene, but as far as Chapel Hill being the next big thing, I never understood what that was supposed to mean. Moist and Alias sign a couple bands, and then, so what? Things moved on."

"It was weird", Gentling says, "and I think everybody felt pretty conflicted. You would hear people disparaging commercialism, but you couldn't help getting a little excited: 'Screw this commercialism, but it would be cool if somebody signed us!' [The name Big Stardom] was complete hipster t-shirt-level irony, but at the same time, it was very consciously promoting the music. It had this carnival atmosphere and you couldn't help but have fun." Within a year, that carnival atmosphere in Chapel Hill was made manifest in a new band called Squirrel Nut Zippers.

In 1993, Bowie was spending a lot of time in Boston with his girlfriend, Mary Timony of Helium. Its culture provided a contrast to Chapel Hill's. "In Boston", Bowie says, "there was more of a history of successful college radio bands— Juliana Hatfield, Galaxie 500, the Pixies, as well as The J Geils Band and all those bigger acts. It seemed like a town very aware of its history. There was a battle of the bands every year that was taken seriously, while [in Chapel Hill], it would have just been laughed at. People here had a bit more of a scornful reaction to any pretension of success in a traditional way. That was the slacker period, where if you were trying too hard to do anything, you might get made fun of."

Squirrel Nut Zippers weren't afraid to be seen as trying hard, and would become one of North Carolina's more successful alternative acts until Ben Folds. "We toured

and did in-stores in any town we could", singer/banjoist Katharine Whalen says, "and tried to get on the radio station there. We went to our local branch of distributors and did a lot of glad-handing. We had a lot of fans on the business side who would make the extra effort to help us out."

But they still reckoned with the fraught indie ideology of the day. "It really did feel like hooking up with a major was 'selling out,' a term that was frequently tossed around back then", Ballance remembers. "That was something we tried to be hyper-aware of not doing because it really changed the way people perceived you. You wanted to be like Minor Threat, not like the Cure."

Squirrel Nut Zippers' travelling carnival act stood out in a scene dominated by mock-surly rock and punk-derived bands. "To me, Archers sounded sort of like a bridge between us and Superchunk", Bowie says, "because they had some of the song structure of Superchunk, but with Eric Johnson doing some Polvo-y stuff on top of it." But where was the bridge to Squirrel Nut Zippers?

"They were a Mammoth band", shrugs Bowie. "You know—on a big label. I thought they were really good and cool, but I didn't really get into them because they had their own audience—the Zen Frisbee, non-indie-rock thing. I thought they were more artsy types, probably all painters and stuff."

"We had different scenes we hung out in, as far as socialising goes", Whalen says of her indie rock contemporaries. "I've always lived out in the country, while a lot of those folks lived in houses together in town. I definitely hung out more with the Zen Frisbee people and their entourage, who were all artists and poets and stuff. Plus, Zen Frisbee was not successfully touring the nation, but Superchunk was. When people are either on tour or at home trying to deal with their cats, you don't see them—you just see their posters."

Raised in the mountains of Hendersonville, Whalen moved to Chapel Hill with her mother when she was 15. She fell in with musician and record collector Dexter Romweber around the time he formed Flat Duo Jets in the early 80s. Flat Duo Jets were the definitive band of the Triangle's rockabilly pocket, alongside the long-running Southern Culture on the Skids. "That's sort of where I got my information about early rock and R&B", she says, "and his drummer, Crow [Smith], blew my mind playing Benny Goodman live at Carnegie Hall."

Whalen didn't become a musician until her early 20s, when she started dating Jimbo Mathus, formerly of Metal Flake Mother. "They were a great band", says Whalen. "Ben Clarke was pretty much the main songwriter, a fabulous guitar player. He'd come out of a heavy-duty hardcore scene, but the stuff he was writing was really beautiful and melodic. Randy Ward, another boyfriend of mine prior to Jimbo, was the other guitar player, and Jimbo was the drummer who wrote maybe a third of the songs. They had a unique sound, very fresh, slightly to the surf-rock side."

The genesis of Squirrel Nut Zippers was in a Metal Flake Mother song, "Wash Jones", penned by Mathus. "Jimbo heard it this other way in his head", Whalen remembers. "He taught me to play banjo so I could play it while he played the piano part." Whalen, like Ballance, came to playing and performance simultaneously, and working with pedigreed musicians such as Mathus and Tom Maxwell (formerly of glam-pop favourites What Peggy Wants) was daunting. "They told me it was just a performance-art piece we were going to do for two nights and then I would never have to do it again", she says.

Instead, they added more members and became a working band with alarming speed. "I immediately had to be a professional touring musician", Whalen says. "I literally kept a chord ahead of the songs they'd write for me to play. Years later, we were touring with the Dirty Dozen Brass Band, and I asked them about this creeping

Chris Phillips of Squirrel Nut Zippers during recording sessions for the album *HOT*, 1994.

Jimbo Mathis and Katharine Whalen of Squirrel Nut Zippers during recording sessions for the album *HOT*, 1994.

horror I had all the time that I was going to fail. One of them told me to learn 40 jazz standards and I would never worry again. Once I did that, I felt confident."

After releasing one single with Merge, Squirrel Nut Zippers signed with Mammoth and released albums throughout the 90s, their profile peaking in 1996 with jazz-pop hit "Hell", which prefigured a national retro-swing revival. "Seven Mary Three was sort of [Mammoth's] successful band before us", Whalen says, laughing. "Later, it was us financing the new office furniture. I think we were different enough from everything else that we were kind of fresh. Some of the indie rock stuff was more to the grunge end of the spectrum, a little darker. We were real positive and I think people wanted to feel good, go dancing, have cocktails."

The Zippers eked out a final album in 2000, *Bedlam Ballroom*, before calling it a day. "We'd finished our contract", Whalen says, "and I had been touring with my daughter. Once she started walking, I just didn't want to do it anymore. Jimbo was the only songwriter because Tom had left acrimoniously, and I don't think he had any more of that material to write from the heart. I like it better being off the road and doing different community gigs. I don't know that I ever felt like a local musician because we travelled so much, but I have pretty much only a regional career now, which is cool—I'm one of those people on the scene. It just happened for me backwards and inside-out."

Polvo played the last show of its original run in 1998. "We just had a sense that we'd done our thing", Bowie explains. "Dave was starting grad school in New York, and I was still in Boston most of the time, and we'd just made a record"—1997's *Shapes*—"that felt more like a hodgepodge of individual projects than a cohesive band effort. We felt like we had a good ride and it wasn't really sad. I was at the end of my twenties and was busy trying to figure out personal things more than worrying about music."

Archers also split in 1998, exhausted from their relentless touring schedule, with Eric Bachmann tugged toward his quieter Crooked Fingers project. "I don't think the ethos here has changed", Gentling says of Chapel Hill now. "It's still the Cradle and we'll see Frank [Heath] and a lot of the staff we've known for a long time. But it's different in that now we'll only recognise ten per cent of the faces instead of 60 per cent. The town has changed, and so much other music came after us, which all colours how you hear it."

Meanwhile, Superchunk and Merge Records carry on, having weathered the shifts from under- to aboveground, physical to digital; from indie rock's last hermetic days to its modern borderless ones. The label is still home to some of the Triangle's nationally recognised indie bands, such as Mount Moriah and The Love Language. "In some ways", McCaughan says, "we weathered them by not doing anything differently. Obviously you have to do different things in terms of distribution and promotion, but we never changed the basic idea behind the label. We just put out records we like and don't spend a ton of money doing stuff that may not work out."

An interview with Matt Gentling
(Archers of Loaf)

Tell us about coming to Chapel Hill and forming Archers of Loaf.

We formed around '91. Basically, it was one of those deals where we all kind of knew each other from Asheville. Our high school bands had played together and I knew Eric Johnson from common friends. I knew Mark Price quite well, and we all had common friends with Eric Bachmann. Mark and Eric and I had gone to the same high school and Bachmann went to the one across town. We all went off to college at various times, but transfers landed us all in Chapel Hill simultaneously. Eric Johnson was on the bus on campus in Chapel Hill, and he looks over and there's Bachmann. He recognised him from Asheville and introduced himself and they talked about playing some music together. Through my sister, who was going to Chapel Hill at the time, Bachmann found out I was transferring from a school up in Maine, got my phone number from her, and called me about playing some music. They had a bunch of songs already written by the time I rolled in. This was late summer of '91. We were sitting around Eric Johnson's apartment playing music and working on songs, and I was in another band with Clay Boyer, basically my first band from high school who were all in Chapel Hill as well—at that point is was called Kangaroo, although I originally I think it was called Rain, how's that for a high-school band name?—and Clay actually did play a couple parties with us. But it was getting too tough for him to reconcile the two band schedules, and he was a little more devoted to Kangaroo at the time.

Was that the band with the future Mayflies USA guy?

Yep, Matt McMichaels. Matt taught me how to play bass, the reason I ever picked it up. He and Clay and I were in Kangaroo together. Clay left Archers, and we were looking at booking some shows, and I hung on in both bands for a while before staying with Archers. Clay suggested Mark Price, who lived in Asheville but came to visit me a good bit. He came up one weekend to visit and literally got home to find out that he'd been laid off from his job. So he said to hell with it and moved to Chapel Hill to play drums with us. That happened right at 1992, beginning of January. We started playing more shows and getting out of town. I took my final semester off to go on our first glorious tour of Florida, where we were out for more than three days and did eight shows with Bicycle Face, an interesting band, a three-piece, a little Rockabilly-ish—a guy named Mitch McGurt was sort of their singer. Brian Husky was the bass player—he's a pretty successful actor now, a comedian. They were all hilarious guys, so biting and caustic onstage. We were worried we were going to get beat up in Tallahassee because there were all these frat guys—I say "all these," there were about four—it was us, Bicycle Face and Zen Frisbee. Bicycle Face was talking smack about Jimmy Buffet and getting the crowd riled up. We left town that night. [*Laughs*] My mom was terrified. You'll never go back to school! But I did come back and finish in the summertime. After that, we were committed. Fall of '93 we did our first long tour, a seven week tour. It just about killed us. I loved it, but man, it was so hard and things were falling apart, we were broke and starving, but it was really fun. The booking agent we had was a wonderful woman, real sweetheart, and absolutely horrid at booking. In Connecticut I saw some graffiti behind the door of the coffeehouse were we played at Trinity College that basically said, "Fuck so-and-so", this women. I grilled all the guys, did you write this? It turns out it was another band she had been booking where it hadn't gone so well either. It was not her cup of tea, and to her credit she got out of booking almost immediately after that debacle of a tour. We weren't allowed into Canada, so we were starving in New York because a guy that worked for Caroline and distributed us in Canada who had a farmhouse in upstate New York in the dead centre of nowhere let us camp out and do our laundry and drink beer. We camped out there and wrote a couple songs like "Lowest Part is Free". We had shows cancelled on us we were never told about, it was just a mess. I look back on that tour I enjoyed it so much, but luckily it didn't stay like that. We got fiscally liquid by I think mid-'94. We did a tour opening for the Lemonheads, and that was the first tour where I remember getting home and getting a check that actually paid all our bills. I actually broke even. I wasn't living off those 25-cent Little Debbie snack cakes, which I lived off of for like a month until on the farm I got sick. I can tell you from experience you can only live off those things so long before you break down. I was working at a bike shop and the owners were super cool, really flexible about our schedule. You'd build up a little cash to pay your bills and rent go back to tour, come back broker than a joke and rush back to work to pay it off, then repeat.

Chapel Hill employers now are used to that rhythm, especially at places like Acme.
Those businesses were all built by music the kind of Chapel Hill band type people after they either became successful in music or gave up on trying to make a living on that. But really there wasn't any of that yet, people worked at Carolina Coffee Shop or one of the pizza places or VisArt Video, those were the options you had back then. Andrea's married to Mac, she wasn't a musician but part of a community. They do society a favour by keeping these music people off the streets. It's sort of a halfway house for otherwise dysfunctional members of society.

When you formed you were the new band in town, and it wasn't long before you were [the] hot band in town.
I hadn't really thought about it much, but I think it's probably the case. We were accepted in town, we weren't the black sheep, but I did feel we were different—this bunch of Asheville guys that didn't quite get it. People were extremely nice to us and it wasn't like we were snubbed or anything. But I think some people were frustrated by the fact that we did pretty well and it didn't seem like we were around to build that up. I can understand that, I think it's valid.

Do you have insight on why Archers took off quickly? Showing up at [the] right moment?
I think that's a lot of it. Part of it is, I felt this way at the time and do more strongly now, but I think Eric Bachmann is one of the most talented people, and the fact that I got to be in a band with him is huge. But also Mark, our drummer, is sort of this underrated guy. He's got this arrangement talent, so much of the arranging is him. He would keep us on task. You'd get into this orgy of coming up with cool parts and he was kind of the disciplinarian. And then EJ had a ton of input in terms of guitar parts—he's just weird, like an evil genius. We'd have a basic song structure we really liked, but he'd be quiet and not playing. We'd take a break and then [he'd] say, "Well, I'm going to sit here while you

guys go to the beer store", and by the time we got back he'd have all this amazing stuff, or come up with the nucleus of a song. Having those three guys, there was a lot of talent there. I don't want to sound like I'm tooting our horn too much but I think they're amazing. The other thing that came from us was a willingness to go out and suffer on the road We never got tired of it—part of it is just being young, and it's cool, new horizons, driving through towns you've never been to, and that kind of fuels you even though you're broke and hungry, not living comfortably. It was fun enough that we kept at it where other folks might've got discouraged. If you go out and play and play, it makes you better at playing your own damn songs, but it also makes more people aware of you, and our species like familiarity [laughs]. You get your songs beat into their heads and eventually they come around to maybe liking them, regardless of whether the song had any merit. But I'm really proud of the songs we did.

How aware were you of indie or college rock?
Semi-aware. Bachmann was really into a lot of that New Zealand stuff and My Dad is Dead. He was a little more tapped in. The rest of us were more into the stuff that influenced us through high school—EJ loved the Pixies and Big Country. I really loved the Replacements and punk stuff. Mark had a pretty broad palate from prog rock to some jazz fusion. Mark and Bachmann had probably the most sophisticated musical education; they actually kind of studied it a little bit.

Bachmann played sax in high school?
He did, and Mark studied music and percussion. He had his chops, you know. We were somewhat aware of local bands, we were all big fans of Metal Flake Mother and the Polvo stuff. I hated Polvo the first, like, three times I saw them and then something clicked and I fell in love with them. Their stuff was just so out there it took me awhile to digest. So we really admired those bands. I remember liking the 3Ds a lot from New Zealand. We all liked Treepeople. Bachmann made us aware of Mudhoney, and I think he saw Nirvana when they first came through.

Did you guys get to open any big shows in the time when that was happening?
I missed a lot of that stuff. Eric saw Nirvana right around *Nevermind*. I remember seeing Young Fresh Fellows when they came through, I thought that was a pretty big band. There were like 20 of us there. It was a Sunday night. They made us all squeeze together so they could take a picture of us. They put on a great show. We didn't open for any though. The Lemonheads was the biggest thing we did until '95 or '96 when we toured with Weezer. We opened for Flaming Lips, which was huge for us, we were huge fans. Butthole Surfers we considered them pretty legendary and opened some shows for them. The Veralines, a big deal to us from New Zealand, were kind of our first real show with Mark.

Anything in particular about Chapel Hill that allowed you to thrive and shape you?
If you take away much convention and canon and have a million people playing music together, where there's not really an established taste, whatever you can sort of lump together as a Chapel Hill sound, I think, kind of grew up on its own. I never felt that you'd be laughed at or ridiculed or ostracised for departing from some protocols in terms of how you were supposed to sound.

Right, those indie bands all sound quite different, from jazzy to punk and so on.
That's true and can't be overstated. The bands that kind of had success definitely tended to sound within a certain set of parameters. The ones who didn't, who I think were real important in terms of what Chapel Hill was musically back then, like BoBo the Amazing

Rubber Faced Boy. Those guys played everywhere and they would always bring in all these local people. Nobody ever heard of them outside of Chapel Hill and I don't think they had a lot of ambitions around making it. They were all over the map, a little artsy, but a party band, rock, they just didn't give a damn. They'd try anything, didn't have cool instruments, just gleefully weird and not too calculated in terms of packaging themselves or creating an image. None of those guys went on to play with other people too much. You also had Zen Frisbee, Blue-Green Gods—they listened to pop music and jazz, like Coltrane and stuff, yet wrote the most dissonant weird dirgey music. They were always trying to play parts a little beyond their technical prowess. So they wrote these gorgeous songs, just sloppy and full of mistakes. They didn't give a fuck and every time I saw them, they'd always play first. They had this nihilistic vibe to them. Todd Goss, the singer, had this record label called Jettison and put out tons of singles, their own and others. He was thin as a beanpole and strong as an ox, just way into pro wrestling, had dreadlocks that obscured most of his face, one eyeball glaring balefully between them, real strong accent, "Well, you can see by looking at me, I'm not really employable." So it's people like that who I feel were really the more interesting ones to talk about. But they just weren't digestible on a larger scale. Blue-Green Gods aren't likely to wow a whole bunch of people out of the gate, you kind of had to live with them awhile to see what they were about. They were influential in their ethos and aesthetic and that they had a record label.

But if bands who broke out had certain parameters they fit, what was that Chapel Hill sound?
Mainly it was sort of straight-ahead rock, kind of a pop format, but played with a lot of dissonance thrown in. If you look at Superchunk, they just had real noisy guitars and quiet vocals, and straight-up high-energy rock. There was a self-effacing quality to a lot of it too. People were tired of the sort of grandstanding of rock, that comes and goes. People get tired of the self-effacement and want somebody to be unapologetically aggrandising then. But at the time people craved something more down to earth and folksy in a lot of ways. The bands that did pretty well out of Chapel Hill stirred a lot of that up. The bands who didn't still had a lot of that stuff, but maybe the dissonance covered up the pop.

Squirrel Nut Zippers were off on a whole other track—how did they fit in your world?
I knew Don, their original bass player, a little bit. Tom Maxwell from Teasing the Korean, who became What Peggy Wants—a really amazing and popular glam-pop band—Tom was involved in Squirrel Nut Zippers out of the gate. We knew him. One of the guys from Metal Flake Mother was involved on the ground floor, and we considered them to be one of the more awesome bands to put anything out there. When Metal Flake Mother put their album out, you'd go to a party and it would be playing on the stereo and everyone would be excited about it, which was really cool. When Squirrel Nut Zippers came out, I guess it wasn't that much of a surprise because you had these kind of erudite dudes who had put out some stuff that people liked. "Have you heard what so and so is doing now? It's this weird circus music." A lot of rock guys didn't know what to make of it but that was part of the attraction.

Did they seem like a whole other world or just another thing in the hodgepodge?
I'd say somewhere in between. They were definitely different, but compared with the amount of variation in style that was already there, it wasn't *too* far out. But it was new and interesting.

What about your relationship with Superchunk and Polvo in those days?
We didn't get close to Superchunk until we had a couple albums out. They were doing real well and out of town a lot, but another part—and I don't have any good explanation for

this—is that they weren't on our radar a whole lot at first. We didn't really listen to them. I'm not sure why. It took me awhile to get their stuff, to understand it or dig it. Once we were travelling and touring a lot, we opened for them a couple times and wound up becoming good buddies with them. Now I absolutely love those guys and I've travelled around with them a fair amount. Early on, it took us awhile. Polvo, we latched onto not necessarily immediately, but by the time *Cor-Crane Secret* came out, I think we were all really blown away by them.

Then who were your comrades on the scene?
The Bicycle Face guys. Picasso Trigger. EJ and I both hung out with them a lot and played a lot of shows with them.

Talk a bit about climate when major labels were sniffing around.
It was weird. I think everybody felt pretty conflicted. What you would hear would be people disparaging it for being commercialism, and I think a lot of that was valid and true. But you couldn't help getting a little excited, like maybe somebody will pay for me to put out my music! You'd have mixed feelings about it. "Screw this commercialism, but it would be cool if somebody signed us." I think a lot of people felt that way. I remember it being around the late summer of '92 when Kelly Cox got the Big Stardom Record Convention going, completely hipster t-shirt level irony, but at the same time very consciously promoting the music. He actually helped start the Moist/Baited Breath record label that didn't last very long but put out the Metal Flake Mother album. He had some ambition and a weird mixed interest in promoting the music, but enough cynicism to do it tongue-in-check. He invited all these journalists to come stay and sleep on people's bedrooms and couches and floors, to stay with the bands. It was really weird, almost a little self-defeating. We'll put you up but all I have to offer is this shitty fold-out couch. There were volleyball games, music in every single club in town, I feel like it was around 100 bands. It was huge, almost every band in existence at the time. It had this carnival atmosphere and you couldn't help but have fun. Admittedly the promotional aspect kind of receded to an afterthought, although it was kind of in the back of everybody's minds, maybe this will lead to being able to put out our music.

Was the industry there?
Yes, on a smaller level. It wasn't really the big labels, but I think it did lead to that. It put Chapel Hill on the radar of people outside the region.

What else helped do that?
Frankly, bands like us getting out of town and touring.

What about coverage in *Spin* and places like that?
I feel like a little bit, but I think it was limited to maybe one or two bands like Superchunk, and again, I think that owes more to their touring than anything. Polvo, out of nowhere, blew everybody's mind showing up in some magazine or other with like a three-line blurb. *Rolling Stone*, at the time, they wouldn't print anything about a small band. I don't think people put a whole lot of thought into the major press—everybody would jump up and down and pat each other on the backs for a minute, but it would be forgotten almost immediately. I don't think anybody in bands thought anything would come of it. Maybe people on the business end did, booking or labels.

Were there important labels besides Merge, Mammoth and Moist/Baited Breath?
Jettison Records was huge in terms of being emblematic of what was going on, and one other

label I'd emphasise the heck out of is a Greensboro one called D-Tox that was run by Eric Shepherd and he was the guitarist in band called Geezer Lake, another band we palled around with quite a bit, an amazing prog rock band and wonderful guys. D-Tox put out a lot of singles, including a Superchunk single. There was a lot of reciprocity between those labels. Jettison was friends with them and they put out some Blue-Green Gods singles. D-Tox put out a great compilation of local bands called *Pyloric Waves*, and Jettison put out one called *Falling Off the Planet*. A lot of local people listened to those and it was a great outlet for bands who never surfaced other than that, shoulder to shoulder with Superchunk and bands like that.

Were there ways in which [the] local music scene was negatively affected by national attention?
Minor ways. There were frustrations of bands that didn't really take off as others did well. Plus, we fared pretty well which took us out of the town altogether, we'd be home for a week and gone for months. The same was true with Superchunk. So you weren't part of that community as much anymore. But generally I think it was pretty positive. You get your ass out of the way and that makes room for other local bands.

What was your relation to the bands that followed you in Chapel Hill—White Octave, The Comas, Sorry About Dresden?
I don't know if I could speak to that because again, we were gone all the time. Capsize 7, we kept in pretty good touch with them. Bands like The Comas, we kind of kept in touch with because they were good friends with us, but we would never get to see them. I still stay in touch with Andy and Nicole. Andy lives in Asheville and still writes music. He's got a band called the Electric Owls, though he's mainly into his visual art. But the Electric Owls stuff is some of the best music in the past couple years, I feel like.

Was what they were doing different or a continuation?
I would say a continuation. People get bored with trying to replicate things, so the aesthetic would change in terms of the songwriting and style of playing.

Poppier, less dissonant?
I think it got poppier, a little mellower maybe. But the aesthetic of doing business and how you represented yourself as a band, I don't think that ethos changed.

Why does this area sustain a thriving music scene?
I think it's pretty boring—the availability of these sort of hand to mouth type jobs you can pick up quickly and put back down at a moment's notice, then come back and find another one later, these light service industry jobs. And then having colleges all around, you get all these people who are curious about art.

Venues that were important, including party houses?
Cat's Cradle obviously. Frank was just a linchpin for the whole thing. He really cared about the music and had the wherewithal to allow it to happen. Then there were little clubs like La Terraza, a little upstairs place, where they'd let anybody play and it was great. Low-key and the beer was cheap. The Hardback Café used to put on shows, they had a neat policy where they wouldn't give you a percentage or part of the door, they'd say we'll give you 60 bucks to play here, which was huge money for a band playing your first shows. The Brewery in Raleigh, the Fallout Shelter, the Trim Shop in Greensboro was a neat legally ambiguous place where the cops would shut it down and it would pop up in another part of town. Under the Street in Durham was a really neat place—just places that would allow bands with no obvious promise to play. That seems different

today. With so many bands around, clubs are not willing to take a chance and let things happen. You need to have a draw. Whereas back then it was like "Ehhh, fuck it, we won't really pay you much of anything", and bands didn't expect anything back then. All the houses had names. I lived in the Purple House because the landlord had gotten a deal on purple paint, and there was the Pink House, and the Polvo house, those guys all lived together.

Archers have done reunion shows in recent years. How does it feel compared to back then?
It feels the same in the sense that it's still the Cradle, so it feels familiar. A lot of the same guys are there. We'll see Frank and a lot of the staff we've known for a long time. It's like a little reunion. My old roommate Alex Mayolo still plays in a bunch of bands there. So we see a lot of old buddies. But it's different in that only ten per cent of the faces we recognise, where it used to be 60 per cent. A lot of the bands are different and the way people listen to the music is different. They hear it with different ears maybe. There's so much other music that came after it, the town had changed, everything feels a little different, and that all colours how you hear the music.

An interview with Laura Ballance (Superchunk/Merge Records)

How did you get into Chapel Hill music scene?
I moved to Chapel Hill to go to UNC. I had gone to high school in Raleigh for one year before that, and in high school I had started hanging around with the local punk rock kids there, some of who introduced me to the guys in Corrosion of Conformity. Sometimes, me and some other people would drive over to Chapel Hill to go see shows at the Cat's Cradle or at the Point, which was in a sort of triangle-shaped building near Crooks, which became Go!. Before it was Go!, it was the Point, where some well-intentioned hippie would have punk rock shows sometimes. I remember going there to see Melvins. It wasn't very well or officially set up—I don't know if they even sold beer. Anyway, I met some Chapel Hill people on our expeditions from Raleigh, and then I came to UNC and started living there. The longer I was there, the more embedded I got in it.

Before you started doing Superchunk, you were involved in some impromptu party bands?
Yes, and Mac was in all of them from what I can remember. I was in a band called Metal Pitcher, that was me and Mac and Jeb Bishop, a Raleigh guy who was in Angels of Epistemology. He lived in Chapel Hill for awhile too. I was in a band called Quit Shovin', with Mac and Jonathan Newman. In order to make me feel better about the fact that I didn't know how to play an instrument at all, they both played instruments they weren't used to playing. Jonathan who was a drummer played guitar and Mac who was a guitarist played drums and I played bass. We would play at parties in Chapel Hill sometimes, there was this one house where they always had parties with tanks of nitrous oxide.

When all these improvised bands solidified into Superchunk, were there other bands that inspired you or did you just want to make the kind of music you liked?
It seemed like a fun thing to do. A lot of my friends were making music in bands. So it seemed like fun even though I was terrified. I don't think I would have kept doing

it except that Mac really put the pressure on. I was just so scared, I would have some serious panic attacks trying to stand onstage and play in front of people, even at parties.

Were there a lot of women on the scene at the time performing?
There were as many women around as men, though maybe there were more guys in bands. Angels of Epistemology had several women in it. There were the Black Girls, which was Dana Glitter and… I can't remember the name of the other two. I guess a lot of these bands I'm talking about are Raleigh bands. In Chapel Hill, I can't think of any bands with girls in it from that time.

But those Raleigh bands played a lot in Chapel Hill right?
Yes. A lot of those shows were at the Brewery, which everybody went to. Somehow it seemed like the Cradle wasn't doing as many punk rock shows as the Brewery back then.

So you didn't have a huge awareness of "indie rock" culture when you started playing in these bands?
Yeah, it wasn't even "indie rock", it was just punk rock, music that wasn't top 40 or classic rock. It was whatever music you were capable of making. Obviously none of us in our minds had made up a name for it. I guess it's not obvious— it actually doesn't seem to occur to people, that you're not making up a genre for yourself. You're just making whatever music you feel like or are capable of making. It's hilarious, the different names. When Superchunk first started people said it sounded like the Buzzcocks. Which is absurd, really. [*Laughs*] I love the Buzzcocks, but what about us sounded like the Buzzcocks? That Mac had a high, squeaky voice? I don't know. The first thing I remember being called after punk rock was college rock. Then there was another name that people in Chapel Hill used... [young rock]. Eventually it became "indie rock", and now that term is completely meaningless. It used to mean on an independent label, basically—you were not major label material, you were lesser. [*Laughs*] Now people call everything indie rock.

Right, we tend to think retroactively that all these so-called indie bands had common cause and influences, but that was a later construct.
Definitely. Some of the bands had a more jazz influence, or were just really weird. Angels of Epistemology and their strange skronkiness, I don't know what those guys were listening to that inspired them, but it wasn't straight up at all. Wwax, too, was pretty weird at the time.

Did bands like Superchunk and Archers feel separate from bands who were local kings before, like Arrogance and Pressure Boys?
I didn't know those bands at all. I don't know if I ever saw the Pressure Boys. You know who I saw a lot was Zen Frisbee and Flat Duo Jets. Those were my favourite Chapel Hill bands early on. But the whole—I don't know what you call it—the time of ska-influenced thing, I don't know about. I've never even heard of Arrogance. I guess they were before my time.

Did Pressure Boys feel like a whole separate thing than what you were doing?
I guess, definitely. But that may have just been the time that I arrived. I moved from Atlanta in 1985, so I missed some of that. If you talk to Mac, probably the Pressure Boys had more influence on him, seeing them in high school.

Archers and Polvo get lumped in with you. Squirrel Nut Zippers was another band that broke out of Chapel Hill, but they seemed quite different.

I also feel like they were a tiny bit later. Our contemporaries, it feels like it was mostly Polvo and Archers, and we would tour together and do stuff like that eventually—not the entire time. And then there was the Sex Police, our contemporaries but also in a different scene—sorority girls went to see them. [*Laughs*] And that mattered back then, which is so funny!

So did you share any camaraderie with Archers and Polvo while a lot of attention was on Chapel Hill?

We had a closer relationship, I think, with Polvo. We were friends with them already before the band; they all were in our neighbourhood. We knew Ash and Dave just from hanging around. The Archers guys, they moved to Chapel Hill from Asheville. My impression at first was that they wanted to "make it". So you're looking at them out of the corner of your eye like "What are you doing? You moved here for this?" [*Laughs*] At first, we didn't really know them that well, and they signed to Alias, and at some point, we realised "Oh my god, we should have put out your records. Too bad you signed that contract!" But who knows, maybe for them at the time they thought it was the best thing. They didn't know what they were getting into. I wonder if we had been a little quicker to warm up to them and talk to them about it, if they would have put their records on Merge instead. And you know, we put out Polvo's records, back in the old days. Merge was way smaller and we didn't really have a staff, and Superchunk would be on tour a lot of the time. I think they might have felt like they would be second fiddle to Superchunk. At some point they jumped to Touch and Go, which was painful for us at the time. We… we didn't like it. [*Laughs*] It made us a little upset. We just assumed we were putting out the records and they never voiced their concerns to us and let us talk about it with them. But it's always like that—friends have a hard time talking about business.

Is that all smoothed over?

Oh yeah, totally. I mean, we're putting out their records again. And we toured with them still while they were putting out records with Touch and Go.

What has Merge's role been in local music, choosing to stay indie when you had option not to?

At that time, it really did feel like hooking up with a major was selling out. This was a term that was frequently tossed around back then. You're just going for the bucks, signing the death certificate of your band for the money. That was something we tried to be really hyper-aware of not doing because it really changed the way people perceived you and your band. It took away some of your legitimacy. You wanted to be like Minor Threat, not like the Cure. [*Laughs*] It wasn't punk rock to be on a major label. And there was this thing of independence, being able to make your own decisions, not having anybody else holding the money reins, have influence over what your decisions were. That was just really important to us.

The bands who came along as the millennium turned—Sorry About Dresden, The Comas, The White Octave—what was your relationship to them?

I feel like at that point, we were like old people. Who knows what they thought about us. Some of them had seen us play when they were kids, and they were good bands. By that point, we toured so much, I feel like we were gone so much of the time that in a weird way we became distant from what was going on in town. I didn't always go out and see bands play all the time, I didn't know everybody any more. There were all these new people. I wasn't tied in as I would have been if I hadn't been on tour six months a year.

Do you have insight on why this area has been able to support a thriving music scene—economic factors, cultural, geographical?

The obvious ones to me are the fact that there are three universities close together so you have a lot of young people in a small area. There's something about universities that helps support music scenes, partly because they have radio stations. And we happen to have three good college radio stations here. Also, we had the good fortune of having more than one rock club that punk rock bands could play at. The Brewery, the Cat's Cradle, Point—it's funny, by the time I got here there weren't any shows in Durham usually. I'd heard there used to be—people talked about St Joseph's, an old church where there used to be punk rock shows. And one time, there was sort of a reggae club I saw a band play at in Durham—it may have been Bad Brains. And there was a place called Under the Street that had shows sometimes, I saw Sun Ra there. But it was more likely I'd end up in show in Raleigh or Chapel Hill.

What other scenes was Chapel Hill connected with back then?

There's always people moving here for college, but I feel like the scene here at that time had close times for sure with DC and Chicago. There was a sense of community between bands and labels and you wound up being friends with people in the scenes in those cities, from going to play there and having common interests. I was doing an interview about Rocket From The Crypt the other day and talking about how back then, it felt like a so much smaller of a community that if you were into another band, you would write them a letter and send it to the address on the back of their seven-inch, and maybe you'd put your record with it, and then they'd listen to it and write you back! Now I feel like everything's gotten too big, there's too much. You can't do that anymore, everybody's overexposed. But back then, we wound up knowing Ian McKaye just because we were in a band. Getting to know Drive Like Jehu because they were in a cool band that sounded awesome, and they liked Superchunk and wrote us asking to do a tour of the East Coast, and we wrote them back and said yes. It was really tied together just by our weird interest in making weird music, which doesn't seem weird at all anymore.

What people outside of bands were really important in Chapel Hill scene?

Lane Wurster and Chris Eselgroth worked for Mammoth, but their office was separate the Mammoth offices, and they had their office in the same building where we had Merge for a long time. They did a lot of design for us and helped us out a lot once we had full-length records to manufacture. There was also that guy Kelly [Cox] who started a label a year or two after Merge that didn't last very long, but they had the Big Record Stardom convention, a little music festival that lasted a couple days. It had Madonna on the flyer. And a person that needs to be appreciated—obviously Frank Heath was really important—but Maura Pautrick worked door at the Cradle for 12 years or something. She was awesome. She really cared about music. She was an important person in the whole picture because she was a presence at the club for so long. Gail Murrell also. They were never in bands, but it was their way of participating. They spent a lot of late nights and long hours supporting the scene. And Billy, the bouncer at the Cradle—such a sweetheart.

CHICAGO, ILLINOIS

ILLINOIS

"WE AREN'T ANYTHING."
A DRAG CITY
RECORDS PRIMER

KEVIN McCAIGHY

"I'll be the first to admit that luck has played a huge role in the Drag City story."
Dan Koretzky [1]

Despite being America's third most populous city, Chicago's independent music scene has lagged behind smaller locales such as San Francisco, Seattle and Washington DC, its notoriety dependent upon individuals such as Steve Albini and Billy Corgan rather than a network of locally committed musicians. The second tier elite of hardcore bands like Strike Under, Articles of Faith and The Effigies had unfortunately withered on the vine without the kind of support available elsewhere in the US underground. In the post-hardcore era of the late 1980s and early 1990s, it was incumbent upon fans themselves to take control of whatever the next phase of independent music would be. One such pairing were two friends from Chicago, Dan Koretzky and Dan Osborn. Both in their early twenties, they initiated the Drag City label in 1990 from earnings from their respective jobs in record distribution and video editing, guided purely by their own idiosyncratic musical tastes. Their first run of releases by the likes of Royal Trux, Pavement and Smog would set the trend for the independent rock revival of the 90s. An inventive, highly articulate trio of bands, they embody an experimental, not to say ad hoc approach to rock music that reflected the post-hardcore diaspora. When asked what common ground he shared with his label mates on Drag City, Silver Jews front man David Berman remarked "I know all the bands are obsessed with reading and literature... there's an intellectual streak in all your bands and American rock is all about glorifying stupidity for the most part."[2] Drag City has flourished precisely because it has eschewed local allegiances for a broader view of what independent music can and should be. And unlike their close compatriots Bettina Richards at Thrill Jockey and Tom Hazelmyer at Amphetamine Reptile, Drag City has not become largely synonymous with certain music genres, like post-rock or noise rock. Nor have any notions of world domination led to the kind of after-the-fact apologies that have dogged Sub Pop's fortunes since their grunge heyday.

Drag City is one of the most successful independent US labels because of its willingness to embrace music from across the world, and re-orient its focus accordingly. This primer aims to illustrate that widescreen worldview by illuminating some of the more occluded treasures of the Drag City discography as well as a few of its acknowledged classics, ranging from a colossal compilation by Royal Trux—the most important band in the label's history—to their monastic Japanese brothers in the ethereal psychedelic rock collective Ghost. Their hometown roots are more than covered by writer/illustrator Steve Krakow, who in addition to publishing the brilliant esoteric periodical *Galactic Zoo Dossier* is a first rate chronicler via his *Secret History of Chicago Music* comic for *The Chicago Reader*. From adopted outsiders like Scout Niblett to the fierce abstractionism of US Maple, these ten dispatches more than convey the longevity and power of what I consider the finest American independent record label of the past quarter century.

"The odd things that's cool... is that Drag City doesn't say 'This is what we are'. It says kinda like, 'I don't know what the fuck we are. We aren't anything.'"
Jennifer Herrema [3]

Royal Trux
Singles, Live, Unreleased
1997

"Royal Trux is an entity, that's the way we've always been."[4]

The story of Royal Trux is, in effect, the story of Drag City Records. Originating from the ashes of Pussy Galore in the New York noise scene of the late 1980s, guitarist Neil Hagerty and singer Jennifer Herrema assumed a regal position from the outset, embarking upon a 13-year career that was one of the most reckless, extravagant and experimental witnessed in rock at the close of the twentieth century. Drag City's very first release in 1989 was "Hero Zero"/"Love Is..." Royal Trux's debut seven-inch single; a howling tranche of maniacal trash rock that presages the entirety of their illustrious musical career. The band's career outside of their full-length album releases can yield a greater understanding of both their music and the environment in which it was created. To that end, their consequent leaps forward (and their often truculent ventures backward) are collected on the vast *Singles, Live, Unreleased* compilation, a 32-track riot of action, intuition and no little experimentation. This crucial early period saw Neil and Jennifer progress from the thin but promising material of their 1988 album debut into fully-fledged composers, honing their writing and production skills in seclusion before drip-feeding the results out on small runs of seven-inch vinyl, letting them detonate out in the world. The non-chronological running order divorces each pair from its mate—"Steal Your Face" from "Gett Off", "Back to School" from "Cleveland" etc.—and scatters them among Peel session tracks and live rarities never previously heard. The version of "Teeth" from *Dante's Vendetta* on cd is among the most vehement of clutch of live tracks present. The list of cover version crimes is almost infinite, but Neil and Jennifer's taste with regard to covers is exquisite, encompassing Milton Nascimento ("Faca Amolada"), The Godz ("Woman", here retitled "Womban"), Jefferson Airplane ("Law Man") and "Suicide is Painless (Theme from M.A.S.H.)" are acts of obscurantism as well as eerie taxidermy, consummately filling the lifeless space of the originals whilst leaving you in no doubt that the vessel they inhabit is reassuringly dead. "Vile Child" and "Lucy Peaupaux", two outtakes from *Twin Infinitives* are among the most rewarding of the self-penned material, reiterating the prominence of that album to any understanding of the group. Royal Trux takes its place at the heart of a key trio of groups organised around personal and artistic partnerships that include Boss Hog and White Zombie. Their signature early albums—*Soul Crusher*, *Cold Hands* and *Twin Infinitives*—are all exemplars of non genre-aligned experimental rock that is currently without the acclaim they deserve. Their finest single is again split apart: "Mercury", an atonal blues-dirge duet of super-stoned proportions, is the kind of mess that two screeching Bowery bums would invent spilling out of some early morning dive. Neil's higher vocals flop and flail over Jennifer's unutterably harsh yelling, while some evil synth glowers in the background. It was like shock treatment. "Shockwave Rider" is another experiment that bore fruit, an impossible funk/hip hop groove snakes and shakes behind one of Neil's most rhyme-busting vocals. Lean guitars burn up the highway, Jennifer's cruise control drawl is laconic in the extreme. Released just as their major label experience was coming to a close, *Singles, Live, Unreleased* is a valuable repository for all of the Royal Trux's early work, setting the seal on their swerve-turns and false finishes in readiness for the most productive and imperial phase of their career.

Plush
More You Becomes You
1998

"It took me a long time to come to the conclusion that the songs were gonna be heard in this way. I fought against something that I created, but I knew this was the only way I could get the songs to work." [5]

The one man enigma that is Liam Hayes AKA Plush would be assured of a place in the pantheon of great Drag City releases even if he had never produced anything other than his 1994 seven-inch "Three Quarter Blind Eyes"/"Found A Little Baby". The supernatural wonder that encompassed this daring brace of songs whetted many an appetite for what would come next. What no-one expected was a seductive, intimate suite of songs that would hold the listener in thrall to their beauty. "More You Becomes You" is as fragile as a cobweb, with Hayes' soothing, aching vocal at its commanding core. "Virginia" is a fragmentary show tune, a lament that feels as its place at a downbeat finale has been denied. Instead, it finds itself as a baleful opener, a drowsy slice of solitude that breaks open the beguiling splendour of the title track. Its evening sprawl attunes the listener to its rhythm, singular and sparing. Hayes' nasal moans are in themselves an uncorrected expression, lingering in their own space, seemingly unheard. That shell is broken by "(I Didn't Know) I Was Asleep", a magnificent climb towards a pinnacle as Hayes' attempts at the word "so", at first faltering and then exultant are moments of sheer ecstasy, albeit of a timorous variety. "The Party I and II" are eerie droplets of nightlife and a soul bared too easily—an evocation of the outsider's curse. The album's centrepiece is "Soaring and Boring", which rivals Laura Nyro in its elliptical lyricism and carefree (though minor key) execution. Its lovelorn grandeur evidently impressed someone enough to feature both it and Hayes in the Hollywood adaptation of Nick Hornby's book *High Fidelity*. Its place in the film seems bathetic, but Hayes' fleeting appearance transcends his surroundings and all the more forcefully foregrounds the greatness of song itself. "See it in the Early Morning" is its polar opposite, a crestfallen snapshot of a loner delivered in an anguished falsetto. Hayes' long, sorrowful delivery of the solitary word "yeah" intimates that there isn't much time or energy left. "Save the People" is another allusion to Nyro, imploring yet not desperate, a slow-motion display of stride piano and gossamer arrangement that comes to rest alongside the crepuscular chords of final track "The Sailor". It ripples with a twilit gravitas, sensing that the end is upon us. Hayes provides the vocal anchorage, a transfixing presence with his entreaties to "find our secret hideaway". A heart-rending suite of minutely crafted songs, *More You Becomes You* has lost none of its magical attributes. Factually the album barely touches 29 minutes: in reality, the album lasts an eternity.

The Nig-Heist
s/t
1998/2011

Question: "I never understood why [Black Flag] would take Nig-Heist or Tom Troccoli's Dog along as support... there were indeed some bad vibes at the centre of the whole operation."[6]

Answer: "The Nig-Heist... was a natural outgrowth of Mugger's personality and the musical interests of the Black Flag road crew (Mugger, Spot, Davo and others)... they cut quite a profile in... depressing and reactionary situations. And if you didn't know they were crew, you'd take them for stars."[7]

In the annals of provocation, almost nothing possesses the toxic power of this irredeemably heinous release. At a time when rock'n'roll stand accused of being terminally co-opted and diluted beyond all recognition, where the impact of taboo symbols and transgressive actions have been denuded of all meaning, it takes a slice of vinyl that is so vicious, so deranged and so righteously offensive to shake anything loose from within our fried out synapses. The sole album by The Nig-Heist, made up of members of the notorious SST road crew, remains one of the all-time great seismic shocks of modern culture. A true product of its time and of its lustful and transient membership, it casts a pall over all who hear it. And consequently, you are demonstrably better for it.

Conceived by Mugger as a band parallel to his duties as Black Flag roadie and all round SST employee, The Nig-Heist took off as early as 1981 with the scorching "Walking Down Your Street" seven-inch. A raw as glass debut, it was a gut wrench track in the LA aftermath of the Germs' demise. (Germs insider Rob Henley was involved in the original "The Nig-Heist" track that features on the *Chunks* compilation). But the following full-length was something else entirely. When Michael Azerrad asserts that The Nig-Heist "may also have been some sort of manifestation of Black Flag's collective id", he is dead on.[8] The cover alone makes that abundantly clear: "The cover was Spot's idea: Chatty Cathy going down on Knucklehead while he pulls her string, perfectly drawn by Kurt Markham's girlfriend Nancy Maurer." [9]

The twin obsessions of sex and money dominate proceedings, from the insolence of "Life in General" with its bellowed chorus of "money is sex/and sex is life!" to the scabrous lechery of "Hot Muff". Mugger's adolescent vocals heckle and sneer, lurking behind primitive expressions of desire that are nothing if not universal on their coherence. Indeed, this is the very ground on which David Lee Roth staked his claim to rock'n'roll infamy. If you think the likes of "Balls of Fire" and "Surfbroad" are beyond the pale (and hey, why wouldn't you?), consider the thematic delights of Van Halen's 1981 album *Fair Warning*, released at the time The Nig-Heist album was being recorded. The former prom queen debased by porn in "Dirty Movies" and the litany of women who look "so fucking good!" in "Sinner's Swing" have been recast as the prey of the Black Flag road crew. Mugger even appropriates Roth's vocal style, aping his falsetto wail during "Balls of Fire". The album's second side is a hardcore blast—"Woman Drivah" and the hot-rod galvanised "Hot Rod" keeps the pressure on and is sonically in sympathy with their big brother band's *My War* era. Drag City deserves immense credit for keeping this decidedly unrighteous cacophony in print for so many years. It deserves your opprobrium and undying respect.

US Maple
Acre Thrills
2001

Furtive, oblique, recalcitrant; US Maple are all of the above, and more. This native Chicago quartet was responsible for some of the most wilfully obtuse and utterly sharp rock music to have emerged from the Drag City label. Their early works—*Long Hair in Three Stages*, *Sang Phat Editor* (both released on cult Chicago-based label Skin Graft)—were the product of a vital, wrenching approach to rock music, in pursuit of non-rock forms using the very guise of rock'n'roll itself. This was not deconstruction; this was a disassembling, a stripping down for parts and taking what was optimal. As singer Al Johnson explained in an interview with *The Wire* magazine:

"... early in 1995 the four of us met... to discuss a way in which to erase the rock'n'roll from our collective minds. Having grown up in Chicago during the late 70s stamped a delicious hard rock imprint into everyone concerned. So we set out to devise a method for reorganising the rock'n'roll, keeping what we feel are its most important core elements; terror, mischief, song, scummy chops etc.."[10]

No other group was as forensic or as intuitive as US Maple in heading for musical hinterlands only previously touched by the likes of Captain Beefheart and the Magic Band. That precedent, such as it is, boils down to at best one or two tracks from *Lick My Decals Off, Baby*, specifically the glorious guitar improve piece "The One Red Rose I Mean". Guitarists Todd Rittman and Mark Shippy and drummer Pat Samson take whatever imprint that piece left in its wake and run it into the ground, firstly on *Talker* 1999, their sepulchral and charred debut for Drag City, and then their magnum opus, *Acre Thrills* released in 2001. That powder blue sleeve interrupted by magic marker scrawl contains the most focused and rewarding compositions of the band's career. "Mr Digital" is anything but; instead it's a hard analogue scrabble of forced guitar prods and vocal rebuttals, parched and (seemingly) incoherent. Similarly, "Obey Your Concert" is a comedic hurtle through misheard conversations and counterclockwise guitar refrains. These are just some of the qualities that led Sasha Frere Jones to describe the band as "...

odder than a nine dollar note but as visceral as AC/DC".[11] In that vein, US Maple's spectacular re-rendering of AC/DC's "Sin City" is still one of the great unknown cover versions, a serious display of 'scummy chops'. What really distinguishes the band is its extraordinary singer. In Al Johnson, US Maple possessed a voice so dishevelled and so fraught that it seems to lose its way at every intake of breath. Johnson rivals the monstrous Peter Thomas of Pere Ubu for twitching, perspiring charisma; his lyrics breathe down your neck and cajole ever moment of attention from you. Often sinister, nearly threatening, always sardonic, Johnson's lyrics are a constant source of humour and wonderment: "Is he jelly king, am I my brother's flag?" ("Total Fruit Warning"); "And you say it's time to breast" ("Babe"); "Let's chain across a super floor" ("Chang, You're Attractive"). The glory of US Maple rests in all its glory on the signature track "Make Your Bedroom Great", a sweeping sigh of a melody carried out with boundless efficiency and no small amount of cheer. It is their very finest moment.

The Fucking Am
Gold
2004

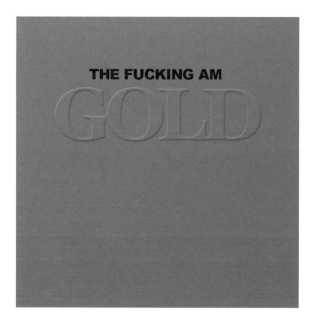

The Chicago independent music scene has been well served by both Drag City and its close cousin, Thrill Jockey for the past two decades. Founded in 1992 by former A&R woman Bettina Richards, Thrill Jockey's affiliation with the post-rock scene was concurrent with Drag City's devotion to all branches of independent rock. Their longstanding work with Trans Am has paid rich dividends, and their close links with The Fucking Champs (in terms of both personnel and a broadly conceptual approach to making music) allowed for a cross pollination of ideas that would lead to some extraordinary music. Their *Transchamps* EP in 2001 was a fitful but intriguing first attempt at collaboration. By 2002, the Champs' aggressive, metal-oriented style and constant inversion and reiteration of riff rock forms had reached a zenith with the release of *V*, and after the departure of founder member

Josh Smith were at something of a crossroads. Similarly, Trans Am's singular post-rock structures had given way to a wider, more electronics-based dynamic, resulting in the brilliant but criminally underrated electroclash odyssey *TA*. What followed was one of the great Drag City masterpieces: *Gold*. The title is no statement of hubris: the crunching impact of the Champs' guitar style meshes perfectly with Trans Am's expansive sense of electronic melody. The euphoric opener "Bad Leg" is an acute demonstration of the collaboration's wider aspirations, a synergistic deployment of both band's resources for maximum effect. The searing twin guitar harmonies of Tim Green and Tim Soete are ably augmented by Nathan Means' synthesizer beams, but this album bears no trace of hierarchy or neat compositional divisions. "The Gauntlet", with its treated vocal intimidation and smeared electronic drones appears to be pure Trans Am, but melodic neon guitars coolly undercut its mood of alienation. The drumming of guest musicians Jon Theodore is one of the album's greatest attributes. An ex-member of cult Chicago rock group Golden as well as a touring drummer for Royal Trux, Theodore's considerable skills are put to the ultimate test here, and at no stage is he less than outstanding. The casual trickery of his fills on "Powerpoint" are in contrast to his best Brian Downey impression on "Doing Research for an Autobiography", a rollicking boogie track that is so smooth and easeful that it managed to ignite the true spirit of Thin Lizzy in everyone present. Phil Manley and Tims Green and Soete are channelling their inner Scott Gorham for the duration, and are clearly enjoying every second of their interplay. On "Taking Liberties" everyone is so in the pocket that vocalist Jillian Iva is able to steal the plaudits right out from underneath them. Her show-stopping performance at the core of this straight up hard rock nugget is the most impressive of the sundry guest contributions. The album's concluding trilogy is the masterstroke, building from the soft shimmer of "Acoustico Gomez" into the swarming stoner-esque rock of "Elastico Gomez" into the climactic riff hypnosis of "Electrico Gomez". A cascade of guitar insurgency and electronic symmetry, *Gold* deserves to be regarded as one of the last decade's most neglected masterpieces.

Galactic Zoo Dossier

The work of artist and writer Steve Krakow first came to my attention via the brilliant but short-lived pro wrestling fanzine *CLAW HOLD!*. An article entitled "Rockin' Wrestlin'" ran down the various highlights of rock music's dalliance with wrestler such as "Exotic" Adrian Street, Hulk Hogan and the legendary Michael "PS" Hayes in an exuberant and witty upper case alongside deftly drawn visuals of each grappler. The mere fact that Krakow would recommend Hayes' outrageous *Off the Streets* album was enough to hook me into his later work in the magazine extravaganzas known as *Galactic Zoo Dossier*. Taking its name from an album by Arthur Brown's Kingdom Come (the death mask-sporting court jester of UK prog), its nine issues span over a decade of independent, underground and extreme music, as well as a good old fashioned rock collector fetish for the deluge of great neglected bands that occupy rock's great history. Each issue is a mine of information, a labour of love wrapped in a sleeve of eye-watering intensity. The image of a cloak-sporting guitarist in vivid purple and yellow that adorns issue 5 (Winter 2001) is one of the most striking Krakow has ever devised; its contents veer between adoration of past greats such as The West Coast Pop Art Experimental Band and Eddie Shaw of The Monks to interviews with contemporary groups like Electric Wizard (coinciding with the release of their classic album *Dopethrone*). This issue also heralded the start of the "Damaged Guitar God" cards; a series of specially designed and collectible cards featuring the very best guitar heroes from all over the world. With each set of exquisitely rendered portraits and couple with concise appreciation Krakow continues to outdo himself, chronicling the achievements of Pip Proud, Robert Quine, Matt Bower, John Morton, Gabor Szabo and Helios Creed to name but a lauded few. He has recently branched out into a newer series of "Astral Folk Goddesses", featuring the likes of Judee Sill, Dorothy Moskowitz and June Tabor—another lovingly crafted series gratefully received. Krakow was also ahead of the curve in his appreciation of Sixto Diaz Rodriguez (issue 6, Summer

2005) well before *Searching for Sugarman*. The core of Krakow's obsession is on local underground scenes that remain undocumented; whether they are located in Detroit, Dorset or Dusseldorf, he will seek to capture them with his accessible and immediate draftsmanship. More recent issues have expanded into book form and have included greater contributions from guest writers, notably Scott Wilkinson and Byron Coley. The rate of publication is slow (five issues in 11 years) but each successive monument to the obscure overwhelms any lingering impatience. Krakow's attention to detail, the magazine's sumptuous production values and fascination-triggering visual and prose styles have given immense amounts of pleasure to similarly obsessed readers around the world. Long may he continue to do so.

Ghost
Hypnotic Underworld
2004

Drag City's patronage of non-US bands is best exemplified by their enduring collaboration with Japanese psych-rock unit Ghost. Beginning with a reissue of their stunning debut album in 1997 (originally released on P.S.F. in 1990), theirs is a fruitful partnership that continues to produce rich results to this day. In his exhaustive discography of P.S.F. Records, Garry Davis observed of the group's development:

"Starting as a loosely organized improve group in the 80s, their gradual transformation into a somewhat more song-oriented entity has seen them blossom into one of the most essential 'psychedelic' bands of modern times (their take on the genre being quite updated and unconventional—not throwback material at all)."[12]

Their evolution under the esteemed leadership of their founder and lead vocalist Masaki Batoh led the group away from the more devotional aspects of their earlier works, and towards a more refined and intoxicating hybrid sound which culminated with their 2004 album *Hypnotic Underworld*. Their previous album *Tune In Turn On Free Tibet* (1999) opened with a gargantuan title track, and *Hypnotic Underworld* follows that example, reveling in an epic four-part sequence that gradually girds its sonic loins through spacious and ethereal drifts, eventually arriving at a woozy aural bliss state suffused with blaring saxophone interjections and stark atonal piano. Its labyrinthine structure builds to a climactic frenzy at the conclusion of "Aramaic Barbarous Dawn"—another clue to the progressive intensity woven by the group's elite players. The complex interplay of Takuyuki Moriya's bass sturdiness and Kazuo Ogino's melodic sharpness at the piano is a delight, notwithstanding the contributions of one of the Japanese underground's greatest musicians. Michio Kurihara has been an exalted member of so many extraordinary groups and collaborations that it is difficult to pick just one example of his genius. However, this album possesses one such example in its searing centrepiece "Hazy Paradise". As a slice of modern psychedelia it is unsurpassed; Batoh's lilting falsetto is borne skyward by Kurihara's soaring, scalding guitar tone. It is a sound so pure and resonant that in my opinion easily surpasses the work of Kurihara's avowed hero, the late Quicksilver Messenger Service guitarist John Cipollina.

The baroque pop atmosphere is deepened by the reverie "Kiseichukan Kite" and the thrilling "Kite", both haunting and flecked by dissonance that casts doubt upon their supposed easefulness. Batoh's lithe vocal style is both affectless and poised, his lugubriousness fully countered by the mystic shriek magic that Kurihara unfurls at the climax of "Kite". Ghost are a group that make every grandiose statement appear effortless, every minute glimmer of melody seem intrinsic. The late Doors shuffle groove of "Ganagmanag" is a poignant maze of flute and flutter, a gorgeous oasis within its multifaceted surroundings. The bouzouki canter of "Holy High" is the brief respite before the heavy-hitting splendour of the album's finale. "Dominoes— Celebration for the Gray Days" is a spectacular burst of rock theatre entirely befitting an album created and realised on a truly vast scale.

Monotonix
Body Language
2008

You wake up in a pool of your own sweat, muscles aching as never before. Your head is throbbing from the most concussive hangover you have ever experienced. Scratches and stains cover what is left of your clothing. What has happened to you? Only when your hands twitch does it register that something is seared into the flesh of one palm; a scorched CD jewel case emblazoned with the words barely visible beneath the encrusted dirt—*Body Language* by Monotonix.

Monotonix were a force of nature, their recordings mere souvenirs of what had to be experienced live—a never forgotten head rush of mischievous garage mayhem that both shocked and captivated everyone who was exposed to them. The group was formed in 2005 in Tel Aviv, a remarkable place of origin for what was to become one of the most astonishing live acts of the last decade. To that end, *Body Language* adheres to the Mike Watt maxim that everything, even records, are meant to act as flyers for live shows. It kicks off with a prime piece of fatback garage rock in "Lowest Dive" as the vast weight of Yonatan Gat's effusive guitar raunch piles up behind Ran Shimoni's devastating backbeat. In vocalist Ami Shalev, Monotonix possessed one of the most extraordinary live performers of the last decade. The follically blessed front man was the impish focal point of every show, a prankster who would wrestle with his band, tip over drinks, kick over obstacles and conjure up a spell of pure anarchy that always propelled the band onward. A case in point is their signature track, "Summers and Autumns". Yat's titanic riff remains the most memorable part of any Monotonix show, its strength and deceptive elasticity is held firmly in place by Shalev's caustic rasp, which wriggles dementedly over the ensuing wreckage. Their skeletal line up belied their considerable chops as musicians. Amidst the bad to the bone starkness of the title track are piano flourishes that cannot help but further illuminate its strident structure. Shimoni and Gat are so in the pocket, so in sync with each other, punctuating the bitumen grunt of "Deadly Weapon" so aggressively that it threatens to drive them completely off the rails. Gat's guitar heroics are the perfect counterweight to the showmanship of Shalev, a fuzz ball of perpetual motion that pays off just as handsomely when the intensity slackens. "On the Road" cuts such a rug that, if you're not careful, will set your shoes on fire. Recorded in three days with the help of Tim Green, *Body Language* could be seen as a simple document of what truly was a not-to-be-missed live phenomenon. But that would be as disservice to the compositional skill and dexterous musicianship displayed throughout a record that doesn't even hit the 25-minute mark. Their follow up album *Not Yet* is another superior offering, and their split seven-inch single with RTX was one of the all-time great killer garage band hookups. Their break-up in 2011 was unexpected, and they are sorely missed. A legion of battered, bruised and elated fans salutes them still.

Scout Niblett
"It's Time My Beloved"
2009

"I know most music I love is American, and I do feel displaced. But (in Britain) I'm seen as an American and in the States as a Limey. So I don't feel like I fit any place."[13]

As an artist, Scout Niblett often feels lost to us on this side of the Atlantic; a performer that made her start in music here and entranced so many with her stark early work and compelling live shows before heading for the US to find new challenges for her nascent talents. But the continual development and maturity of her work ensures that she is never very far from anyone prepared to listen. "It's Time My Beloved", her only release of 2009, is a prime example of the leaps forward that her music has taken. "It's Time" places Niblett's keening vocal front and centre. Its delicate, brooding atmosphere with its loping downward guitar figure stings waspishly in the background. The snap of her military snare gives the track a dark momentum, increasing in intensity until the song assumes its fullest scale with a scourging guitar solo worthy of the great mystic guitar master himself, Michio Kurihara. The abrasive sting of "My Beloved" is crisp and stark, a solitary slice of romance with skipping, hypnotic tempo. The plaintive resonance that Scout exhibits on "Kiss", her magnificent duet with Bonnie Prince Billy returns here with a vocal sultriness that bursts with long arcs of anguish cries and passionate pleading. Niblett transforms the phrase "my beloved" into a vow of enduring love so forceful it is a truly raw listening experience. As with "It's Time", the compositional control finally is broken down, as "My Beloved" rushes to a breathless, hectic conclusion, a blaze of scrubbed guitars and collision drums. These songs of endless ardour occupy a finely articulated and intimate space, and are by no means the choicest of her latest works. They merely happen to be my favourites amid a sea of tantalising candidates.

"I do like how, in America, people just do things they want to do much more than people I know here (in the UK). I think we're too aware of what we should be doing with our lives."[14]

Black Bananas
Rad Times Xpress IV
2012

After releasing the stunning *Pound for Pound* album in 2000, Royal Trux unexpectedly split up in mysterious circumstances. Neil Hagerty forged his own path, taking a circuitous route via a clutch of solo works, then as part of Weird War and then The Howling Hex, where he has remained ever since. Jennifer Herrema dropped out of sight altogether, and it seemed that the old fire had died. With her relocation to California and a crew of young guns by her side, notably her songwriting cohort Nadav Eisenman and guitar hero Jaimo Welch, she returned in 2004 with her new band RTX, and a debut album that was part Blue Öyster Cult homage, part *Rocky IV* soundtrack. *Transmaniacon* was a raucous yet utterly calculated quantum leap forward for Herrema and her new cadre of Californian band mates. "Joint Chiefs", their colossal stadium rock reworking of the Royal Trux song classic "Shockwave

Rider" pointed the way ahead. This was Joan Jett-style bubblegum metal to the maximum, with riffs laid out in mountainous heaps of incomparable rock swagger. RTX were a powerhouse unit that cultivated a bubblegum stadium metal sound over three killer albums before the funkadelic fibres twitching at their core instigated their sudden transformation into Black Bananas in late 2011; a move that took everyone by surprise. The promo ad shot for the album (using the album's harshest synth blaster "Do It") was a dizzying collage of neon urban noir and would-be Giallo horror, lashed together with imagery only fans of Stephen J Cannell could love. With *Rad Times Xpress IV*, Herrema and her longhaired honchos fashioned a work of mind-bogglingly infectious space funk: not so much a radical departure as an intergalactic lurch. The album is festooned with grooves so ass-quakingly righteous that they practically squelch beneath your feet, from the cyborg boogie of "TV Trouble" and the hard party anthem-in-waiting "Rad Times". The George Clinton vibrations that permeated the run-out groove of *Transmaniacon* closer "Resurrect" are now all embracing. Always knowingly outlandish, Herrema's dalliance with her auto tuner goes well past the point of consummation on the jaw-dropping "Hot Stupid", just one slice of (beyond) genius hybrid rock that is as infectious as it is ridiculous. The rock hard mind crush of "My House" mines that same free-wheeling style of unreconstructed rock, where Welch is able to showcase his instinctive talents with a display of furious guitar flash. Black Bananas mines an even richer seam of skewed space funk, hard rock dynamite and pro wrestling theatricality than anyone thought was possible. Time has been kind to Herrema, and it's only going to be more interesting from here on in. Here's to whatever comes next.

Notes

1. Howland, Don, "Drag Kings: Chicago's Drag City is America's Best Record Label", *SPIN*, November 1993, p. 101.
2. Howland, Don, "Drag Kings...", p. 102.
3. Howland, Don, "Drag Kings...", p. 152.
4. Neil Hagerty, Royal Trux interview, *The Wire,* issue 199, September 2000, p. 27.
5. Plush interview with *NME*, 12 September 1998, p. 22.
6. John Spencer, JSBX tour diary, *The Stool Pigeon*, October/November, 2012.
7. Carducci, Joe, "The Nig-Heist", *Life Against Dementia*, Redoubt Press, 2011, p. 219.
8. Azerrad, Michael, *Our Band Could Be Your Life*, London: Back Bay Books, 2001, p. 51.
9. Carducci, Joe, *Enter Naomi*, Redoubt Press, 2007, p. 50.
10. Al Johnson, US Maple interview, *The Wire*, issue 185, p. 15.
11. Frere Jones, Sasha, "Hairballing America", *The Wire*, issue 185, p. 15.
12. Davis, Garry, *Arcane Candy*, fanzine issue 2, 2003, p. 31.
13. Scout Niblett interview, *Comes with a Smile*, issue 12, Summer 2003, p. 47.
14: Scout Niblett interview, p. 47.

SEATTLE, WASHINGTON

"IT'S NOT WHY
WE'RE DOING THIS/
WHY CAN'T YOU
FUCKING GET IT?"
THE GITS "SLAUGHTER OF BRUCE"

PAVEL GODFREY

This is about underground bands from Seattle and the scene they created. It is not about grunge, at least not directly. That story is important, but it has been told many times over, and it doesn't come close to compassing the incredibly rich, potent underground scene from which Mudhoney, Soundgarden, and Nirvana first emerged.

Grunge was simply *a* Seattle sound, one among many. And while grunge was a uniquely American aesthetic, traceable back to The Stooges and The Sonics, it emerged from an environment where British music was taken seriously—more seriously, perhaps, than in the rest of the American underground. The swinging, choppy rhythms of bands like Soundgarden, Mudhoney, and TAD had roots in dark UK post-punk. The punk-metal hybridisation of Nirvana was anticipated by a generation of hardcore bands who looked to Bristol and the Midlands more than to DC and Los Angeles.

If there is any polemical thrust to what follows, it is not against grunge or the grunge bands, but against the way we have inadvertently reduced the history of Seattle music to the history of a single label—Sub Pop. It's important to broaden our perspective on what happened in this city between the mid-80s and the mid-90s. Some of the bands covered here achieved notoriety in their time, and some have been mentioned in the extensive writing on grunge, but none of them have received the attention they deserve. Let's focus on some new characters and follow them through a decade of heavily amplified creation and destruction.

Post-Punk Prehistory

Seattle in the early 80s did not have cohesive punk and art-rock scenes in the way that Los Angeles, Washington DC, and New York City did. It was too small, and too culturally isolated. But that sense of inhabiting a shared space and sharing a common calling gave the Seattle scene its own unique strength—a spirit of openness, adventure, and exchange. Daniel House of Skin Yard and C/Z Records remembers this atmosphere fondly:

"Seattle had such a wealth of different kinds of bands. And before it got really popular, what was really fun was that different kinds of bands would all play together on the same bill. So you might have a total thrash metal band playing with a wavy 80s pop band playing with a rockabilly band, and then maybe you'd have an electronic band or a surf band. We would all go to each other's shows. It hadn't started to get quite as factioned out."

Much has been written on the foreshadowing of grunge by a chaotic noise-rock band called The U-Men, but The U-Men also need to be understood in their contemporary context, as Americans who were paying careful attention to British post-punk and goth. Indeed, this was one of the major tendencies in Seattle's pre-Sub Pop underground. Producer and Skin Yard guitarist Jack Endino quips: "In 1985, post-punk wasn't very 'post' yet—it was current!" The U-Men were by no means the earliest band influenced by this sound: "One of the biggest bands in Seattle circa 1982 was The Blackouts, who were explicitly post-punk/goth.... And they left town and mutated into Ministry!"

The Blackouts started making neurotic, noirish new wave in 1979, but they were already working towards something harder and stranger. By 1980, when they released the *Men In Motion* EP, frontman Erich Werner used a bizarre, whooping vocal style, and played guitar with a clangorous attack that suggested the Gang of Four. Roland Barker was making the switch from sci-fi synthesizers to saxophone, which he played like an ancient ram's horn without losing his subtle popcraft. Their drummer, Bill Rieflin, could pile on weight in staggered rhythms then switch to a disco beat in an instant, but on the record it sounded like he was holding back.

The Blackouts found their stride on the "Exchange of Goods"/"Industry" single, which was recorded in the fall of 1981 and released later in the year on a British label, Situation 2. Barker's brother, nicknamed "Ion", had replaced their original bassist, and he played powerful, pitch-black riffs that reeked of The Birthday Party and dub reggae.[1] The whole band seemed to go unhinged, throwing out their pop structures and locking into Rieflin's militant dance grooves. This new style was almost certainly influenced by Killing Joke, and it paralleled the work of PiL and Liquid Liquid, but there was nobody who sounded *like* The Blackouts. Werner and Barker had a *sui generis* way of shaping melodies, voice and saxophone intertwining in a Dionysiac wail.

Daniel House encountered The Blackouts at their peak, and speaks about them with a reverence he reserves for few other bands:

"I remember seeing them in '81 or '82. I saw them every chance I got. It was mindblowing, it was unlike anything I'd ever heard. Their sense of urgency and the things they did rhythmically... Bill Rieflin was such a great drummer. They were incredibly dynamic musically and as performers."

But at the height of their success in Seattle, The Blackouts left the city looking for a wider audience. They migrated to Boston, where they recorded the brilliant, industrial-leaning *Lost Soul's Club* EP, and then ended up adrift in San Francisco, where they ended the band in 1985. But it would be wrong to say they split up. Rieflin and the Barker brothers realigned with Al Jourgensen as the new industrial-punk version of Ministry.

Back in their hometown, The Blackouts had helped inspire a circle of young bands to explore the "angular" riffing and dark atmospheres of post-punk. Their rallying point and practice space was a large, leaky-roofed house on a slumlord-owned block about a mile north of the happening U District. "It was known to us as the Death House", recalls Endino, "because in 1982–83 a band called The Death Of Marat rehearsed there, and a few of the members lived there." Daniel House played bass in The Death of Marat, and Alfred Butler (later of Vexed) played keyboards. According to Endino they were "pretty terrible", and House's own opinion is not so different: "We were a band with lofty ambitions. We were writing stuff that we really couldn't play. We had a handful of fans, but not that many. We were definitely in the art-rock vein, but very noisy, and had weird punk overtones as well."

The Death of Marat left no recorded legacy, and was less significant as an artistic endeavour than as an opportunity for its young members to cut their chops and explore new sounds. Their peers included The Altered, which featured Milton Garrison (later of Vexed) on guitar and Hiro Yamamoto (later of Soundgarden) on bass, and another Milton Garrison project called In Vitro Pope. These groups were constantly exchanging ideas. "When our friends were in any band", says House, "we'd go see each others' new band."

The other early group to emerge from the Death House milieu was, of course, The U-Men, who formed in 1981. Their guitarist, Tom Price, lived at home, and in their early days they practiced in its basement. The U-Men were too rock'n'roll to be a goth band *per se*, but their songs bore what Endino calls "an unmistakable Birthday Party influence". They spent several years honing their sound and playing live to riotous crowds, then released a shockingly mature self-titled EP in 1984. "Shoot 'Em Down" channels the drunken dissonance of Nick Cave and company: vocalist John Bigley rasps his lyrics while Price's skittering guitar plays against a swinging bass riff. "Blight", though, combines this decadent clamour with beautiful, phantasmal melodies and surging hardcore riffs. It is easy to hear how this band paved the way for Mudhoney and Nirvana, but equally easy to hear their debt to The Blackouts and their kinship with dark Los Angeles bands like The Gun Club and Christian Death.

The rise of the U-Men and their galvanising effect on the Seattle scene is amply chronicled elsewhere. What is forgotten is that the noisy, brooding Anglophile aesthetic of the Death House seeped into the roots of grunge. Jack Endino, however, remembers:

"Really early Soundgarden, before their first record, had a definite Bauhaus/ Chrome taste to it. And you can hear it on the very first Nirvana recordings I made in January 1988, which are on side two of *Incesticide*. Nirvana used to refer to them as their 'new wave' tunes, which I thought was a funny description because they obviously meant post-punk."

The Accused

We move, now, from the dreary walls of urban rental houses to the deep green woods of Whidbey Island, northwest of Seattle. Whidbey was, and still is, sparsely populated by Navy families, fishermen, and retirees. Here, in 1981, a young guitarist called Tommy Niemeyer formed a band with his buddies Dana Collins on drums and Chibon "Chewy" Batterman on bass. They were in their early teens, and the only punks on the island. That was as good as painting targets on the backs of their jackets: States Niemeyer:

"They'd put us up against the wall between classes and say 'If you come to school tomorrow wearing that Sex Pistols shirt I'm gonna kick your ass'. And they were serious about it. The look in their eyes was beer-soaked hate. 'Too Drunk To Fuck' was the shirt that really got 'em going."

That sense of being surrounded and hounded might have something to do with the band's confrontational name—The Accused. Some people play music to be part of a scene, but The Accused were a scene unto themselves, writing songs together for kicks, and their mere existence was an act of resistance.

There was no place to play on the island, so they started gigging in Seattle, where they recruited John Dahlin as their vocalist. At this time, bands as disparate

as The Fartz and the Fastbacks were spearheading a strong punk scene. The Accused got their 'in' through The Rejectors, a more experienced South Seattle group who took the younger band under their wing. They would set up in a venue, tell the promoters there were some kids who wanted to jam, and then let The Accused do a quick opening set on their gear. The openers quickly won an audience in their own right, playing furious sets for kids their own age, a few of whom would go on to form Green River.

While most American hardcore bands emulated the spastic attack of Minor Threat or the distorted garage rock of early Black Flag, The Accused were fascinated by Discharge and the UK-82 movement that flourished in their wake. "We wanted to be as heavy as *Hear Nothing, See Nothing, Say Nothing* by Discharge", recalls Niemeyer. "Or as crisp and ripping as *Troops For Tomorrow* by The Exploited. That album just changed my life."

This Anglophilia was unusual at the time. With their white t-shirts and shaved heads, hardcore kids worked hard to differentiate themselves from the leather-clad flamboyance of British punk. But the bands coming out of the UK midlands were heavier and harder, their minimalist riffs driven relentlessly by the "d-beat". The Accused soaked up this brutality and made it their own.

This might have made The Accused pariahs in a city like DC or LA, but they were not the only Seattle band drawn to the extreme side of UK punk. Their friends The Rejectors used post-apocalyptic gasmask imagery long before bands like Nausea and Carnivore popularised it in the United States. The Fartz's Paul Solger wrote dissonant, grinding riffs that were closer to Rudimentary Peni than Black Flag, and their vocalist, Blaine Cook, spewed vile screams modelled on vocalists like Cal from Discharge. But these Seattle groups were part of a scene that extended down the West Coast. Portland was home to an excellent proto-crust band called Final Warning, and also to hardcore titans Poison Idea, who focused on brutality and heaviness in a way that stood out from the USHC sound. (Their *Pick Your King* EP makes prominent use of d-beat rhythms.) San Francisco had Crucifix, who evolved from martial anarcho-punk towards a chaotic, hyperspeed sound reminiscent of Disorder. All these bands were tapped into an international underground as well as local scenes. They had as much in common with spiky-haired punk bands in Scandinavia, Japan, Italy, and Britain as with their local peers in hardcore bands.

The Accused also stood out for their frank and unrepentant embrace of heavy metal at a time when many punks saw it as the enemy. Almost from the beginning, Tommy says, "We had set our mind on incorporating the more raw, exciting elements of the first Iron Maiden album, Tank, and Venom into our music." Even on *Please Pardon Our Noise*, their side of a 1983 split with The Rejectors, you can hear The Accused hinting at metal with metal palm-mutes and solos. This is most explicit on "But What About Later", where Niemeyer switches from chugging d-beat punk into an epic doom riff (or a teenager's bare-bones approximation of one). The whole record is dominated by his precociously heavy guitar sound.

The Accused really came into their own, though, after The Fartz turned into 10 Minute Warning, kicking out Blaine Cook. Cook, in turn, replaced John Dahlin in The Accused, contributing his gruesome screams and reinforcing their interest in metal. This new lineup developed The Accused's inimitable "splattercore" aesthetic. Blaine wrote gruesome lyrics inspired by slasher films and the brutality of real life, while Tommy matched them with his illustrations of Martha Splatterhead, a fearsome, buxom knife-murderer who was his band's answer to Iron Maiden's Eddie or The Misfits' Crimson Ghost. When The Accused played live Blaine took on a mischievous horror persona, presiding over the circle pit like a hobgoblin dancing around a cauldron.

Jeff Gaither and RK Sloane, *Martha's House of Horrors*. Taken from *Martha Splatterhead's Maddest Stories Ever Told*, a comic book conceptualised by the band and published by Monster Comics in '92.

Musically, "splattercore" was one of the earliest, most extreme manifestations of the crossover thrash movement, but The Accused sounded little DRI or Agnostic Front. Where most other crossover groups were punks absorbing the influence of Metallica and Slayer, The Accused had simply come up in parallel to those bands, listening to the same NWOBHM records. Their fellow-travellers were UK "metalpunk" groups like Broken Bones and Sacrilege, German thrash bands like Kreator, and grinding American hardcore outfits like Septic Death.

The Accused's 1986 debut full-length, *The Return of Martha Splatterhead*, came out on Seattle's Subcore Records as the crossover movement reached its peak, but many of its songs dated back several years. Tracks like "Take My Time" and "Slow Death" must have been named as jokes, because they accelerate to ripping speeds. These tempos were not unheard-of in hardcore, but The Accused *sounded* faster than their peers, partly because they had the chops. Where other bands disintegrated into a chaotic blur, The Accused never lost the driving, Discharge-esque pulse that gave their songs momentum. The sense of speed also comes from an extreme contrast with slower Sabbath-esque riffage, the doom sound that was influencing the proto-grunge bands at the time. "Autopsy" opens with a gnarled, atonal riff that wouldn't be out of place on Melvins' *Gluey Porch Treatments*—an album that came out a year later. The heaviest song on the album, though, is "Wrong Side of The Grave", which springs from a punishing metallic groove into a breakdown that out-moshes the Cro-Mags, every riff anchored around Tommy's crisp chugging on an open E string.

Over the next few years The Accused would become even faster, tighter, and more metallic, but they would also suffer several lineup changes that left Niemeyer and Cook as the core of the band. Batterman left in late 1986 or early 1987, just before they recorded *More Fun Than An Open-Casket Funeral* for Combat Records (a major New York punk and thrash label). They replaced him with Alex Sibbald during the recording process, so Niemeyer had to play bass on some of the faster tracks. Collins stayed behind the kit through the recording of *Martha Splatterhead's Maddest Stories Ever Told*, what many consider the definitive

Blaine Cook and Tommy Niemeyer of
The Accused, Portland 1989.

Accused album, but left after Combat dropped the band in 1988. He was replaced by Steve Nelson, and then by Josh Sinder.

By 1990 crossover was obsolete, but on *Grinning Like An Undertaker* The Accused remained a vital force. Sinder was an exceptionally agile drummer who complimented Niemeyer's nimble picking, and together they wrote intricate, grooving thrash tracks. Jack Endino gave it an armour-plated production. While he had worked with heavy bands like TAD, this was his first proper thrash album, and he was astounded by the band's energy: "After a day in the studio with The Accused, I felt like I drank ten cups of coffee! Just from the music! I couldn't even sleep!"

But it is telling that this album came out on Nastymix, an eclectic hip-hop label founded by Seattle rapper Sir Mixalot. In Seattle, as on Whidbey, The Accused had done their own thing. As their sound took shape, they had alienated some of the downtown punk rockers that were their original fanbase: "Not a lot of people were doing that. There were punk purists that were freaking out. Mark Arm, for one, got pretty bummed out. He was a huge Accused fan until we 'went metal!'"

Niemeyer remembers that "there was almost a weird closed-door club thing that we didn't have the key to", but this may have been exacerbated by the band's own contrarian tendencies. The Accused sought out the outrageous and extreme— "the weirder the better" was their rule—and nothing reflected that more than their gore imagery. This conceit, indebted to brutal comix and lo-fi fantasy art, was more likely to appeal to teenage skaters than to the inner circle of pre-grunge dudes obsessed with Iggy Pop and Steve Albini.

The Accused were further marginalised by the Teen Dance Ordinance of 1985. This law required any Seattle venue holding an all-ages show to post a prohibitively expensive bond to insure against damages. Teenagers were the beating heart of the punk scene, so the Teen Dance Ordinance effectively outlawed extreme punk and hardcore in Seattle. Greg Anderson, who was friends with Niemeyer and played guitar in Brotherhood, recalls their plight:

"It was really rough. It pretty much wiped out the hardcore scene. Any local hardcore shows would have to be really underground, in basements, or you'd

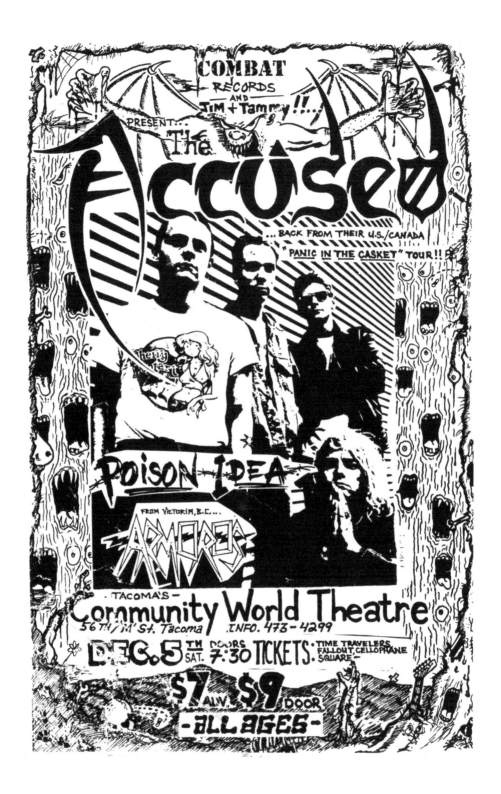

Flyer for an Accused show in Tacoma,
Washington 1987.

Tommy Niemeyer and Blaine Cook, 1989.

By Tom Street.

Legal Representation
Neil Sussman
10727 Interlake Ave., N.
SEA, WA 98133
(206) 363-8070

THE Accused

"KINGS OF SPLATTER"

NASTYMIX

800 Tower Bld.
1809 7th Ave.
SEA, WA 98101
(206) 292-8772

have to go outside the city of Seattle. A lot of stuff happened in Tacoma and Bremerton. And the grunge thing was happening as well. So there weren't any hardcore bands."

With their mix of hard rock, garage, and metal, the bands of the nascent grunge scene were attracting older fans and playing bars. This meant that they were relatively unaffected by the law, and kept playing in the city center even as a huge swathe of the broader punk community was legislated out of existence or banished to the suburbs.

After the release of *Grinning Like An Undertaker*, the seemingly inexhaustible momentum of The Accused started to run out. They were about to lose Sinder to TAD, and Nastymix was spiralling towards insolvency. Niemeyer was playing with a side project called Gruntruck, and starting to enjoy it a lot more than his main band. Labouring under the inebriated auspices of Poison Idea's Thee Slayer Hippie, he laid down the riffs for their final album, *Splatter Rock*. Then, just before The Accused left for a European tour, he quit the band to do Gruntruck full time. The nails were in the coffin.

The Accused perfected a sound that nobody in Seattle directly emulated. They might seem like an evolutionary dead end, but they had a major impact beyond the region, as one of a handful of American bands pushing towards the extremity of grindcore and death metal. And their influence on Seattle has been sorely underrated. In showing that it was possible for punk to get really heavy, and for metal to be really punk, they helped open the door for grunge. A young Mark Arm might've hated The Accused's crossover, but a couple years later he formed Green River, who smashed garage punk into hair metal. The ingredients were very different, but the formula was similar. And suddenly, somehow, it was the cool thing to do. "The irony", Niemeyer notes, "is so frequent and so deep and so blatant."

10 Minute Warning

When The Fartz transformed into 10 Minute Warning they recorded a single tape demo with Blaine Cook on vocals and Duff McKagan on drums. On *Survival Of The Fittest* (1982) they took The Fartz's sound to its logical conclusion—dark, thunderous d-beat hardcore. Then, when Duff started playing guitar alongside Paul Solger, they started writing slower, more sophisticated songs. They kicked out Cook (who continued with The Accused), replacing him with a more rock-oriented vocalist, Steve Verwolf.[2] In the summer of 1984, before recording anything with the new lineup, Duff McKagan left for LA. Bassist Steve Hoffman left at around the same time, so Daniel House stepped in to replace him. For House, this was an opportunity to play with one of his favourite live bands.

As their turbulent lineup history indicates, 10 Minute Warning never fully materialised as a band. They played legendary live shows, but the Verwolf lineup only went into the studio once, in late 1984. The recordings remain unreleased, but Daniel House kindly shared several songs for this project, enough to convey a sense of the music. If 10 Minute Warning had originally worshipped *Hear Nothing, See Nothing, Say Nothing*, they now drew inspiration from the darkest recesses of *Fun House*. "Stooge", built around a frantically looping blues bassline, made that influence explicit. Verwolf sang with an Iggy-esque yowl, drawing out notes and bending pitches in a way that foreshadowed the inflections of Mark Arm and Kurt Cobain. Solger, free from the responsibility of laying down power-chord riffs,

Above left
10 Minute Warning at Metropolis, 1985.

Above right
Daniel House of 10 Minute Warning.

laced the songs with psychedelic leads. There was some metal in the slithering melodies and swaggering rhythms of "Disraeli", but this grandiose, 70s-style metal was distant from the thrash of The Accused, more closely resembling what Soundgarden would play in a year or two. 10 Minute Warning's drummer still used hardcore beats, but now he was playing with them, stretching them out or staggering them, swinging hard. Where before the music had charged ahead, now it loped or prowled.

As a formative band—an idea band—10 Minute Warning resisted reduction to categories. What they were doing was deeply weird. There wasn't a word for it yet, and when there *was* a word it didn't fully encompass what they'd been doing. Given their brief existence and their failure to release any recordings, 10 Minute Warning was one of the most disproportionately fertile bands in rock history. You can hear how their sound formed a blueprint for Green River recordings like *Come On Down*, and you can hear their imprint on early Soundgarden. But the band that directly inherited the strangeness of 10 Minute Warning was Skin Yard.

Skin Yard

After 10 Minute Warning broke up, Daniel House was playing convoluted instrumental compositions in a band called feeDBack with a guitarist named "Nerm" and a powerful, virtuosic drummer—Matt Cameron. But House envisioned a band that would combine the sounds of feeDBack and 10 Minute Warning—"a heavy, psychedelic thing but with a cerebral aspect". He sought a songwriting partner in Jack Endino, a producer who was also an accomplished guitarist.

feeDBack dissolved, and Cameron joined Endino and House in the new project. They jammed extensively, developing polyglot instrumental tracks that Endino half-dismisses as "proggy 'head' music made for our own amusement". These jams developed around Cameron's ability to lock into any difficult riff they threw at him. The band had already written almost an album's worth of material by the time they found a vocalist. While playing a friend's basement party, they asked audience members to try their hands at improvising lyrics. Ben McMillan, an artist and local

Skin Yard, s/t, 1987.

Skin Yard, Love Battery and Hammerbox at the
Central Tavern, 24 November 1990.

scenester, had a booming voice, a frontman's charisma, and the daring to attempt singing over the band's intensely challenging jams. They invited him to join the band, and with his flair for the grotesque, he named it Skin Yard.

The four members came to the band from distinct musical backgrounds, and Skin Yard arose out of the unexplored area where their tastes came together. House was into post-punk as well as prog. Endino loved 70s metal and psych-rock. Cameron was most interested in jazz, while McMillan dug Bowie's more *outré* Berlin albums. "We all liked King Crimson as well as The Stooges", Endino says. These two common reference points could not have been further apart, an early sign of the productive oppositions that would define Skin Yard's music but destroy Skin Yard as a band.

That tension is thinly veiled on their first album, *Skin Yard*, which they recorded shortly before Cameron bounced for the blooming Soundgarden. House and Endino are both quick to point out that, in House's words, "the first record is like nothing else we did subsequently". Compared to feeDBack, Skin Yard was almost a punk band, but they still favoured an intricate, technical approach to songwriting that didn't go over well live: "Audiences (consisting at that time mostly of other musicians) were 'impressed' and clapped politely. You sure couldn't dance to it. It was kind of constipated."

And McMillan, with a booming baritone but no prior experience as a vocalist, found it difficult to sing over the music. Skin Yard was groping towards a vision that hung just out of reach. Still, the first album is an interesting listen on its own terms, a paranoid vortex of spindly leads and "way off-kilter grooves." And it was an illuminating mistake—it gave Skin Yard a clear idea of what they did *not* want to do.

McMillan's role in the band was complicated. With his limited musical background, he at first felt alienated from Skin Yard's involved songwriting process. At times, he seemed like a walking stereotype of rock'n'roll chaos. He frequently missed practices, and drank heavily on tour. But he had a great voice, an innate sense of theatre, and a gift for writing lyrics. Endino got the impression that the singer was, despite his outward bravado, "a really insecure and somewhat neurotic guy", and that insecurity deeply informed McMillan's songs. On "Skins In My Closet", the first song on *Skin Yard*, McMillan sings about our liberating but terrifying potential to shift between social guises, urgently asking "Who am I today?"

At this point, Skin Yard was a twentieth century schizoid band. It was McMillan, with his acute attention to identity and aesthetics, who saw the need for Skin Yard to develop a coherent personality. "He wanted something that would grab people physically and emotionally", Endino remembers. The other guys knew he was right. *Skin Yard* came out in 1986 on House's C/Z Records, but the band was already writing radically different material.

That year, Jack Endino moved into Tom Price's old room in the Death House. Working with Alfred Butler, who was now playing in a band called Vexed, Endino set up a new practice room for Skin Yard in the vast basement: "We began to rehearse there, 20 feet over from where Vexed rehearsed, an arrangement that lasted as long as Skin Yard existed." Shedding their prog skin and grinding out new songs in the bowels of the old house, they channelled the post-punk sounds that had flourished there.

House was a fan of bands like Bauhaus and The Birthday Party, and he was "almost fanatical about early Killing Joke", so it was natural for him to refocus on writing powerful repeating figures. He and Endino contributed equally to the songwriting, but the process often started with one of House's melodic basslines. "I hated Joy Division", says Endino, "but it was interesting not having to be the 'riff'

SKIN YARD

Cruz Records promo.

guy all the time on guitar, it opened up a lot of sonic possibilities." Skin Yard explored these possibilities by jamming. House (or Endino) would bring in a riff or two and the band would use it as the basis for extended improvisation. House recalls how, once every few weeks, "Jack would go through all the tapes from our jams and pull out pieces that he considered the best." In a pre-digital era, combing over all this recorded material must have been a considerable task.

Hallowed Ground, released on Toxic Shock in 1988, is the result of this disciplined process of conceptual and compositional stripping-down. It plays like a dark but revelatory acid trip, or the kind of fascinating half-nightmare that you'd rather not forget. The opening track, "Stranger" turns on the tension between a twitchy riff and a staggering, syncopated mosh breakdown—it's Skin Yard at their most cerebral, and then at their most direct. McMillan sings about a psyche under assault from within, a shadow-self taking shape behind the conscious mind. That neurotic panic, however, discharges into the psych-metal triumph of "Open Fist". Endino unfurls florid solos as McMillan shouts a mystic manifesto: "I made an open fist and punched it into my brain." Again, the mind is challenged or violated, but this time that psychic violence is joyously self-imposed. It opens up the egoistic self to the dizzying possibility of "you and me and us and them... spinning round". Indeed, the listener is spun around by the contrast between "Open Fist" and "Stranger", disoriented and rendered maximally vulnerable to what follows.

The core of *Hallowed Ground* is seven consecutive tracks of madness, some of the heaviest and most harrowing art-rock to come out of America during the 80s. The blasphemous title track is driven by a polyrhythmic pulse that recurs, in altered forms, throughout Skin Yard's discography. Riffs like these exemplify how the band folded the virtuosity of Crimson into the visceral thrash of Killing Joke. "G.O.D." and "In The Black House" are slower songs where Endino layers fragile arpeggios and searing noise over House's heavy grooves. On "Burn", McMillan rants and rages over a set of sadistically dissonant riffs, his refrain a heavily distorted growl. At the three-minute mark the tension is so extreme that the song can only explode, breaking out into a thrashing hardcore beat.

Gregory Gilmore and Ben McMillan.

After all that bizarre and deathly heaviness, "OP4" is a joyful release. On this final track, feeDBack guitarist Nerm joins Skin Yard for a spacious instrumental jam. Pedals blazing, he and Endino trace out arches of echo over a cascading major-scale bassline. This is the psychedelic apex of the album, a vision that brightens even as it subsides.

In a way, *Hallowed Ground* was perfectly timed, because 1988 was the year when the grunge phenomenon truly began. Mudhoney took Seattle by storm with a series of chaotic gigs at packed venues.[3] Sub Pop released a seven-inch featuring "Touch Me I'm Sick" and "Sweet Young Thing Ain't Sweet No More", and then the legendary *Superfuzz Bigmuff* EP. Nirvana released their first single, "Love Buzz", also on Sub Pop. Soundgarden's 1987 EP for Sub Pop, *Screaming Life*, had landed them on Greg Ginn's SST for their debut full-length, *Ultramega OK*. Just a year later, they'd release *Louder Than Love* on A&M, opening up the major-label hunt for Seattle talent.

But the buzz didn't quite touch Skin Yard. In 1989, as people began throwing money at their old friends, they set out on a traditional DIY tour to promote the album. "Back then", House says, "you worked as much as you could leading up to a tour so you could afford to *go* on tour, and the tour usually wouldn't pay for itself. So you'd come back in six weeks and actually be in debt, and have bills to pay." Skin Yard's van kept breaking down because they couldn't afford to repair it properly. Endino and House remember this trip as the "Tour From Hell".

All their frustration and mutual hostility from tour was channelled into the recording sessions for Skin Yard's third album, *Fist Sized Chunks*, which was released by SST subsidiary Cruz Records in 1990. Endino describes it as their "harder/faster" album. This is the closest Skin Yard got to pure body music, lashing out with their sinuous, poly.rhythmic riffs. Looking back on *Fist Sized Chunks*, it sounds like a kind of metal or hardcore, but at the time there was nothing like it. Along with their housemates, Vexed, they foreshadowed the heavily syncopated alt-metal of the 90s. The first track, "Slow Runner", features Tom Niemeyer of The Accused playing rhythm guitar alongside Endino. It's easy to tell who's who—Niemeyer lays down brutal off-time chug while Endino wraps it in eerie harmonies. Niemeyer recalls being "in awe" of Endino, and considers

Above and opposite top
Skin Yard live.

the experience a great honour, which says something about the respect Skin Yard commanded among other Seattle musicians. Even with their nod to thrash, though, Skin Yard kept one foot firmly in abrasive post-punk and psychedelia. Helios Creed, a hero of both Endino and House, joined them on guitar for the epic freakout of "Gentle Collapse".

For Skin Yard, though, the collapse was less than gentle. Unanimously pissed off with one another after recording *Fist Sized Chunks*, they broke up. 14 months later they reformed to record *1000 Smiling Knuckles*, but with McCullum replaced by the classically trained drummer Barrett Martin (later of Screaming Trees). House and Endino agree that this is their favourite Skin Yard album, and Endino thinks of it as the place where the dizzying psych-punk-prog hybrid they'd envisioned on *Skin Yard* really came together. On songs like "Living Pool", for instance, the band lock into their hostile throb without compromising texture and melodicism. The juggernaut title track features a catchy, radio-friendly chorus, but that only makes it heavier. And it culminates in a face-melting guitar solo. Endino comes tearing in on a single note with Sonic Youth-ian skronk power, but then lets it blossom into glorious metal shred.[4]

But Skin Yard's newfound accessibility points to a shift—even as ... *Knuckles* captures all the best qualities of the band, it lacks the roughness and eccentricity of their earlier work. And, more important, it is markedly closer to what people thought grunge was *supposed* to sound like. The production is crisp and up-front, the riffs are a bit more Rock, and you can hear McMillan affecting the drawl of a Layne Staley or a Kurt Cobain (even as he delivers his best performance with Skin Yard). This was clearly a band trying to triangulate between two impulses. McMillan was pushing harder than ever for songs that were "simpler, easier, thicker, and not so cerebral". To House, it seemed that "Ben, more than the rest of us, really wanted rock stardom." While interested in seeing the band succeed, House was personally reluctant to write straightforward rock songs "for the kids".

Even as McMillan and House butted heads, other factors were pulling them away from the band. McMillan had a promising new side project, Gruntruck, and his interest in Skin Yard was waning. House, on the other hand, realised that he could

Skin Yard, *1000 Smiling Knuckles*, 1991.

C/Z Records' *Deep Six* compilation, 1986.

no longer balance touring life with raising a young son and making ends meet. He announced he was leaving the band, but hoped, before he left, to secure them a small development deal with Warner Brothers, record their fifth album, and go with them on a planned European tour.

The rest of the band decided that they'd rather find a new bassist before touring or seeking any kind of deal. Skin Yard recruited Pat Pedersen and they did the tour, but they were haunted by the curse of the Tour From Hell—all their gear was stolen. Upon their return, they recorded *Inside The Eye* for Cruz, and then broke up. That final album came out in 1992, after Skin Yard had ceased to exist.

Skin Yard remained on the margins of the grunge boom. Partially, this was by choice—they were not writing commercial music, even towards the end. But with the alternative rock audience primed for increasingly heavy fare, Skin Yard could conceivably have found a much wider audience than they did. And in many ways they were at the very epicentre of the Seattle scene. They had contributed tracks to the grunge-defining *Deep Six* compilation (1986). Endino produced albums like *Bleach*, *Screaming Life*, and *Superfuzz/Bigmuff*. As head of C/Z Records, House ran the nearest local rival to Sub Pop. So why didn't Skin Yard ever "make it"?

They simply didn't have that iconic Seattle Sound. And this is strange, because if any band sounded like Seattle, it was Skin Yard: Their music was a distillation of all the diversity of the 80s underground scene, linked to Vexed and The Blackouts on the one hand and to Soundgarden on the other. But as the decade wore on, Bruce Pavitt and Jonathan Poneman worked to make "Seattle" synonymous with "Sub Pop". There was a carefully manufactured Sub Pop aesthetic: blue-collar party animals in plaid shirts singing pop hooks over meaty power-chords. It could be, and often was, summed up with a single word: "dumb".[5] That label grossly undersells the intelligence of Mudhoney or Nirvana, of course, but it captures the simple, straight-from-the-groin directness of their music. Skin Yard was not about being dumb. They knew there wasn't a place for them in this world. Asked about his band's position in the changing scene, Endino recalls:

Skin Yard-era Daniel House.

"I don't know where we fit in. We felt like we didn't. We had our own niche all to ourselves at the time. The grunge and indie-rock crowd in 1988 thought we were too metal. But the metal fans thought we were grunge. Sub Pop hated us, because Ben's vocals were too far removed from punk rock for them. The prog influence also scared them away, even though it was OK for Sunny Day Real Estate a few years later."

Of course, Sub Pop succeeded for good reasons—they signed great bands and crafted a compelling image rooted in the Seattle experience. But they were highly selective about how they contributed to and represented that experience. House, like others interviewed for this piece, recalls how Pavitt and Poneman "did as much as they could to try and keep their bands playing with each other". They were cultivating a "Motown sensibility", which entailed founding the label on "a specific music scene, within a specific city, with the same producers". The aim was "to create a very specific regional sound identity". The problem is that this level of control was anathema to the spirit of openness and connectivity that had given Sub Pop bands their distinctive hybrid sounds. Sub Pop created a regional brand at the expense of something that made the region special. It's telling, for instance, that the label's in-house photographer, Charles Peterson, cut most of the background out of his photos to make it look like young Sub Pop bands were already playing to huge audiences. In the same way, Sub Pop was actively reshaping the scene in its own image, promoting their Seattle Sound and inadvertently marginalising bands, like Skin Yard, that didn't fit in.

With their imagery and music, Skin Yard evoked a world that never intersected with the world projected by Sub Pop's "dumb" bands and their imitators. Where grunge guys wrote about girls, partying, and emotional problems, Skin Yard wrote about insanity and revelation. There was a mystical energy in Endino's warped guitar lines, in those insistently throbbing rhythm section grooves, and—perhaps most of all—in McMillan's lyrics. "Psychedelics", says Endino, "moulded a lot of our conceptions about music. Psychedelic mushroom species grow wild here in the northwest. No one talks about it, but it's part of growing up here." It seemed natural to Skin Yard that music should help us "push on through to the other side". But the reigning aesthetic of the moment was inimical to transcendence. People responded to grunge's (stylised and highly selective) image of everyday life, perhaps because there was a kind of inverted glamour to its grit, a romance that seemed within grasp.

Skin Yard could only have come out of Seattle, and yet they were living in the wrong city half a decade ahead of their time. Perhaps they would've made more sense in England, if they'd had more opportunity to tour there. It's certainly ironic that in 1992, the same year Skin Yard posthumously released *Inside The Eye*, Tool put out their debut EP, *Opiate*. While it's unlikely that Tool were directly influenced by Skin Yard, they achieved staggering success with many of the elements Skin Yard pioneered—polyrhythmic drums, psychedelic riffs, goth-metal basslines, and words that caught the shadows on the outskirts of the mind.

Gruntruck

Gruntruck is the closest thing in this chapter to straight-up grunge. They fit into this narrative because they included members of Skin Yard and The Accused, and because of their complex relationship to the commercial orgy that erupted in Seattle. Gruntruck almost "made it", and their struggle to break into the mainstream from a background in two of the city's more left-field bands speaks to the experiences of many other now-forgotten Seattle groups.

In the latter days of Skin Yard, Ben McMillan started learning guitar and writing meaty, metal-influenced rock songs that clearly fell outside the purview of his main band. He started working on them with Scott McCullum. As their side project became more serious, the pair realised they needed a primary guitarist—someone who could contribute to writing and help anchor the riffage onstage. Scott approached his roommate Tommy Niemeyer, who had just played with them on "Slow Runner", and who, in The Accused, had been rhythm and lead guitarist rolled into one.[6] They found a bassist in Tim Paul, a former member of Portland's Final Warning. Having cut his chops on that band's precise crust grooves, he understood how to lock in with an aggressive guitarist like Tommy.

The new quartet chose the preposterously heavy name "Gruntruck". As the name suggests, they embraced the "dumb" aesthetic with enthusiasm—this was the visceral, accessible sound McMillan had sought in Skin Yard. Like Soundgarden and Alice In Chains, they belonged firmly on the "metal" side of the grunge camp. But where those two bands embraced arena-rock operatics, Gruntruck remained grounded, directly linked to hardcore by a chain of thick, low-end power chords.

Gruntruck practices tended to happen right after Skin Yard and The Accused had rehearsed. "We would meet up after our bands practiced", Tommy remembers, "and do some Gruntruck stuff for a few hours a night. We found ourselves doing that a lot, and we ended up with an album's worth of material in no time at all." To him, this was clearly fun, but the fact that he and his bandmates could find it stimulating rather than exhausting presupposes a staggering level of commitment

to music. They would work their various day jobs, run through serious practices with serious touring bands, and *then* work on new material for "a few" more hours. This was far more intense than the low-key, irregular messing around that we usually associate with the term "side project", and yet it felt natural at the time. It's hard to imagine the reserves of creative energy, the level of pure musical obsession, which would make this possible. Gruntruck took form against the backdrop of a city where music had become an urgent collective undertaking, and where that extra time spent jamming seemed like it might—at any second—translate into something big.

A major factor in Niemeyer's excitement about this new band was the songwriting freedom it afforded to him. He had shaped The Accused's crossover sound, but now felt constrained by it: "The rules were getting more and more strict. Practices had to be this and that and this and that, it was all beginning to become routine." The writing for Gruntruck, on the other hand, was open and highly intuitive. McMillan and McCullum clearly had an idea of what they wanted to do, but it had emerged naturally from Skin Yard. They gave Niemeyer space "to just do whatever the song required. The rules were stripped completely away. There was no preconceived idea of what was expected from me as a guitarist." He was used to writing riff-driven thrash, so rock songwriting was "an alien world" that nevertheless felt natural. His playing with Gruntruck "was all just a big release of what I already had in me", allowing him to channel aspects of rock and metal that never quite fit into The Accused.

Gruntruck started playing out almost by accident, and the side project quickly became the main band. Rather than hitting the official bar circuit, they came up through playing "at speakeasies and after-hours stuff", venues frequented by a scene of hard-partying adults that formed a funhouse mirror to the teen DIY underground. McMillan's downtown connections allowed them access to this world. But soon interest grew, and the band started playing "official" gigs. After Skin Yard temporarily split, McCullum stayed out of the band for good. McMillan stayed with them for two more albums, but his energies were increasingly invested in Gruntruck. Niemeyer, for his part, was growing disenchanted with the constraints of playing in The Accused.

Gruntruck's first album, *Inside Yours*, was produced by their friend Jack Endino and released in 1990 by the DIY punk label Empty Records, which also put out material by The Gits. But soon after its release, Monte Hunter of Roadrunner Records saw Gruntruck play live. He offered them a contract the next day. Today Roadrunner is reviled as the label that brought us Limp Bizkit, but in the early 90s Niemeyer knew it as a prestigious Dutch metal label that had put out albums by Mercyful Fate, among others. It had serious credibility but growing reach and resources. For Gruntruck, the decision was an instant and unanimous "Fuck, let's do it!" Like many Seattle bands, though, they were technically under a verbal contract with their independent label. When bands broke these contracts it often led to serious conflicts and feelings of betrayal. In Gruntruck's case, though, it worked smoothly: "Apparently they had a meeting that was good enough for Blake [Wright, co-owner of Empty Records], he seemed pretty happy. They bought the rights to *Inside Yours* and then re-released it. We immediately went into the studio and recorded *Push*."

Roadrunner released *Push* in 1992. Endino returned to the studio with Gruntruck, but this time he co-produced the record with Gary King. They recorded in King's studio, a cavernous room with thirty-foot ceilings, and King's intimate knowledge of the acoustic space helped give the album a massive and unique guitar sound. *Push* is worth examining as a hyper-intensification of certain elements of grunge, and worth remembering as an excellent, unfairly neglected album.

But it starts off on the wrong foot with a song called "Tribe". This was chosen for Gruntruck's first music video, and it encapsulates the awkwardness of underground veterans trying to write for the mainstream. "Tribe" opens with an exciting thrash riff from Niemeyer, but then drops into a lurching groove that, even at the time, must've sounded like grunge-by-numbers. When McMillan comes in you can hear him trying for the yawning grunge drawl. He sings a verse or two about slacking off, and then a seriously goofy chorus: "I just wanna fly my freak flag (x2)/C'mon join our triiiiibe (x2)." It's a little painful to hear one of Seattle's best lyricists deliberately stifling his vision to write an "alternative" manifesto. "Smells Like Teen Spirit" and "Man In The Box" were pop songs, to be sure, but both have smart, evocative lyrics, and neither was a self-conscious attempt at accessibility—if anything, the opposite.

From there on, though, *Push* turns hard rock into total body music, bludgeoning the listener into stupefied submission. There is the sense of being walloped over and over by viscous riff-waves, or crashing headlong through a wall of solid riff. This is the music of "dumb" pushed to a gloriously retarded extreme, music that cries out for the opening of beers and the banging of heads. It was practically fated that "Crazy Love" would become a fixture of the flagship program of "dumb" TV—*Beavis and Butthead*.

This sleeper hit shares a title with dozens of saccharine pop songs, but Niemeyer's whiplash riffage and McCullum's swaggering backbeat suggest the buildup to a bar fight. Affectations abandoned, McMillan sounds powerful, but the song's "chorus", when it comes, is actually instrumental—a bluesy doom-metal riff played at quadruple time, the sort of thing that would be ripped off *ad infinitum* through the 90s and on into today. Here, and on other tracks like "Racked", Gruntruck has a strong affinity with Pantera. Much as they were rooted in grunge and Seattle punk, it's also possible to place them on the more melodic wing of the new "groove metal".

But on the second or third listen you'll hear some more depth to *Push*. On "Above Me", released as the lead single by Roadrunner, McMillan draws one of his most melodic vocal performances from a darkly beautiful chord progression. You can hear him bending his notes like Niemeyer bends his riffs. "Machine Action" is built on a set of throbbing, bass-centric riffs, similar to those on Skin Yard records like *Fist Sized Chunks*, but here their power is magnified through brutal simplification and droning repetition. Niemeyer layers on heavily bent one-note leads and dark arpeggios before building into a frenzy that somehow synchs up perfectly with what's going on underneath. It sounds like a metallisation of Endino's psychedelic playing in Skin Yard, and in this case it is probably safe to assume a direct influence.

With their signing to Roadrunner and the release of *Push*, Gruntruck started looking like the next Seattle band to break out. At this point, Skin Yard had broken up and Niemeyer had left The Accused, so Gruntruck was a full-time concern. The anticipation was only strengthened when Layne Staley chose them to support Alice In Chains on a mini-tour of the northwestern US in the early fall of 1992. Then, in November, Gruntruck rejoined Alice In Chains for a full tour of the US and Canada (which also included the Screaming Trees).

Despite their diametrically opposed backgrounds in punk and hair metal, the two groups developed a strong bond. Staley strongly supported Gruntruck, and Niemeyer would watch the headliners' set every night. This tour was his band's baptism in mainstream rock music, and it came as an "incredible whirlwind of backstage passes, and lighting techs, and guitar techs, and deli trays, and press days...". It was also their point of entry into the carnal carnival that seemed to follow Alice In Chains everywhere.

"To try and learn the word 'no' was very, very difficult. But not so difficult when you're crapping blood and barfing blood at the exact same time on the tour bus. I'm really glad it didn't get better for Gruntruck after that, though, because we wouldn't have known how to say no. If we had gotten big enough to tour on our own, I'd probably be dead by now. It was so good. There was so much of everything. Now I'm glad it didn't happen."

But Gruntruck wasn't wholly invested in this world in the way that AIC was. Niemeyer understood that he was now "part of the machine", and kept his distance from the casual misogyny that prevailed on tour, a "macho rock'n'roll" attitude that he had spent years skewering with The Accused.

The next year, Gruntruck would tour Europe with Pantera, playing to especially enthusiastic crowds in the UK. A European tour marked a coming of age for any American band, especially one from a formerly isolated West Coast scene, and they were touring as the main support for the biggest new metal band in the world. Greg Anderson, who was playing in Engine Kid and had known Niemeyer since their days on the hardcore scene together, wryly recalls his high expectations for his old friend's new band:

"I remember seeing Gruntruck start playing bigger places, they were opening up for bigger bands, they played this place in Seattle called the Warren Theatre. That's when you knew you made it. I saw them open up for Alice In Chains there. And I thought, 'They're on their way. Tommy got his break and his ship came in....'"

As Anderson saw it, the Seattle scene in the early 90s was haunted by a sense of tremendous success being just around the corner, which blinded people to the risks and probabilities involved in the record business. This was a time when a deal from a major label or a powerful indie could just *materialise*, as it did when Roadrunner scooped up Gruntruck, but the "support" of a label could be a double-edged sword. It was too easy to assume that popularity and acclaim would translate into commercial success.

When Gruntruck signed to Roadrunner, they were as uninterested in the "contractual legalese" as you would expect any group of hard-partying punks and longhairs to be. But they knew enough to hire a local lawyer to review the contract for them—"We had heard you could get fucked, and we were wary of it." The lawyer looked it over and, after four drafts, gave them the go-ahead to sign. Gruntruck proceeded to rock out with no reservations. They "did the tours and recorded the CDs and made videos, and we weren't expecting any money of course because we knew those things cost, and we knew that someone was paying for it and it was probably us". This is the critical thing to understand. In most record deals at the time, *the band was actually covering business costs for the label*, in expectation of the sizable return profit that would follow a successful tour, solid album sales, and the use of their music in film and television. Gruntruck was going heavily into debt, but they figured it would all come back to them tenfold.

Then, they noticed that the expected money wasn't showing up. Their wake-up call came through a conversation with Alice In Chains, who had savvy management and were far more experienced in the business end of the music business. Someone in AIC mentioned that they should be seeing money from publishing, especially from the use of "Crazy Love" on *Beavis and Butthead*. Gruntruck called up their lawyer, who checked their contract, and realised that he had made an error. Niemeyer's response, as he recalls it, bears quoting in full:

"So, the bigger we get, the bigger tours we get on, the more videos we do, the more times we get on Beavis and Butthead, the more we... rock out as Gruntruck, the less money we're going to be making, because it's costing so much and we're not seeing any of it?" And he says "Yeah, essentially." So we say, "OK, you're fired."

Gruntruck attempted to open direct negotiations with Roadrunner to resuscitate their contract, but Roadrunner wouldn't budge. At the same time, the band was receiving offers from major labels like A&M, EMI, Capitol, and Warner Brothers, who were eager to buy out their suffocating contract. Representatives of these labels would call them, baffled, to explain that Roadrunner was refusing their entreaties, even hanging up on calls.

Eventually, the band hired a skilled Los Angeles attorney who helped them escape the contract by filing for bankruptcy as a band. But these proceedings took years, and in that time Gruntruck wasn't allowed to exist, because it was, by its own declaration, bankrupt. McCullum and Paul left the band in frustration, while McMillan and Niemeyer were back to playing underground Seattle gigs as "Mona Diesel", just to "make a couple bucks here and there and keep some fans happy". Gruntruck won their bankruptcy and their release from contract. It was a pyrrhic victory. By that time, Kurt Cobain was dead and the grunge bubble had burst, so the majors were looking elsewhere. Gruntruck was bankrupt, without a label, without popular momentum, and without its original lineup. They rallied to release one more Endino-produced EP, 1996's *Shot*, but the moment had passed, as it passed for so many other bands that were scooped up and then steamrollered by the hype machine.

In this age of reunion tours, it seems deeply unfair that Gruntruck will never get a second run. Ben McMillan died of diabetes in July of 2011. He still lived in Seattle.

Vexed

Vexed shared no members with Skin Yard, but they shared a basement, and as Death House bands they shared a musical inheritance. As Skin Yard moved towards metal and hard rock (and, ultimately, grunge), Vexed pursued a radically experimental direction.

The core songwriters were Milton Garrison and Alfred Butler, who started playing together in 1984 after the dissolution of their respective bands, The Altered and The Death of Marat. Butler switched from keyboards to bass, developing a fast and percussive funk-influenced style. Garrison remained on guitar, continually expanding his range of effects. Vexed was originally a quartet, but by 1986 it had cohered as a trio with the versatile David Lapp on drums and percussion.[7]

This lineup did not release a single until 1988, perhaps out of commitment to perfecting their sound, but also because their challenging music did not readily attract record labels. The music demanded to be taken seriously, and Vexed were a force on the Seattle underground, as Jack Endino remembers:

"One of the coolest shows in those years was a Soundgarden/Skin Yard/Vexed show. I think it was 1987. Vexed had a very large live audience, and was one of the best live bands I've ever seen, but have been pretty much excluded from the history books because they do not fit the grunge historical narrative. They were still overtly post-punk (and took it even further!) when the rest of the scene here had gone grunge."

What Endino means by "took it even further" is that Vexed were *using* goth/angular/post-punk music rather than *playing* it. They had subordinated the style to their own ends. Daniel House could easily hear where Vexed were coming from, and yet he was struck by the irreducibility of what they were doing:

"Blackouts were definitely a band that influenced them profoundly. But Gang of Four was another really profound influence, and I think Killing Joke as well. There weren't many bands that sounded like them, and certainly not in Seattle. They really stood out, because they were kind of bombastic and heavy, but super-rhythmic and infectiously dance-y. Most of the bands doing stuff that combined rock with dance were coming out of Chicago on Wax Trax."

But Vexed, with their fluid rhythms and mercurial song structures, were far from the battering repetitions of the Wax Trax sound. Butler was proud that his band was considered both "the most danceable band in Seattle" and "the most challenging band to dance to".

The classic Vexed record is their 1990 EP, *The Good Fight*. It begins with inchoate noise that sounds like the end of an album, as if the band were putting down their instruments, then erupts into a Dead Kennedys riff, which again erupts into a violently swinging punk-funk groove, the kind of thing that makes dancers trip. Garrison repeatedly jabbers a single line: "Don't. wanna talk about it/Don't. wanna think about it, WOOOO." These neurotic, frantic lyrics are part of a submerged political critique—they express the subjective side of life under late capitalism, the unbalanced emotional states that are the natural reaction to an unbalanced world.[8] Garrison's outburst is mirrored by abrupt rhythmic change-ups and a relentless barrage of stuttering, abrasive riffage. And this, the title track, is one of the record's more conventional songs.

What distinguished Vexed from other dance bands and art-noise acts was their sense of beauty and their compositional ambition. They centred *The Good Fight* on two extended instrumental tracks. "A Cruel Accounting" pushes far beyond Gang of Four into a kind of fiendish world-beat, with Lapp playing as drummer and auxiliary percussionist folded into one. When the breakdowns hit it's like getting bounced between walls. "Memories of Things We Never Had", though, is the album's finest track. It opens like a revelation, with Garrison leaping from one brilliant guitar structure to the next. Each seems to echo the riffing style of a different British post-punk band, but Garrison is not playing riffs. These are full melodies, great arcs of sound subsuming every individual element within them. When he steps back, and Butler steps back, it is equally revelatory—we are left for a minute with just the pulse of the drums.

It should come as less than a surprise that *The Good Fight* was a record made purely for the sake of making a record. Luckily, it found its way to Daniel House, who released it on C/Z:

"This was a case of me saying, 'This needs to be heard.' I think that first record is one of the best I ever put out. They went into the studio of their own accord. Jack [Endino] was recording it, so I was interested, but I knew it probably wouldn't sell that well.... I did agree to put the record out, and once I heard what they were doing with Jack I was like, 'Oh my god, this is amazing.'"

In keeping with the singular, self-necessitating nature of the recording session, *The Good Fight* was not a bridge to a broader audience or a national tour. Vexed broke up shortly afterwards, as if with that sonic document they had accomplished their mission.

They reformed in 1992 with Buzz Crocker on drums, recorded a full-length album, and promptly broke up again.[9] C/Z released the record, posthumously, as

Cathexis. The songs were undeniably compelling, and extremely heavy, but they were closer in form to metal and grunge tracks. Vexed's new power came at the cost of the utterly free and open approach they had developed during the 80s. And at this point, the zenith of grunge, the musical climate had shifted so much that their cerebral, lyrical, danceable music no longer made sense to people.

Vexed saw this coming. On "Gang of Youth", the final track of *The Good Fight*, Garrison sings:

"Whatever happened to the last 10 years?
Everything we hated has become so dear...
I'm tired of the same thing over and over again.
I don't like it now, and I didn't like it then.
But what do you do, when it happens to your friends?"

The Gits

When people mention The Gits today, it's usually as a band whose singer was brutally murdered, as a band whose promising career was cut short by tragedy, or as a forgotten punk band with a charismatic female vocalist. All of these characterisations are fair, in one way or another, but they obscure the central truth—The Gits were one of the best punk rock bands of their generation, and their music was in a category of its own. They helped invent the melodic, hardcore-influenced punk that would dominate the West Coast scene for more than a decade, and they did it with an artistry that was lost on most of the bands that followed in their wake. Their music tapped into deep currents of American music and a lost ideal of the rebel West. They radiated an energy and commitment that cut through the slacker nihilism of Seattle's grunge scene.

But, technically speaking, The Gits were not from Seattle. In fact, they arrived in the city as a complete musical unit with a history and a collective personality. Unlike many later transplants, they became a real part of the city's music community, absorbing the spirit of their surroundings and helping galvanise the ailing punk underground. But to understand their music and the role they played in Seattle, it's important to start from the beginning.

Deep in rural Ohio, in the post-hippie haze of Antioch College, the future Gits bonded over boredom and booze as well as punk and blues. Where many bands are alliances of convenience based on participation in a scene, The Gits' friendships preceded their musical partnership, grounding it and giving it character. Andy Kessler (aka "Joe Spleen") and Matt Dresdner were hardcore kids from the East Coast—Brooklyn and New Jersey, respectively. Kessler was a skilled guitarist who had grown up idolising Black Sabbath and Zeppelin before hearing punk and cutting his hair. Dresdner, who had minimal musical experience, simply picked up the bass and turned himself into a proficient fingerstyle player. Steve Moriarty grew up playing jazz drums in small town Indiana. He had his mind blown when the Dead Kennedys played at Antioch and the FBI showed up to videotape the crowd. Vocalist Mia Zapata came from Louisville, where there was not much of a punk scene. She had a huge, soulful voice, and used broken guitars and old pianos as songwriting tools. Mia loved singers like Patti Smith, but also spent a lot of time in the college music library, digging through mouldering records by the likes of Ma Rainey, Bessie Smith, and Robert Johnson.

The initial impetus behind the band came from Matt and Andy. Legend has it that Matt "discovered" Mia's vocal talent at a particularly raucous party, when she

The Gits. By Lucy Hanna.

got up on the table and sang. They called their new group "The Sniveling Little Rat-faced Gits", after a line in a Monty Python sketch, but quickly (and mercifully) truncated the name. By 1985 they were gigging locally and writing original material. In the isolation of Antioch they worked with only the vaguest notion of "punk", adapting to each other's disparate influences and writing without constraint by subgenre or scene.

In the next few years The Gits would take time off from school to play in San Francisco (minus Moriarty, who was temporarily replaced by a local drummer). There, they volunteered at The Farm, a pioneering urban agriculture project in the Mission District that doubled as a European-style punk house. The grounds included a vast warehouse where The Gits saw (and played alongside) bands like Bad Brains, Social Distortion, DRI, Dead Kennedys, Sublime, NOFX, Bad Religion and Fugazi. Their time at The Farm gave them a better sense of where they fit into the international punk scene, and intensified their commitment to DIY practices.

When they returned to Ohio and reunited with Steve, The Gits were finally ready to record. They wanted to retain complete control over the process, and so modelled their approach on the Minutemen:

"They recorded *Double Nickels On The Dime*, like 36 songs, in three hours. Well, we wanted to do it like that, so we just went to a really nice studio where choirs would record, set up our band in the large room next to the grand piano, mic'ed everything up and recorded 17 songs in three hours."

The Gits recorded it all live to two tracks, without second takes, overdubs, or after-the-fact manipulation. They recorded Mia's vocals onto one track and the whole band onto another. This was a perfect realisation of the Minutemen's "jam econo" principle, but The Gits weren't trying to get a raw sound. Their speedy, bare-bones method meant they could afford to book time at a space with excellent facilities, and that is reflected in the clarity and power of the resulting tape.

In dispensing with the technical artifice of "hi-fi" studio production, The Gits managed to record something with a genuine *fidelity*—faithfulness, truthfulness—to the sonic details of their playing together. This process says a lot about the ethos at the heart of the band's music. The Gits were fiercely committed to artistic autonomy, and they were motivated by a radical ideal of Truth. Like the hardcore bands that preceded them, they wanted "to subvert pop music and pop culture and replace it with authenticity and reality". They weren't an overtly political band, but for them the very act of making honest music was a political act—a brick chucked at the rose-tinted glasses of Ronald Reagan, or a pair of giant scissors slicing through the polychromatic veil of MTV.

The Gits called their tape *Private Lubs*, and Steve describes it as "creepy and kind of weird".[10] Mia played a leading role in writing many of these early songs, and they revolve around her blues-cabaret aesthetic. Andy shaped his riffs to her unusual melodies, while Steve pushed the tracks into odd time signatures and tricky rhythms. The strangest moments include the excellent "Monsters" and the less-excellent "Eleven", where overt jazz influences collide with queasy dissonance. The beginnings of The Gits' mature sound can be heard on an early version of "Cut My Skin It Makes Me Human". Here, the rhythms have the loose lope of a country and western song. But on more straightforward tracks like "Kings And Queens", "Tempt Me", and "Looking Right Through Me", it's easy to hear how much Kessler's guitar playing owed to the New York Dolls and Johnny Thunders.

Rather than shopping around for labels they simply pressed 50 copies of *Private Lubs* and sold them directly to friends. When those ran out, they printed another

50 and sold those too. At this point, they knew they had outgrown Antioch and its environs, so they moved to San Francisco.

The Gits knew a lot of people from their days at The Farm, and they expected their music would find a suitable home in the teeming Bay Area punk scene. But when they arrived, they realised that they couldn't afford to live in the city, much less rent a rehearsal space. Where to go? Moriarty had been to Seattle once and loved the mountains. And when he was booking DIY shows back at Antioch, someone had passed him a copy of Soundgarden's *Screaming Life* EP: "I thought it was different, I really dug it. Chris Cornell's screaming and just the dark tone of it. It was hard without being cliché. It wasn't really hardcore, it wasn't really thrash...."

He and his fellow Gits had no idea that the city was bursting with rock'n'roll, but that was enough to give them a good feeling. They headed north.

The Gits arrived in Seattle in the fall of 1989 with a posse of other Antioch punks. The northwest welcomed them with heavy, unceasing rain, but rent was so low that they could all go in on "a four-bedroom, two-storey, hundred year-old piece of shit farmhouse" for a grand total of $380 a month. They called it the Rathouse. "It was falling down", says Moriarty. "There were rats, and like eight or nine people living there at once." Despite the squalor, or perhaps because of it, it was an invaluable resource. The Gits could set up a practice room in the cellar, host friends and touring bands, and throw chaotic parties.

The Gits were eager to start gigging in their adopted city, but it wasn't easy. The Teen Dance Ordinance was in full effect, so all-ages shows were almost impossible to find in the city, and the DIY punk scene was all but nonexistent. Worse, there weren't enough music-friendly bars to keep up with the rapid growth of the underground rock scene. As The Gits' *de facto* manager, the guy who handled the practical stuff, Steve was frustrated by the strange ecology of live music in Seattle:

"There were only two venues. One was Tuesday night, called The Vogue. It held about 100 people: they packed 200 in it. It was a little hole in the wall in the worst part of town. And there was a little beer bar called Squid Row, where there was a stage about the size of a bed. And people would pack in there on Friday nights. So you had dozens of bands, or maybe 100 bands at that point, all vying for two nights a week. You see these pictures from the time that make it seem like it was this huge scene, but if you were there you know it was only 40 people, going crazy."

It took six months of making friends and sending out demos for The Gits to land their first show. Finally, they debuted at a warehouse party with The Cryptkicker Five, a surf-punk band featuring Jack Endino on drums, and followed that up with a proper gig at The Vogue.[11]

But as much as that half-year of waiting around frustrated The Gits, it was actually a crucial turning point for them as songwriters. As the Winter mists rolled in, they holed up in the Rathouse basement to practice. "We just woodshed it", says Moriarty. "We rehearsed every day, sometimes five or six hours, just because we loved it. We wrote the whole time." Those frenzied writing sessions yielded some of The Gits' best songs, including "Second Skin", "Precious Blood", "Absynthe", and "Another Shot of Whiskey". Over the next two years they drew on this new material, and older songs, to put out three seven-inch records on local DIY labels such as Big Flaming Ego, Broken ReKids, and Empty Records. On these releases The Gits defined their mature sound—melodic punk rock with hardcore propulsion and blues inflections.

Early on, Sub Pop invited The Gits to play a major show at The Hub with Nirvana and TAD. Moriarty later spoke with Jonathan Poneman about doing a single for his label, but these tentative overtures never went anywhere. Sub Pop, teetering on the edge of bankruptcy, had no money to risk on new bands. The Gits, moreover, did not quite fit the Sub Pop aesthetic, and took a wary attitude towards the record industry. They were ambitious, but they wanted to succeed on their own terms—to reach as broad an audience as possible while remaining faithful to the DIY punk ethos and (somehow, just barely) making ends meet. Where many contemporaneous bands sought a meteoric rise to fame, The Gits were the rare band that *wanted* to pay their dues in the underground.

With minimal access to coveted bar nights, The Gits had to create their own gigging opportunities. "I realised that in order to get more gigs and play as much as we wanted to play that I would have to get my own club", Moriarty remembers. "I kind of bullied my way into booking an all-ages venue that was a coffee shop and had a big stage in the back. It was a former flophouse called the OK Hotel." The Gits played there regularly, and by setting up the gigs himself, Moriarty built friendships with other bands from Seattle and beyond. He often booked touring bands like Babes In Toyland and Sublime, who in turn would set The Gits up with gigs throughout the western part of the country.

The Gits weren't just networking, though. They were helping to create a new scene in their own image, grounded in the DIY practices they'd mastered in San Francisco and Antioch. Shielded from the Teen Dance Ordinance through some magic legal loophole, the OK Hotel became the center for a resurgence of all-ages shows in the early 90s. The Rathouse became a teeming warren of Seattle punks, and sometimes hosted its own shows. This was quite distinct from the grunge phenomenon, as much as that remained musically connected to punk. "There was the Sub Pop scene, and then there was the underground punk scene", Moriarty explains. "The Sub Pop scene was not the underground punk scene." He sees what The Gits were involved in as "more akin to Olympia", and strongly linked to Portland. There were also parallels to the Bay Area scene and to the network of squats that extended throughout Europe. This new wave of bands was politically conscious, sceptical of "success", and willing to draw sharp distinctions between what was punk and what was not. In a way, this was an underground in defensive formation, struggling to define and sustain itself at a time when Seattle rock was becoming a brand.

The Gits were close friends with 7 Year Bitch, a younger band that played heavy, slowed-down punk. They started out rehearsing in the Rathouse basement, and some members lived there for a time. Three out of four members of the DC Beggars lived at the Rathouse, and guitarist Julien Gibson was especially close to The Gits. They sounded like a weird fusion of Dead Kennedys, GBH, and Iron Maiden. Nothing could have been less fashionable in the early 90s, but they absolutely ripped. Other Gits allies and gigging partners included Treepeople, a brooding indie band co-fronted by Doug Martsch before he founded Built To Spill; Gas Huffer, a garage punk act led by Tom Price of The U-Men; Christ On A Crutch, a heavy hardcore band with a young bassist named Nate Mendel (later of Sunny Day Real Estate and Foo Fighters); Subvert, a thrashing crust band from Tacoma (which would evolve into Christdriver); Metal Church, a veteran power metal band that had completely missed the grunge boom; and Portland groups as divergent as Poison Idea and Heatmiser (the latter co-fronted by Elliott Smith).

As The Gits came into their own they also developed friendships with some of the grunge guys, independent of the divide between their scenes. When Nirvana was slated to drive to LA for the *Nevermind* sessions, Sub Pop was too broke to cover their gas money. They were able to afford the trip because Moriarty and his DIY comrades booked them a packed fundraising gig at the OK Hotel.

The barrage of Gits singles in 1991 had paved the way for an official debut full-length. They were approached by Slim Moon of Kill Rock Stars, already a well-established indie, and by Fat Mike of NOFX, who had just started his own label, Fat Wreck Chords. Both were friends who came up through the same DIY channels, but neither was located in Seattle. The Gits wanted to work with someone local, and they chose C/Z Records.

Daniel House had taken over C/Z from Chris Hanzsek and Tina Casale in 1986, just after they put out the poorly received but hugely influential *Deep Six* compilation, effectively ground zero for the grunge movement. *Deep Six* included Skin Yard, Soundgarden, Melvins, Green River, Malfunkshun, and The U-Men. The future owners of Sub Pop picked up on the common threads between these bands, extrapolating an aesthetic that would influence their label's signature sound. House, when he inherited the label, moved in a different direction, away from grunge. He made C/Z into a reflection of the musical diversity and cooperation that defined the Seattle scene in its early days. The Gits respected this, and Steve Moriarty saw C/Z as a serious contender to Sub Pop:

"For a while Daniel House had the best bands in town. Sub Pop was almost out of business. The bands that were selling the most records were C/Z bands—Treepeople, Hammerbox, Monks of Doom. He had compilations with bands like Nirvana and Soundgarden. His label was the shit, and we thought we might as well go with this guy."

In addition to those bands, which were all poised on the edge of alt-rock success, C/Z worked with punk stalwarts like Coffin Break and supported challenging, uncategorisable groups like Vexed, whose music, in House's own words, "clearly wasn't going to sell very well".

Frenching The Bully came out on C/Z in 1992. It is tighter, faster, and more aggressive than The Gits' demo, a fact which reflects Andy Kessler's increasing involvement in the songwriting process. As much as he loved the Dolls and tuneful UK bands like The Undertones, he was more drawn to extreme hardcore groups like Discharge, Cro-Mags, Misfits, and Portland's Poison Idea. The dissonant, thrashing power chord riffs on songs like "Insecurities" and "Here's To Your Fuck" are straight from this tradition, but its influence is everywhere. Kessler injects aggressive picking patterns into highly textured playing on "Absynthe" and Moriarty matches them with his slowed-down, swinging version of the d-beat. Dresdner provides a counterpoint with a bold, jazz-inspired walking bassline.

The final track, "Second Skin" is *the* definitive Gits song. Here, the band strikes the chord of yearning that resonates throughout their music, and—characteristically—find a way to do everything all at once. Kessler's dark harmonies mirror Mia's lyrics, which delve into her sense of vulnerability but emerge with steely resolve. Another band might have written it as a ballad, but The Gits roar ahead like Motörhead. Mia considered this song a breakthrough; she was struck by its wild, "desperate" feeling, the crystallisation of a mood they had already been working towards. The Gits' songs carry a sense of peril and potential, the sense that something vital is at stake. At a time when slacker nihilism was the reigning ideal, The Gits believed that how you lived your life mattered.

The Gits' move towards a more straightforward sound was inevitable, given the values enacted in their first demo. After recording those early tracks, they had continued the process of cutting out what Moriarty calls "all the extraneous bullshit" that got in the way of authentic, truthful expression:

"I would venture to say that there's not a false statement or contrived sentiment in any of the lyrics that Mia wrote. And the music works that way as well. That's why

The Gits' kit.

you won't hear any guitar leads, that's why you won't hear any drum solos and showboating. If it works for the song, it works great."

There's only one ballad on *Frenching The Bully*, a reinterpretation of "It All Dies Anyway". Mia improvises on pre-written lines, bending pitches and dressing up melodies, drawing out some notes and compressing others. Gradually, she escalates from a frank, conversational tone into full-on, howling blues rapture. While many singers in punk (and pop) simply "do vocals", producing a fairly standardised sound in rhythmic intervals, Mia had mastered the hard work of *singing*, giving shape to the air pouring out of her lungs. In song after song, her lyrics return to the idea of openness—to pain, to joy, to love, to the struggles of others—and you can hear it in the way her voice "opens up" throughout the track, her power increasing in proportion to her naked vulnerability.

Frenching The Bully was favourably reviewed in American publications and major British magazines like the *NME*. But The Gits found a more receptive audience in Europe—where they had just completed an extensive DIY tour—than in many parts of the United States.[12] Despite the respect they received from other Seattle bands, they never really came into the view of the hype apparatus. For instance, a cover story in *The Rocket*, Seattle's monthly music newspaper, was a sign that a band had risen to prominence within the city's increasingly crowded rock scene. The Gits never made the cover—they were passed over for newer bands, groups that were easier to market or more likely to make the jump to the mainstream.[13] They had struck the glass ceiling that shielded the alternative scene from straight-up punk bands.

At the same time, The Gits' cautious alliance with C/Z Records was deteriorating. This tension is detailed in other places, but it arose, in part, from a clash of expectations. They were looking for the kind of equal-footing partnership and handshake-deal treatment they would have received from friends at DIY punk labels like Broken

Above left

Mia Zapata.

Above right

Mia and crowd.

ReKids and Kill Rock Stars. Daniel House, on the other hand, felt that the band never trusted him sufficiently, and that they were too hostile to the "business" aspect of the music business. Regardless of its DIY roots, C/Z had to pay bills, pay staff, and turn a profit—or at least break even. House irked The Gits by trying to place them on highly eclectic bills. This choice reflected C/Z's catholic approach to genre, but The Gits wanted to gig with bands that shared their influences and ideals.

They had financial concerns as well—they weren't seeing the royalties they'd expected, in part because they were getting billed for C/Z's marketing campaigns, and they wondered whether the marketing was having enough effect. They saw more in royalties from the limited vinyl pressing of their record, by Broken ReKids, than from the CD put out by C/Z. "By 1993", says Moriarty, "after four years of virtually starving, we had to find ways to make money. At that point the Seattle scene had blown up, and major labels wanted to sign us, so we started talking to some of them about our third record." The goal wasn't to become rock stars, but to pursue a sustainable, relatively autonomous career in music: "We were thinking 'We're not gonna be stupid, we're gonna get this money and be able to play music. We'll get an advance, we'll do the record for $2000, we'll take $40,000 and be able to live for a year and tour.'"

With this money, and with the logistical support that a major label could provide, The Gits hoped they would have more freedom to do what they wanted to do. Never ones to do anything by halves, they figured that if they couldn't climb the indie ladder they might as well leap to the top.

In the spring of 1993 The Gits went into the studio with to record what would be called *Enter The Conquering Chicken*, their second album for C/Z. They knew they had to prove that they could connect with listeners beyond the punk scene and the Seattle underground. "We experimented a bit more with a pop sound", says Moriarty, "but maybe we didn't put enough thought into it." The urgency remained, and the sense of melancholy was stronger than ever, but the new album was not a unified statement in the way that *Frenching The Bully* clearly had been.

The group tried to approach accessibility on their own terms, fleshing out the classically Rock sensibility that was always implicit in Mia's melodies and Kessler's guitar work, slowing down the tempos, and focusing more on introspection than vituperation. The album opens with "Bob (Cousin O)" and "Guilt Within Your Head", midpaced tracks that easily fit the "alternative rock" rubric, but also help place The Gits in a lineage of hard-edged Americana that includes Neil Young, Tom Petty, X and The Gun Club. The Gits explore lower tempos with a gracefully executed Sam Cooke cover and the surging, distorted balladry of "Precious Blood". Yet these songs are interspersed with goofy filler like "Italian Song", and they sit uncomfortably alongside the gore-splattered hardcore of "Sign of the Crab".

The album's most important track is "Seaweed", which succeeds as a pop song without sacrificing any of the drive of The Gits' earlier material. Mia sings about leaving a lover who is bringing her down, but she lets this generic trope bleed into her crystallised memory of swimming in a lake with some members of 7 Year Bitch.[14] She recalls the initial shudder of dread at the touch of slimy seaweed, turning it into a metaphor for the fear she must overcome:

"I feel the seaweed creeping up my skin
It's like a monster that's reaching for me
With the passion of life I've got left I'm gonna use it to sacrifice myself
Well, I dove down into the seaweed
Scared once before, but not anymore
As it twists and turns me away from the surface
Here's my chance of letting it go."

As on "Second Skin", Mia's lyrics have a grim, metaphysical quality. Insisting once more on the need to "sacrifice [her]self", she shows the intertwinement of fear with courage, of vulnerability with strength, and of death with life.

And yet the song has none of the brooding quality of "Second Skin"—it represents the moment of triumph over obstacles that Mia lived for, and often sang about as "release". There's a surreal quality to the riffs that compliments her free-associative imagery, and a motion from clipped arpeggios to full-on thrash that doubles the emotional trajectory of her narrative. Kessler and Dresdner's mere choice of notes is enough to evoke anxiety and serenity, regret and affirmation, sorrow and joy. "Seaweed" could only come from a band that had developed its own harmonic world—a distinctive set of chord structures that unifies the individual songs and gives them an underlying mood. This is the sort of thing that music writers recognise when it's obvious, in bands like Sonic Youth and My Bloody Valentine, but overlook too easily in bands with simpler setups and more straightforward styles. The Gits were masters of texture, atmosphere, and expression in a way that was almost unparalleled on the punk scene at the time.

The Gits had almost completed the record by the middle of June. Then they made a short tour down the coast to LA, where they met with various suits from major labels. On their return to Seattle, Mia was going to return to the studio to polish up some of the vocals (she had been battling a cold during the original takes). On 6 July, the night before that last session, she met Valerie Agnew and other members of 7 Year Bitch at The Comet to swap stories and celebrate a successful tour. Mia left after midnight but before the others, heading home to get some rest. The next day, nobody could find her. When the police did find her, Mia was dead. On the walk home she had been viciously assaulted, raped, and strangled.

The three surviving Gits made it their mission to find the killer and honour Mia's legacy. Friends and fans from the entire Seattle music scene lent their support, even as the police investigation cast suspicion on all of Mia's male friends and acquaintances. There was a strange, contradictory phenomenon of alienation and unity—the scene was coming apart because people didn't know who to trust, but it was united in grief for Mia and hatred for whoever had killed her. On their first full-length album, *Viva Zapata*, 7 Year Bitch paid tribute to Mia while capturing the loss and trauma that her murderer inflicted on them and on the entire scene.

Andy, Matt and Steve could not continue as The Gits without Mia. They tried out some other local vocalists—Steve even wrote to PJ Harvey—but in the end, he says, "We couldn't emotionally deal with having anyone else sing." The band wanted to play a release party for their final record, and they knew they had to face their loss together: "We were grieving, so we would drink and play music really fast and loud. A lot of it was really angry at first." *Enter The Conquering Chicken* came out in March of 1994, some nine months after the murder. They'd written some new songs: straight-up hardcore, stark and brutal but recognisably Gits-ian. The rock and the blues and the melody were stripped away but not erased completely, revealing how much this band always had in common with Poison Idea. Andy stepped up to do vocals, his NYHC bellow speaking for everyone who felt the loss and wanted to see justice done.

The surviving Gits and their fans felt that the police weren't doing enough—that they had written Mia off as another dead punk, a casualty of her own nocturnal lifestyle and ne'er-do-well friends. Andy, Steve and Matt hired a private investigator to press ahead with the case. But they needed money to finance the investigation, so they kept playing benefit shows as the "Dancing French Liberals of '48". The bizarre name indicated that this wasn't The Gits, nor was it anything else—it was just three guys who needed to play. They toured nationally and released an album. This trio also collaborated with Joan Jett, playing as "Evil Stig"—"Gits Live" spelled backwards. Evil Stig played a number of packed benefits and even recorded an album for Warner Brothers, but the publicity they garnered did not translate into the hard cash needed to pay the investigator. In the end, all the money came from DIY shows organised by the Dancing French Liberals and by readers of *Maximum Rock'n'Roll* around the world.

Then, the members went their separate ways—working on their own music projects, building new careers, and trying to deal with the grief as best they could. They wouldn't see the end of their story until 25 March 2004, when conclusive DNA evidence led to the conviction of Jesus Mezquia. He wasn't one of Mia's friends; he was a fisherman by trade and a predatory sociopath with a history of violence against women. Mezquia was sentenced to serve a 36-year prison sentence. It was a victory for Mia and everyone who loved her, but it was no triumph. The memory of The Gits is haunted. If there was any victory, it's in the music.

7 Year Bitch

One of the bands hit hardest by the murder of Mia was 7 Year Bitch. With her, they lost a close friend, a mentor, and a stalwart supporter. And it had been little more than a year since they lost their first guitarist, Stefanie Sargent. Wracked with grief and enraged at a world that had taken two friends from them, 7 Year Bitch refused to go silent, and they refused any attempt to "transcend" an insurmountable sense of bereavement. Instead, they faced the pain head-on and produced one of the realest, most confrontational albums to come out of Seattle at the time.

7 Year Bitch was entwined at the roots with The Gits. Valerie Agnew was part of their original Antioch College crew, and in 1989 she moved out to Seattle with them, taking up a room in the Rathouse with her then-boyfriend, Steve Moriarty. Inspired by The Gits and other bands represented at the house, such as DC Beggars and Big Brown House, she decided she wanted to learn drums. She got some lessons from Steve, but she knew that "the only way to figure it out was to play with someone else"—she wanted to learn to play as part of a rhythm section. Valerie, like Matt and Andy of The Gits, had grown up on the East Coast and hung out with hardcore kids in high school. But as much as she liked Bad Brains and 7 Seconds, her musical center was in heavy hard rock—the outlaw thunder of AC/DC and the working-class thrash of Metallica.

Working at an organic food store in the Pike Place Market, Agnew shared shifts with Selene Vigil. Like her, Vigil had never been in a band, but she wanted to try singing. They started playing with guitarist Lisa Orth and a bassist named Cheryl, and called the new group Barbie's Dreamcar. At their first gig they opened for a band called Steelpole Bathtub, and Agnew remembers being so nervous that she played the whole show with her snares loose and rattling. But this was punk—picking up an instrument and learning on the fly.

At Pike Place, Selene and Valerie struck up a friendship with Elizabeth Davis, who worked at a restaurant upstairs and regularly came into the shop to buy fig bars. She always wore a Metallica necklace, so they recognised her as a kindred spirit. It turned out that Elizabeth was a bassist. She, too, had recently taught herself to play, but was already accomplished enough to play hyperspeed Slayer songs in an all-female thrash metal cover band. Elizabeth grew up in a family of music-loving Seventh Day Adventists, playing various instruments in high school band. But she questioned their religion from the beginning, and at the age of ten she encountered the music of KISS—her gateway into the "heavy, dark, evil" world of heavy metal and hard rock.

When Barbie's Dreamcar ran out of gas, Valerie and Selene persuaded Elizabeth to start jamming with them. Soon they were joined by Stefanie Sargent on guitar. She had been a street kid in San Francisco, where she made friends with everyone on the punk scene, and then moved up to Seattle, where she stayed at the Rathouse. She already had some guitar experience. She was charming and extremely popular, but also toughened by years of hard living. Her taste was rooted in the political punk of the Bay Area and the bilious, heavy hardcore of NYHC bands like Cro-Mags.

The new group was booked to play their first show at a Books To Prisoners benefit at the OK Hotel, organised by Steve Moriarty and others from the Rathouse. Hurrying to make flyers, they had to come up with a name. Ben London, the singer of Big Brown House and Alcohol Funnycar, suggested "7 Year Bitch" as a throwaway joke. It was funny enough for the flyers, and catchy enough to stick.

Above left
Elizabeth Davis (-Simpson) of 7 Year Bitch.
By Lucy Hanna.

Above right
Selene Vigil of 7 Year Bitch. By Lucy Hanna.

At their debut performance it was apparent that 7 Year Bitch needed some more practice, but rather than letting this discourage them the band took it as a challenge. They became much more serious, writing new songs and honing their set in the Rathouse basement, which was directly under Mia's room. "She had to hear us learning how to play", says Davis (now Simpson), "and she still said 'Keep playing, keep doing it, don't listen to anyone that tells you you're not good.'" Her encouragement was vital for 7 Year Bitch, and it paid off. They re-emerged with a killer set at the Rathouse on New Year's Eve of 1991. The Gits and The DC Beggars played with them, and the show turned into a kind of impromptu rally/party against the Gulf War, Selene leading the crowd of wasted punks in time-honoured protest chants.

Later that year, the band released their first single, "Lorna" on Rathouse Records. This label was less a business than a tool for DIY, an in-house imprint that allowed the Rathouse bands to control the release of their own music.[15] "Lorna" is fast and tense, built around the grinding interaction between Elizabeth's intricate minor-key bassline and Stefanie's fierce, down-slashing chords. There's Slayer in the bass and Sonic Youth in the guitar, but it all comes together as punk rock. Selene uses a kind of punk recitation, almost rapping, to sketch the story of a self-possessed, sexually liberated woman who gets her head smashed through glass. It raises dark questions: was it a window on the world, or a mirror? Was she shoved into it for having a mind of her own, or was she pushed to some wild act of self-mutilation? Backed by an equally fearsome track called "Dead Men Don't Rape", the seven-inch stood as a statement of hard-edged, matter-of-fact feminism. Seattle scenesters quickly realised that this band was a force to be reckoned with, and Daniel House approached them about recording for C/Z. In the spring of 1992, 7 Year Bitch recorded six tracks for their debut EP, which would be called *Sick 'Em*.

At this point, the band's songwriting process was immediate and intuitive, inseparable from the fun of playing together. But looking back on those sessions, Agnew realises that everyone else's parts were coming together around Elizabeth's basslines:

"I don't think I knew at the time how good she was at writing songs—that she could hear all the parts in her head, that she had an idea of the whole song. She wasn't ever explaining that or trying to get us to do a specific thing, that early on. She had a vision and therefore had a clear enough, heavy enough riff for us to follow it, so it wasn't just meandering all over the place."

In Davis, the band had a songwriter of a rare calibre, capable of "hearing" an entire track in her head and then communicating that insight to her collaborators. It's common practice in punk to just throw some riffs together, but Davis knew how to communicate an underlying idea through her various riffs, endowing 7 Year Bitch tracks with a sense of internal, musical motivation.

Davis, however, saw herself and Valerie as a unified rhythm section: "I like the way that the drummer and that bass player play *together*, you know? It's more that kind of a thing than a particular bass player." She taught herself to play by following the locked-in bass/drum grooves on AC/DC and Stooges records, and the spirit of both bands is apparent in the minimalist stomp of *Chow Down*. There's more explicit Stooges influence in the bluesy, thrashing verse riffs of "Tired of Nothing" and "Gun". But Davis was also deeply into the dark, fractured rhythmic structures of The Birthday Party and The Jesus Lizard, influences that she shared with older Seattle bands like Skin Yard and Vexed.

As central as the rhythm section was to 7 Year Bitch, Sargent played with a brash style that set *Chow Down* apart. "She had a fierceness to her", says Agnew, "and it came out through her guitar"—as meaty, highly distorted power-chords played with furious intensity. Davis remembers that Sargent didn't have to double-pick on fast, strummed hardcore riffs. Instead of picking "down-up-down-up" she could play "down-down-down-down", hitting each chord as hard as she did the first time:

"It changes the sound of things, it's way more rad.... We did a split single with this London band called Thatcher On Acid. They told us, 'Yeah, we had to change it around because our guitar player couldn't keep up with Stefanie's down-stroking.' Stefanie definitely came from that super-fast hardcore punk style. That was a big influence for her."

Scott Benson's production seems like a deliberate response to Sargent's playing. The bass riffs rumble and the beats hit hard, but it's the guitar that dominates the record with sheet-metal clangour and mighty fuzz. Sargent contributed two excellent songs of her own, "In Lust You Trust" and "Sink", both of which open with slithering Melvins-esque metal riffs. Tracks like these suggest that, if 7 Year Bitch were playing today, their take on punk might be classified, as with Melvins, as "sludge". Indeed, every member of 7 Year Bitch was a serious Melvins fan, and the two groups were friends.

Early in the summer of 1992, *Chow Down* was mixed and readied for release. Meanwhile, 7 Year Bitch flew to New York to play a storming set at the New Music Festival. They returned to Seattle a band on the rise, planning their first tour. But on 28 June, Stefanie Sargent was discovered dead in her apartment from a combination of heroin and alcohol.[16] Like The Gits, 7 Year Bitch weren't just a group of collaborating musicians, but friends and allies, so this hit them hard. It's impossible to imagine how Stefanie's death affected them, so let's not attempt it here.

Just as the band was finding their stride, it had been broken. But after a period of doubt, they decided to continue playing. They found a new guitarist in Roisin Dunn, whom they already knew as a friend, and who could step naturally into Stefanie's place. Later that year they authorised C/Z to release all their recordings as an album-length compilation called *Sick 'Em*, which they dedicated to Sargent. By the summer of 1993, they were back to gigging and working on new material. Then, that July, Mia Zapata was murdered. In little more than a year, 7 Year Bitch took two shattering blows. But if the first shook their resolve, the second ultimately strengthened it—they had to carry on for Mia, who had encouraged them, and they had to give form to the pain, to turn it into something meaningful and then blow it all to hell through shivering amplifiers.

The resulting album was *Viva Zapata*, which C/Z would release in 1994. As Kurt Cobain, Eddie Vedder, and other idols of alt-rock built a glorified image of inner turmoil, 7 Year Bitch produced a document of loss. Selene thoroughly subverted the prevailing format, stripping away layers of apathy, irony, and cool until what was left was real, hard, and almost uncomfortable to hear. On "Derailed", she sings about forcing herself to relive the darkest moments and face the ugliest truths. It's masochistic but not nihilistic—this is her way of mastering the "memories of tragedies", transmuting them into wisdom. Consciously or not, Selene is channelling Mia's philosophy of sacrifice and struggle, carrying on her friend's legacy even in her mourning.

There are some bad songs on this album—the anti-heroin, anti-catchy vamp of "Hip Like Junk", the goofy feline pissing match of "Cat's Meow"—but they're so far removed from the centre of *Viva Zapata* that they simply don't matter. That centre is "M.I.A.", where the music and lyrics came together to capture everything 7 Year Bitch was feeling. "It's mad, and it's pointed, and it's kinda evil-sounding", Davis says, with some justified pride. Valerie had been honing her chops with drum lessons, so Elizabeth wrote the riffs in a tricky time signature and helped her counterpart work out a brutally subtle drum part: "I love where the snare placement is. The riff stays the same but the snare timing changes, and it changes the feeling of the riff." When the riff drops out and Selene sings "It's dark now", she sounds utterly alone. But when the rest of the band comes back in, grinding up a dissonant scale, their force has redoubled. The song closes with a chilling declaration: "Does society have justice for you? If not, I do."

While 7 Year Bitch were a punk rock band, tracks like "M.I.A." and "Rock A Bye" (their ode to Stefanie) have little to do with any notion of "rock". They are so dark, so dramatic, and so rhythmically fluid that the closest parallel is early Neurosis. This is no coincidence—Neurosis, like Melvins, were friends of and influences on 7 Year Bitch. It is important to remember, then, that as much hype as they received at the time, and as catchy as songs like "Lorna" were, 7 Year Bitch were in touch with the chthonic underside of punk-metal.

Recording *Viva Zapata* for C/Z gave 7 Year Bitch the opportunity to work with Jack Endino, who accentuated the dark, heavy side of their sound. He worked closely with Roisin, who was relatively new to guitar, to create her massive Sabbathian tone, and he built up the sound of the band as a whole. At the same time he cleaned things up, toning down the gonzo scuzz of *Chow Down* to emphasise Davis' elegant minimalist forms. Endino took 7 Year Bitch seriously as musicians in a way that music journalists, who fixated on their gender, had not:

"He was so cool to us. We had been dismissed by the press quite a bit for being girls, or for having songs that were short and fast and simple, but Jack Endino really appreciated stuff that we did. He would comment on it, like 'Yeah that's a really cool time signature', or 'That's an interesting change right there.' It felt really validating to be respected by someone like him."

7 Year Bitch initially had a strong relationship with C/Z, but by the time they were writing *Viva Zapata* that relationship was unravelling over many of the same issues that frustrated The Gits. Word of 7 Year Bitch had passed through strange channels, including Courtney Love, to Danny Goldberg at Atlantic, and he pursued them assiduously. Buzz and Dale of Melvins, who were experiencing their own major label woes, warned the younger band not to sign. But in the end the promise of label support and economic security won out, and 7 Year Bitch signed to Atlantic as they sat on the floor of the studio, Endino looking on like a presiding sage.

The story could end here, because in a way the rest of it is depressingly predictable—"underground band signed to major label in Seattle frenzy records middling commercial album and breaks up"—but 7 Year Bitch inverted this trope even in adhering to it. Normally, majors neglected artist development, rushing out albums by new signees in hopes of scoring a quick hit and confirming the value of their investment. In this case, though, it was the band who rushed their third album, *Gato Negro*, recording before they had played the songs enough on tour. Goldberg and his colleagues actually encouraged them to wait, but to no avail—7 Year Bitch acted under their own direction.

Often, underground bands that signed to majors made doomed attempts—under label pressure—to write catchier songs, alienating their fans without striking pop gold. But in this case, 7 Year Bitch adamantly refused to write a "radio friendly unit mover", and sought out the production skills of Billy Anderson, who was recommended to them by Neurosis, of all bands. He helped them bring out the distorted snarl in tracks "24,900 Miles Away" and "Disillusion", but this wasn't what the label wanted in a single, and it wasn't what the public wanted in a hit. Sales of the album were disappointing.

7 Year Bitch lost momentum. They had opened a stadium for the Red Hot Chili Peppers and toured large venues with the mighty Rage Against The Machine, but the headliner of their final tour was Everclear. After this, Roisin threw in the towel. She proved difficult to replace, and Selene was already living in Los Angeles. The band broke up just before a trip to Brazil, where they were scheduled to play with the excellent street-punk band Ratos de Porão.

At the time, 7 Year Bitch received a lot of attention for being an all-female band. This was understandable, but it tended to obscure the more important fact—they were a *really* good band. It also led to their being lumped in with riot grrrl. Agnew stresses that her band supported the movement, but was not a part of it. For her, the difference is that those bands espoused an "academic" feminism, a programmatic effort to change the rock scene and fight patriarchy in the public sphere, while 7 Year Bitch simply lived their lives as feminists and allowed those principles inform their music. If riot grrrl wrote "about" being autonomous women, 7 Year Bitch wrote "from" the perspective of autonomous women.

The feminist radicalism of 7 Year Bitch was not in what they questioned, but in what they took for granted. Their genius was to hold up a distinctly female mirror to the cocksure swagger of rock'n'roll and the tough-guy aggression of hardcore. They played with the boys' club on its own terms, but not as boys. In "Gun", Selene sings about standing up to thuggish bullies (cops?) by staring them down with a loaded weapon.[17] In "The Scratch", she brushes off a cowardly suitor and then sings, "I will. Have my. Cake and. Eat it. Too. Just like you." Rather than condemning male sexual entitlement, she asserts her own symmetrical entitlement, the right to enjoy life as she pleases, with whomever she pleases.

Engine Kid

By the time *Viva Zapata* came out in mid-1994, the spell of the Seattle Sound was lifting. The major labels still hovered around the city, picking off what new talent they could, but the feeding frenzy was dying down. The bands from Seattle's mid-80s scene were either broken up or touring stadiums, and the die-hard punk community had started to come apart in the wake of Mia Zapata's murder. In this post-grunge malaise, though, a band called Engine Kid signalled the continued vitality of the Seattle underground even as they looked beyond the regional scene.

Engine Kid did not sound like a grunge band, or any kind of Seattle band. They charted a strange path through a thicket of emerging subgenres: indie rock, post-rock, post-hardcore, screamo, emo, math rock, sludge, and even death metal. It was as if "Seattle" was a musical idea they were running from or trying to overcome.

The band's guitarist and lead songwriter was Greg Anderson. Today, Anderson is the head of Southern Lord Records, the partner of Stephen O'Malley in Sunn0))), and the former guitarist of Goatsnake. But he came to Engine Kid from the Seattle hardcore scene. He started going to shows as a high school freshman in 1985, and quickly started hanging around with older kids in a band called False Liberty, who were vaguely political and extremely fast. When their guitarist left, he joined the band. Anderson was a huge fan of The Accused, and he looked up to Tommy Niemeyer as a friend and mentor: "If it wasn't for Tommy, I don't know if I'd be here. He's the one who inspired me to play guitar. He made me tapes of Poison Idea and English Dogs and Discharge, and it was the first time I'd heard stuff like that."

Tommy's crucial recommendations, as well as his band's vicious thrash attack, helped the young Anderson see vital connections between metal and hardcore (this wasn't obvious to everyone, back then). When he started playing guitar in his own band, with the drummer of False Liberty, they juxtaposed the insane speed of Siege and DRI with big, slow pit riffs inspired by Sabbath and St Vitus. Their overall aesthetic, however, came from Boston tough-guy hardcore. They called themselves Brotherhood (after a DYS song), they wore gym shorts, and they were the *only* straight-edge band in late-80s Seattle.

Brotherhood had an uphill battle. They were radically out of step with the inebriated state of the city; their music sounded nothing like grunge or even punk rock, and their existence coincided perfectly with the Teen Dance Ordinance, which made it almost impossible for them to play out locally. The hardcore scene was crippled: "Besides us there were maybe one or two other bands. We were right in the middle of this lull." But, true to the hardcore ideal, Brotherhood prevailed against the odds to record a seven-inch and a demo. Out of the blue, Greg got a call from his old friend Tommy, who asked them to open for The Accused on an American tour in early 1989. The bands toured together for a month and a half, opening up pits across the country, then returned to Seattle and broke up. Later that year a German label called Crucial Response released their two recordings as *Words Run... As Thick As Blood!*

Greg, sick of straight-edge and increasingly interested in other forms of music, briefly moved to San Diego, where bands like Heroin, Rocket From The Crypt, and Drive Like Jehu were beginning to shape the "screamo" sound. Greg was paying close attention to these bands, and to related music coming out of DC's Dischord scene. When he returned to Seattle he cut his teeth on these more melodic sounds in a short-lived "emotional hardcore" band called Galleon's Laugh, which he formed with Nate Mendel from Christ On A Crutch. They broke up within a year. Mendel went on to Sunny Day Real Estate while Anderson formed Engine Kid with bassist Brian Kraft and drummer Chris Vandebrooke.

Anderson's musical horizons were rapidly expanding beyond hardcore, and hearing Slint had been a revelation for him. He was an enthusiast, a consummate fan, and he knew he wanted to do something in a similar vein, exploring deliberate tempos and extreme dynamic contrasts. So, as he frankly acknowledges, "Engine Kid was really, really influenced by Slint." They were also influenced by Chicago noise/post-punk bands like Rapeman and Bastro, and by the angularity and distortion of the "San Diego Sound". That didn't stop some people from pegging them as a Slint-worship band, however, a reputation that unfairly saddled them for most of their career.

In 1992 Engine Kid put out a debut seven on Anderson's DIY label, Battery Records, but Daniel House soon approached them about signing to C/Z. With his background in post-punk and prog, he was naturally drawn to their labyrinthine rhythms and crystalline harmonies: "Engine Kid just kind of came from a different place. I was really into Slint, and obviously they were really into Slint. They were the only band around doing anything like that. But when they got heavier they were that much heavier. And live there was such an intensity...."

Engine Kid were stylistic outliers even within the third generation of Seattle groups, so it meant a lot for them to be recognised by someone from the core of the old scene. And, in a way, the band made sense on C/Z's roster:

"At that point we felt like we were connected. 'OK, Daniel House from Skin Yard who has this label, he's given us the stamp of approval.' We didn't really fit in with bands like The Gits or 7 Year Bitch, but that was something cool about his label—there was diversity there. At that time, Sub Pop's new signings were going elsewhere. C/Z was almost like this outcast label that stepped in and scooped up the good Seattle bands."

In 1993, C/Z released Engine Kid's *Astronaut* EP, followed by a full-length album they called *Bear Catching Fish*. *Astronaut* was vulnerable to kneejerk Slint comparison, but Engine Kid was already a distinct entity. The difference was apparent in the quality of the sound alone. Where Slint spun webs of trebly guitar, Engine Kid moved from reflective arpeggios to crushing waves of warm distortion. Engine Kid had Slint's delicacy but none of their nervousness.

Bear Catching Fish saw the band distinguishing themselves from their initial inspirations. "Treasure Chest" opens with a wall of roaring noise, quiets down, and then builds to a kind of ecstatic Sabbath riff. "The Rockford Files", written by Kraft, sounds like Sonic Youth playing on Napalm Death's guitars. Anderson acknowledges that, from the beginning, Engine Kid were approaching post-rock with a metal mentality: "We were still really into the heavy, dark side of things, Melvins and St Vitus and stuff like that, but putting a different twist on it." They recorded the album in Chicago with Shellac's Steve Albini and he helped reinforce the more abrasive side of Engine Kid's songs without compromising their poignancy.

The record's liner notes explain that they "drove 1400+ miles from Seattle to Chicago to record in the basement of some guy's brick house. Go figure." They might have driven even further for a chance to record with Albini, but the broader point is that this was a band on the road: "All we did, basically, was tour. That's probably one reason we broke up, actually. We just spent too much time together in a van. We'd come home from tour, live on someone's couch for a month, and then be off for the next one, trying to string these things together as close as we possibly could."

In other words, they were "Engine Kid" in an almost literal sense of the word.[18] They mostly played DIY shows at houses and small bars, events organised by local bands and committed scenesters. But they did progress to larger venues. "Near the end of the band", Anderson recalls, "we were headlining tours and able to bring out 150-200 kids, which to us was really good back then."

Touring was simply what this band did, what they loved to do, but there was a broader significance to their road-dog habits. Engine Kid, like Brotherhood, was oriented outwards, and they were adapting to the increasingly de-localised nature of music scenes. The band had strong friendships and musical affinities with Seattle groups like Silkworm, Treepeople, and Sunny Day Real Estate, but they were also part of a national scene with no single regional center. Simultaneously, they inhabited their native city and a cross-country network of bands, labels, and local scenes. To cover this broader space, the group had to stay on the move.

Engine Kid's migration patterns also helped them adapt to life in Seattle as grunge bloated then declined. Since they were frequently on the road, they were able to keep some distance from the destructive commercial hype cycle and the solidification of various musical clichés. But Anderson remembers playing out frequently in Seattle, as well:

"By that time we were all over 21, and that's where the scene was, with C/Z and Sub Pop and whatnot. There, it was more common to do the bar shows than it was all-ages shows. And actually, there weren't many bands that could pull off doing both. I was excited that we were one of those bands. We could play the OK Hotel and do well, but we could also go and play the Crocodile and do well. I was proud at the time that the kids were still into what we were doing, and that the over-21 crowd was into it as well."

Anderson's perspective confirms what other accounts have suggested, that even after the revival of the DIY scene through bands like The Gits and venues like the OK Hotel, Seattle remained a bar town.

After finishing work on *Bear Catching Fish*, Engine Kid changed direction. Kraft and Anderson decided to part ways with Chris and recruit their friend Jade Devitt as the new drummer. Chris had from the indie rock school, and was technically skilled but not the hardest hitter. Jade, on the other hand, played aggressively, and Anderson was excited at possibilities that opened up: "The band kind of changed. It might not be apparent to a casual listener, but we felt it had changed. We had a better drummer, who hit harder, and we were playing heavier. It was not a drastic style change, but it was definitely important for us as a band."

At the same time, C/Z was stricken with financial problems, and effectively closed down without warning. Engine Kid had to find a new label, and they turned to Revelation Records, an East Coast institution known for championing the "youth crew" hardcore sound. Anderson had befriended Jordan Cooper while playing with Brotherhood, and he knew that Revelation was branching out into more experimental territory by signing bands like Iceburn, a Salt Lake City group who played withering, technical "jazzcore". Engine Kid was a natural fit, and Revelation agreed to release their next full-length.

Going into this recording, Engine Kid were absorbing two new and seemingly contradictory influences. On the one hand, all three started getting into jazz. Anderson says they favoured "late 60s and early 70s Miles Davis, John Coltrane, and fusion bands like the Mahavishnu Orchestra". Exploring this new horizon dovetailed with a dramatic swerve from the straight-edge towards the wavy line: "We were smoking massive amounts of marijuana for the first time in our lives. Really getting into weed." On the other hand, Anderson was falling under the spell of the most brutal and extreme music he had ever heard—death metal. Since this was probably *the* decisive turning point in his career, and a big change for his band, it's worth quoting him at length here:

"At the time there were a bunch of death metal bands actually signing to major labels. They started making records that were produced really well, I couldn't believe how incredible they sounded. There was Carcass, and Morbid Angel, and Entombed, and Cathedral as well, though that was a lot slower and sludgier. I'd never heard insane guitar sounds like that. It was because these bands got some budget and went into a studio and spent some more time. I was really into how incredibly heavy that sounded, and that's the direction I wanted Engine Kid to go in. I started kinda forcing death metal into the equation of what we were doing. And, unfortunately, that wasn't really a mutual feeling amongst all three of us...."

Revelation released *Angel Wings* in 1994. Amusingly, the first part of the record seems to dramatize Engine Kid's stylistic shift. They begin with "Windshield", a sensitive, pretty emo/indie song that calls up memories of "sleeping in the summer rain" and poses the perennial question, "Can I drive you home?" It's closer to verse/chorus pop than anything Engine Kid had done up to that point. Then "Holes To Fight In" blows it all to hell. It opens with huge major chords shaded like a sunset, ringing out until Anderson drops into distorted chug. Kraft curls his melodic bassline around it, rising to a wordless scream, and then everything explodes into convulsive doom-hardcore and yowled vocals. You can practically see the circle pit open up. And in less than two minutes, Engine Kid have foreshadowed some of the most iconic sounds in the next decade of heavy music: the micro-riffs of Mogwai, the textures of Pelican, the roiling rhythms of early Kylesa, the violent passion of Planes Mistaken For Stars; it's all there, and more. This track even hints at the drone power Anderson would later unleash in Sunn0))).

It'd be difficult to argue that this relatively obscure band from Seattle had a direct influence on all those groups, but *Angel Wings* was bursting with cool ideas whose time had not quite arrived. Engine Kid's jazz tendencies were evident in Kraft's cycling basslines, sometimes reminiscent of a young Dave Holland, and in moments of light, tight ensemble playing like the jam that opens "Jumper Cables". The album closes with an extended cover of John Coltrane's "Olé" that brings out its latent heaviness. *Angel Wings* passes from plaintive indie through storming sludge and on into abstract art-music.

This small masterpiece of an album signalled great things to come, but the other members of Engine Kid were not as into their new sound as Anderson was. They also saw that other bands from their circle had developed a much more accessible sound, and no longer had to live on couches and in vans:

"Jade, especially, wanted to go in a more melodic direction. He was roommates with the Sunny Day Real Estate guys. He was really into them, and he saw what was happening with them. That band just exploded in the mid-90s in Seattle. Those were all friends of ours, guys we'd all played in bands with, so it was like 'Oh, this is what these guys are doing, and this is how popular they became....'"

Once more we see how the booming music industry of the 1990s exerted an almost gravitational pull on Seattle, reshaping the music community in its own image. Just *knowing* there was a chance to break out of voluntary poverty and relative anonymity affected people's thinking. Of course, this is not to suggest that Anderson's bandmates wanted to pander to the mainstream—they genuinely loved what Sunny Day Real Estate was doing, and they had genuine musical differences with Anderson.

On Engine Kid's final recording, the "Heater Sweats Nails" single, it's easy to hear why the trio had to part ways. The title track bore almost no resemblance to the kind of music the band had set out to play. It was full-on sludge, dark and crushing downtempo hardcore that wore its metal influences on its sleeve. It indicated where Greg was going, but this was not what Brian and Jade had signed up for, and not what they wanted to do. The B-side, "Husk", is like a musical trace of Engine Kid's breakup. Anderson plays in the fragile, shimmering style of post-rock, but his melodies are darker now. Kraft sounds a droning bassline, and Devitt plays with carefully restrained power. The track swells ominously and then, tension undiminished, fades away.

End

These bands are unified not only by their musical and personal ties, but by the situation they faced. They saw their world reconfigured by the attention of major labels, the media machine, and the broader American culture industry. Suddenly, they might have the chance to make a living doing what they loved, or to reach broader audiences, or just to get their albums released. And yet their artistic decisions placed them all on the periphery of this revolution. They didn't fit the grunge bill, and they played music that was too rough, too strange, or too honest to market easily.

If Seattle was the city where "punk broke", then it was also the city where punk was broken, momentarily—where it buckled under the weight of commerce and contradiction. No urban scene had faced this kind of pressure before, and few American indie bands had been faced with the same set of opportunities, temptations and traps. Almost everyone quoted here had his or her own way of saying what Greg Anderson put especially well:

"There was so much money coming into Seattle, all these big league major labels were just coming in and throwing money around—publishing deals and record deals and all these things that were so foreign and new. So it was like, 'Well, it happened to this band, so it's not out of the question that it's gonna happen to our band', you know? I think that attitude killed a lot of bands…. People went for the gold, so to speak, but it just wasn't realistic. It all came and went. You see what your roommate or neighbour's doing and you think, 'Aw shit, I could do that!' But obviously it's not gonna happen for everyone."

Ten years ago, these bands had all faded into relative obscurity, their work remembered by dedicated fans who understood the music because they'd *been there* for it, whether they were in Seattle or beyond. Their records were artefacts you had to hunt for. Today, the Internet gives us a total retrospective view of the last half-century of popular music. If you look for it you can hear it, or buy it, or read it. The music of the Seattle underground is very much present and accessible, in some cases more so than it was in the 1980s. And now, with some historical perspective, we can hear its real significance.

Thanks to the collapse of the majors and the radical decentralisation of the music industry, musicians can live with the kind of autonomy and sustainability that bands like The Gits and Skin Yard struggled to secure. It's still not lucrative to play heavily distorted guitar music, but it's possible to build a worldwide following and pay (most of) your bills without compromising your integrity. The underground bands of the Seattle scene are long defunct, but they took the first, fraught steps towards building a world where the mainstream is just an embarrassing footnote to the underground. In the end, punk wins.

Notes

1   Lee Lumsden, liner notes to *History In Reverse*, Spring 2004.

2   Prato, Greg, *Grunge Is Dead: The Oral History of Seattle Rock Music*, Toronto: ECW Press, 2009, 64–5.

3   Azerrad, Michael, *Our Band Could Be Your Life: Scenes from the American Rock Underground 1981–1991*, 1st ed., Boston: Little, Brown, 2001, p. 426.

4   While Endino's playing with Skin Yard often verged on noise-rock, his influences as a lead guitarist were surprisingly classicist, dating back to his youth: Robert Fripp and Robin Trower, Tony Iommi, Jimmy Page and, "looming over them all", Tony McPhee of The Groundhogs.

5   Doug Pray, *Hype!*, 1996.

6   *Gruntruck Documentary 1992*.

7   Justin Vellucci, "Interview with Vexed", *DOA*, January 16, 2006.

8   Cluster, Dan, "Milton Garrison Interview. Part II: The Vexed Years", *Noise*, 10 July 2010.

9   Vellucci, "Interview with Vexed".

10 In 1996, Broken ReKids re-released these demo tracks on CD and vinyl as the *Kings And Queens* album. George Horn of Fantasy Studios mastered the original two-track recording, bringing out the warmth and youth in Mia's voice.

11 Steve Moriarty, "The Gits Timeline", *The Gits*.

12 Moriarty, "The Gits Timeline."

13 Yarm, Mark, *Everybody Loves Our Town: An Oral History of Grunge*, 1st ed., New York: Crown Archetype, 2011, p. 327.

14 Kerri O'Kane, *The Gits*, documentary, 2008.

15 In 1991, for instance, Rathouse released the *Bobbing For Pavement* compilation, a kind of *Deep Six* for the resurgent punk underground.

16 Haberstroh, Joe and Patrick Macdonald, "Guitarist Sargent Found Dead", *The Seattle Times*, 30 June 1992. http://community.seattletimes.nwsource.com/archive/?date=19920630&slug=1499798

17 The lyrics here are by Davis, though.

18 There are three songs about cars on their final full-length, but these are far from "Pink Cadillac". On these tracks, Engine Kid blurs the distinction between the metal guts of the vehicle and the machinery of the soul.

PHOENIX, ARIZONA

"A HALL WHERE WEIRDOS
SOMETIMES WRESTLE/
A FITTING PLACE FOR US
FREAKS TO NESTLE."
JFA "MAD GARDEN"

NOEL GARDNER

Regional music scenes can be and often are wonderful things, of course: wells of creativity, culture and inspiration. Nevertheless, there is potential for these scenes to become victims of their own success. Most typically, this happens when one or other act takes on the appearance of figureheads. They attract copyists who see a way to snag some quick-fit popularity, and invariably dilute whatever made the scene so thrilling to begin with.

With this in mind, the music that emerged from Phoenix, Arizona in the 1980s was all the more remarkable. Pretty much none of the bands involved sounded like any other, and although the scene in the city mushroomed due to the explosion of punk rock, it was far from a given that a 'punk show' in Phoenix would consist of music that conformed to the tropes of the genre. Some of the bands involved made records which stand among the most revelatory and least tethered documents of the American underground in that decade.

No legitimate rock stars or globally recognised icons emerged from Phoenix punk; no rabble-rousers to rally round a la Dead Kennedys, Black Flag or Minor Threat. Apropos the point about figureheads and copyists, maybe if one of the bands involved had somehow started to shift serious units, it might have shifted everyone's focus. But what were the chances of that happening for the Sun City Girls, who from their misleadingly gendered name onwards needled and provoked audiences while creating unruly beauty from improvised, globally influenced clatter? Or for Mighty Sphincter, who specialised in truly unhinged gothic discordance that ranks with the cream of 80s 'deathrock' while remaining totally punk in its attitude? Or the Meat Puppets, whose love for all manner of canonical, well known big hitters was belied by an unfathomably weird acid-dipped outlook on life?

As it happened, the Meat Puppets *would* go on to enjoy a dalliance with the rock mainstream—but not until the 1990s, after Nirvana's *Nevermind* had served as a catalyst for major labels to sign myriad bands from similar backgrounds. By this point, the Phoenix scene as it had existed in the decade previous was but a distant memory. All relevant parties had broken up, moved away, returned to obscurity or sunk into personal turmoil. However, the documentary evidence left behind on vinyl, cassette and master tape sounds everlastingly fresh. If the Phoenix underground of old is underappreciated today—and it is—it's because there was no easy way of grouping the bands together, not because said bands weren't terrific.

In pondering why Phoenix produced such wild and woolly music in this period, it's tempting to resort to geographical and social cod theories. Located in the southwest of the USA, in a state whose landscape is typified by vast expanses of desert, blisteringly hot and humid summers are the norm. For residents, the only thing to do is roll with it. "The summer lets you know what nature is all about," says Dan Clark, a Phoenix scene lynchpin whose CV includes The Feederz, Victory Acres and Mighty Sphincter. "It doesn't give a damn whether you're alive or dead. It gets so fucking hot it's funny. To this day I can't work if I'm not pouring sweat."

"Of course", counters Richard Bishop, one third of Sun City Girls and now a solo artist and member of Rangda, "when other people try to describe us, the first thing they all mention is how sun-damaged we were. That's just a way for them to say that they didn't understand what we were all about. I'm OK with that."

Historically, Arizona has tended towards social conservatism, and since the Second World War has usually been a nailed-on Republican victory come election time. During the Reagan era 1980s, it may have felt like a bellwether for the United States as a whole. Alan Bishop, brother of Richard and also a Sun City Girls member, recalls:

"There was definitely a confrontational tension in the air during that period, especially regarding the police. They always used helicopters to fly over and patrol the city and shine spotlights on people to intimidate them as they walked the streets at night. It was easy to stand out in Phoenix and create situations everywhere that bordered on confrontational. It was a way of life."

In spite of considerable population increase throughout the 60s and 70s, leaving it the ninth largest city in the United States by 1980, Phoenix was timid when it came to embracing the counterculture. Alice Cooper, then known as plain old Vincent Furnier, fronted a garage band called The Spiders; acerbic glam/proto-punk conceptualists The Tubes were a merger of two Phoenix combos. In both cases, they moved to California in the late 60s to further their career ambitions. The birth of punk failed to quell this trend.

The first punk band to form in the city was The Consumers, prog rock enthusiasts converted on exposure to Sex Pistols and Damned 45s. A less then sympathetic environment greeted the band: the sleeve notes for *All My Friends Are Dead*, recorded in 1977 and released in 1995, talk of pissed-off rednecks threatening members with knives. Dan Clark formed its *second* punk band, The Exterminators, "after seeing The Consumers having to play three sets a night". This was par for the course in the city's bar band culture.

"The shows then were all confrontational. There were no punks other than us and a few others. Some of the weirder artsy gay crowd would show up, but it always wound up with about ten of us against 50-plus cowboys or bikers." The Consumers split for Los Angeles shortly after recording what would become *All My Friends Are Dead*, as did The Exterminators' drummer Jimmy Giorsetti. He would shortly reappear in the Germs, calling himself Don Bolles (after a Phoenix journalist who was assassinated in 1976) and playing a key role in the invention of hardcore.

The Feederz, formed by Clark and his friend Frank Discussion in 1978 (Clark: "We met on the dancefloor at a Consumers show. I recall coming up from a pile of bodies and I had the distinct feeling that somebody was on acid"), upped the outrage quotient to a degree that has scarcely been equaled since, let alone at the time. They were also the only 70s Phoenix punk band to survive the transition between decades. Their debut show was marked by Frank firing blanks from an assault rifle at the audience; his departure from Arizona was forced in 1981 by a warrant for his arrest, the result of a prank which faked documents purporting to be from the state's Department of Education. In between, the band penned debut single "Jesus", which can still out-blaspheme any black metal you care to name, and played live shows that might be best described as sticky situationism.

Above left

Frank Discussion of The Feederz at Mad Garden with rat and hammer. Pope Paul Bernsten, centre, looking on, 7 November 1981. By Neal "Doc" Holliday.

Above right

The Feederz, "Jesus", 1980.

Frank is generally assumed to be the brains behind the Feederz' anarchy, but Meat Puppets bassist Cris Kirkwood, who started dabbling in Phoenix punk in the late 70s, differs. "The Feederz was so much [Clark]. Wearing clear suit bags; shave your head and dump honey and a bag of live cockroaches on it—Dan's idea!"

Clark: "We both loved that stuff. We both had snakes, fish and lizards, ferrets, rats and whatnot as pets. So we were very accustomed to preparing dinner with and for rodents, insects and our cold-blooded friends. This lent itself to using hordes of crickets, baby mice and rats in the shows." During this era, both lived in a rambunctious commune known as the Hate House.

"It was a neat little explosion of an art scene, one that was definitely brought about by punk rock", recalls Cris Kirkwood, who rehearsed there early on with the Puppets. "It attracted all these freaky people, and a lot of them were really not that stable! But that's not necessarily [indicative of] punk—it's just the times, and Phoenix, and how people are. It was just a dwelling that stayed in the hands of a succession of people until it fell prey to the same thing everybody else did. Weirdness."

"Hate House was absolutely crazy", confirms Clark. "In Phoenix in the summer with swamp cooling you don't keep your windows and doors closed. So we had a big house, downtown with doors wide open. This was pre-AIDS so the 70s drug and sex culture was still in full swing. My brother [Doug Clark, frontman of Mighty Sphincter] had it for a while and painted the indoors black and covered it with spider webs. We had the Bad Brains stay there and they wouldn't come in—they slept in their van. The Gun Club, 45 Grave and SPK all stayed there. 45 Grave had a New Year's LSD party that I'm sure many would like to forget, full of naked, sweaty, blazing monsters."

Lorraine and Charlie Monoxide (scene regulars)
outside Hate House. By Robert Steinhilber.

JFA, *Blatant Localism*, 1981.

Meat Puppets, *In A Car*, 1981.

"A lot of the people back then were doing a lot of drugs", confirms Lucy Lamode, singer of outrageous new wave curios Killer Pussy. "I didn't participate, even though it was all around me, but I never judged anybody for what they were doing."

Hate House founder Rick Bertoni, who died of an overdose in 1991, fronted a band called The Deez. "He got bored easily and we only did a few shows", says Don Redondo, who promptly became one of the founder members of Jodie Foster's Army, more commonly known as JFA. Their name was a tribute of sorts to John Hinckley Jr, an unwell Texan who a matter of weeks prior to their early '81 formation had attempted to assassinate President Reagan to impress Jodie Foster. (The actress would later acknowledge the band, rather more approvingly than she did the gunman.)

Having become friends through skateboarding—all members skated, and continue to 32 years later—JFA transferred the energy they expended on the ramps to their music. Before the year was out they had a debut seven-inch, the *Blatant Localism* EP on the Placebo label. At a time when punk's mutation into hardcore was a rapidly spreading infection, and the idea of impact through velocity was gaining traction, cuts like "Out Of School" and "Cokes and Snickers" were faster than nearly anything else yet heard. One notable rival in this area, in fact, were the Meat Puppets, whose 1981 debut EP *In A Car* (five songs, five minutes) was blisteringly speedy. "There was nobody else [playing fast] except the Meat Puppets and they were new too—their early shows were *gnarly*!" enthuses Redondo.

Hardcore ferocity was a passing phase for the Puppets, comprised of the Kirkwood brothers plus drummer Derrick Bostrom. Their self-titled debut LP, released by Greg Ginn's SST label in 1982, was tangentially related to the movement, but equally indebted to prog rock, psychedelia and bluegrass. By its follow-up, *Meat Puppets II*, two years later—perhaps the most treasured part of their catalogue, thanks partly but by no means wholly to Nirvana covering three of its songs on their *Unplugged* live album—they had put away punkish things near-entirely. Cris Kirkwood:

"Well, on one hand we were hardly ever punk rock *enough*... by the time we started playing in bands, in late '79, punk bands were only supposed to look that

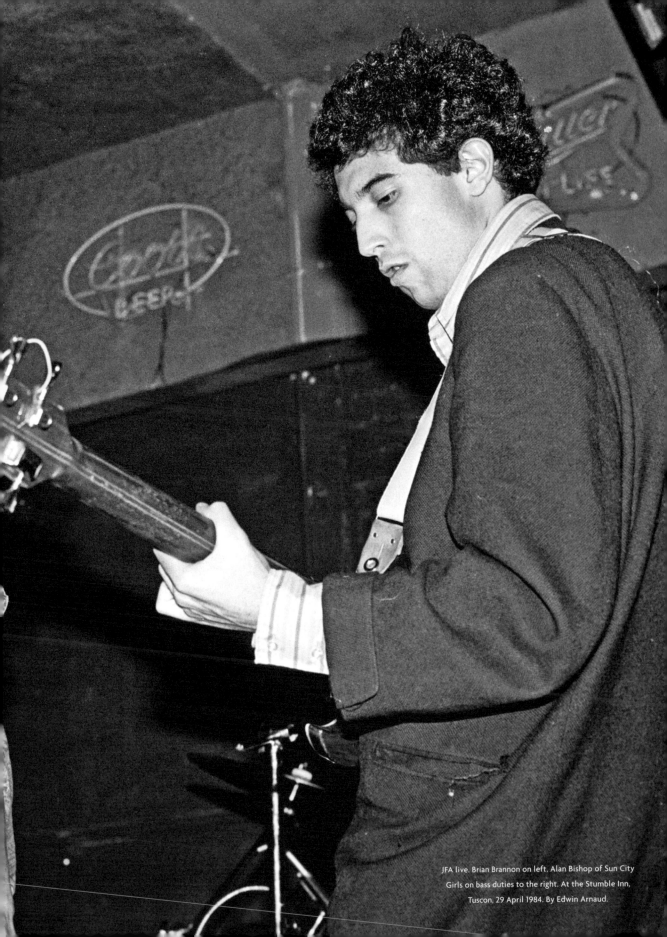

JFA live. Brian Brannon on left, Alan Bishop of Sun City Girls on bass duties to the right. At the Stumble Inn, Tuscon, 29 April 1984. By Edwin Arnaud.

one way, and then hardcore started developing and all that kinda stuff. And we just did the crap we wanted to do. The artier side of punk rock allowed for this."

The Meat Puppets were pretty much unique among Phoenix bands, in that all of their releases appeared on out-of-state labels. Despite their image as slightly oblivious banjo-owning goofballs, they had some pretty neat connections. Bostrom, present at Phoenix punk's inception, stayed in contact with LA-bound Consumers frontman David Wiley; a track from an early Puppets tape surfaced on a Los Angeles Free Music Society compilation. "Then we met the people from Monitor [another LA art collective], who had their own World Imitation label", Kirkwood relates. "That's who put out the first seven-inch. At one point Black Flag came through town and we played with them; they asked if we'd like to do a record [on SST]."

By the time of that debut album, Phoenix had enough individual sproutings to make it clear a new scene was forming. The Brainz' self-released single (released in 1979), equal parts Sabbath and The Sonics, was notable for featuring three future members of Mighty Sphincter in its lineup. Grant And The Geezers gigged with visiting punk icons including Black Flag, The Misfits and TSOL, despite playing a moderately punked-up strain of rockabilly. Jr Chemists played ultra-basic strum-pop with a preteen outlook, which predated Beat Happening by a good two years. They featured Michael Cornelius, who would join JFA on bass immediately after their breakup in early '81, and released a split single with Tucson's similarly amateurish Les Seldoms.

Phoenix bands with female input were few and far between (a discrepancy also found in most other scenes, it should be said), but Killer Pussy, fronted by Lucy Lamode, packed enough vampishness and sexploitation into their songs and shows to compensate. The Hate House scene was crucial to their formation: Lamode's first band, The Roll-Ons, featured Frank Discussion, while Feederz drummer John E Precious came aboard when she formed Killer Pussy. Yet what might have stalled as a localised in-joke ended up being anything but. For a period in the early 80s, the group enjoyed considerably more fame and notoriety than any other products of Phoenix punk.

"I was eighteen when I started Killer Pussy," remembers Lamode. "We weren't serious; we were just having fun. We decided to record an EP called *Teenage Enema Nurses In Bondage*. The guys in the band were good friends with Freddy Snakeskin, a radio personality on [Los Angeles station] KROQ. They knew him from when they went to high school together in Phoenix. They sent him a copy, he started playing it on the radio and people went crazy for it!"

California subsequently became Killer Pussy's secondary—perhaps even primary—market, their hugely arch pop with a John Waters-esque taste for sauce playing well among LA's fast-moving brashness. Their claims to fame/infamy, as recounted by Lamode, are legion and sometimes surreal. At one gig in Anaheim, their support act was Spinal Tap—the movie was being filmed at the time, so no-one knew who they were. Bret Easton Ellis namechecked *Teenage Enema Nurses...* in *Less Than Zero*, his debut novel. The band counted Dennis Hopper as a celebrity fan, and when he took up painting in the early 80s, his portfolio included *Killer Pussy*—a nurse-costumed Lamode in "the classic *Attack Of The 50 Foot Woman* pose". The band hooked up with actress Edith Massey, a staple of John Waters' movies, for three live performances in 1984; Massey and Lamode duetted on "These Boots Are Made For Walking", and these were Massey's last public appearances before her death a few weeks later. Additionally, claims Lamode, "the number one Halloween costume in LA in those days was to dress up as a sexy enema nurse".

Killer Pussy, *Teenage Enema Nurses In Bondage*,
1982.

Lucy Lamode of Killer Pussy inside chicken wire
cage at Mad Garden, 1981. By Neal "Doc" Holliday.

Opposite top
Derrick Bostrom of Meat Puppets at Nino's,
Tuscon, ZA, March 1984. By Edwin Arnaud.

Opposite bottom
Cris Kirkwood of Meat Puppets at Nino's,
Tuscon, ZA, March 1984. By Edwin Arnaud.

Previous
Curt Kirkwood of Meat Puppets at Nino's,
Tuscon, ZA, March 1984. By Edwin Arnaud.

Killer Pussy's OTT sexuality permeated *Bikini Wax*, their sole album from '83. The lyrics to songs like "Boys", "Pocket Pool" and "Dildo Desire" are barely even subtle enough to qualify as double entendres; the music is colourful new wave daftness influenced by girl groups, rockabilly and synthpop. "I came from a very strict Italian Catholic family and was not exposed to a lot of things—especially sexual things", Lamode says. " I didn't have my first sexual relationship until I was 21, so yes, in a way it was an act, because I wasn't some nasty porn-queen sex addict like someone who didn't know me might think. But the moves and the stage presence and the way I spoke to the audience... that was the real me."

Attitudes were even inclusive enough to embrace someone like Eddy Detroit, a one-time White Panther in the Motor City itself who hung with Nico and Mary Hopkin during the 70s and moved to Phoenix in 1981. His *Immortal Gods* LP, privately pressed the following year, features Dan Clark and two Sun City Girls among others. Partly inert acid-folk, partly rollicking ritual chant-pop and lyrically fixated on Satan, *Immortal Gods* is a lost outsider classic in the best sense: one of uncompromising oddness rather than a point-and-laugh car crash.

An avant-garde scene was also gestating at this time, formed around a small but dedicated core of folks. David Oliphant, who moved to Phoenix from upstate Flagstaff, was certainly one of the keenest. His first solo project, Destruction ("the idea was a general destruction of limitations, not objects"), evolved into a band featuring Sun City Girls' Alan Bishop among others. After this came Dali's Daughter ("sound art and noise") and Maybe Mental, which ended up releasing several tapes and a split LP with the formidable Controlled Bleeding. Maybe Mental was of a piece with the dread end of the era's DIY cassette culture: what would come to be dubbed dark ambient, or industrial before that mutated into something MTV-viable. *To Cease Burning* (1985) is a minor classic of oppressive synths and cold sweats.

Oliphant: "Growing up, two of my most influential composers were John Cage and Stockhausen. Within a few years my exposure to punk was the discovery of bands like Chrome, Throbbing Gristle, SPK and many others. At the core of what might be called the punk rock attitude was the lo-fi do it yourself mentality, which motivated me to start experimenting with sound."

International Language, who sporadically featured David Wiley, had almost nothing formally released but commanded considerable respect. "They were a great electronic dance band with a Pere Ubu feel", says Dan Clark. "George [Dillon, frontman] was a great poet in Phoenix and helped finance cool stuff."

Brian Brannon, JFA vocalist: "The early 80s were a golden age for Phoenix punk. Everyone was going in so many different directions and no one thought twice about International Language playing some weird industrial music stuff, and then having Grant And The Geezers go on afterwards and throw down some tight rockabilly jams."

Another ensemble sucked in by this gravitational pull were Sun City Girls, whose very earliest performances took place at open mic/free improv nights in nearby Tempe. Some of them were hosted by Alan Bishop, bassist of the trio—although this role was but a fraction of what one might see him do onstage, likewise his guitarist brother Richard and drummer Charles Gocher. "I think the open mic scene allows for a greater sense of freedom, looseness, and immediacy of performance", Alan says. "You're allowed 10 to 20 minutes to give what you got, so one becomes quite aware of the moment and tendency for maximising it."

Before SCG hit the studio in earnest, the Bishop brothers spent just under a year as members of Paris 1942—a quartet also featuring Jesse Srgoncik, another local

Sun City Girls, 1983. By Neal "Doc" Holliday.

scene perennial, and Moe Tucker of The Velvet Underground. The group formed a decade after Tucker had quit the Velvets, while their unedifying reformation was still another decade away, which might explain why Paris 1942 is just about the most obscure branch of the VU rock family tree. Nevertheless, their self-titled LP—recorded in 1982 but unreleased until the mid-90s—is a compelling test of the garage ethos's limitations. At times it cribs from the VU/Modern Lovers book of detuned tunefulness; elsewhere, not least on a cover of Syd Barrett's "Long Gone", P42 take apart rock convention in a way that feels like a harbinger of the first few Royal Trux albums.

Alan Bishop: "Jesse Srgoncik was the catalyst. He was working at a record shop where Moe shopped and one day he asked her if she wanted to start a band and she agreed. I had no idea she was living in Phoenix—I don't think she ever went out to shows. She was corresponding by mail with other musicians at that time—Jad Fair and the former Velvets, among others. And she released that self-produced LP *Playin' Possum* around this time. The band lasted from late 1981 to August 1982, when she left her husband and split to Tucson with her kids. Most people still don't even know P42 existed. Someone just put out a compilation of Moe's post-Velvets material without including any P42 tracks, and P42 was the main relevant stuff she did post Velvets."

Sun City Girls zealously recorded jams and live performances onto cassette, several of which they would release in limited runs during the 80s. Their three long players during the decade—an eponymous 1984 debut, '86's *Grotto Of Miracles* and *Horse Cock Phepner* the following year—are by no sensible standards sanitised for the format. Alan had moved to Morocco for a couple of months in 1983, during which he jammed with and recorded local musicians. These, as with scores of similar recordings from other African and Asian countries, would later be released on Alan's Sublime Frequencies label, founded in 2003. More immediately, it made its presence felt on *Sun City Girls*, notably with "Helwa Shak", a remarkable North African reimagining of jazz-punk. Disquieting sound collages ("The Burning Nerve Ending Magic Trick") and satirical conspiracy rants ("Uncle Jim") seemed to come from somewhere more directly American, but equally likely to fuck the assumptions of the uninitiated.

Horse Cock Phepner, from its inexplicable title onwards, hundred-hand slaps the listener with waves of profane surrealism. It was released into a mid-80s underground that also housed GG Allin, The Mentors, The Nig-Heist and other wilful provocateurs—but sounded like men trying to ascend to the next plane, not wallow in the swill. A vicious cover of The Fugs' "CIA Man" gives half a pointer as to where SCG's heads are at—beatnik-y free expression exacting revenge on the culture that let it happen—but comparisons are mostly odious when talking about this anti-rock rock classic. Richard Bishop says: "*Horse Cock Phepner* captured a lot of what was going on politically at the time, even though that wasn't the intention. It was probably the most 'political' album to ever come out of Phoenix." At one point, this manifests itself in a lyric about Mr T ejaculating in Nancy Reagan's hair.

David Albert, who ran a local recording studio named Gilamonster, moved into the label business in 1980. Issuing Feederz' aforementioned "Jesus" 45, Red Squares' splendid "Modern Roll" and a split between perky 2-Tone merchants The X-Streams and keyboard-heavy new wavers The Nervous, his was Phoenix's first punk label, although he never settled on a name—the labels read Anxiety, Nanxiety and Gila Bite Records respectively. After it fizzled out, "Jesus" was licensed to Placebo—a new label ran by the entrepreneurial, tireless and sometimes controversial Tony Victor. Its initial function, to release The Teds' likeable new wave EP *The Eighties Are Over*, proved a red herring. Victor was shortly partnered by Teds drummer Greg Hynes (whose nickname, Mr Wonderful, was borrowed by David Foster Wallace, budding writer and Phoenix scene fringe member, for a short story in his debut collection. Michael Pemulis, a central character in Wallace's acclaimed *Infinite Jest*, was a nod to a local, Placebo-signed singer-songwriter circa 1987).

Giving JFA, Mighty Sphincter and Sun City Girls their vinyl debuts, Placebo quickly established itself as *the* means of getting yourself heard if you were part of the Phoenix underground. Says Richard Bishop:

"No other label would have had any interest in Sun City Girls. We were not a money-making band. So without Tony's help, who knows what would have happened to us? It is my opinion that if Tony Victor wasn't around in Phoenix there would have been no scene whatsoever after 1982. He made everything work."

Victor also cornered a fair chunk of the local gig promotion market from 1981 onwards, most infamously at the Mad Garden. This was a spit'n'sawdust wrestling venue (leased by Barry Bernsten, Victor's uncle) lent a unique factor—among punk spaces—by the ring in the main room. Bands set up and played inside the ropes, while punters scaled the fence around the ring before hurling themselves off. It provided a focal point for Phoenix punk and hardcore, although like the Hate House before it, unruly attendees were pretty much a given. This eventually led to its closure in 1984, Bernsten deciding that his efforts to defy the authorities and keep it open weren't worth efforts expended. JFA penned a hearty eulogy,

Above
Mad Garden outside (top) and in (bottom).
By Neal "Doc" Holliday.

"Mad Garden", on an '84 EP of the same name; prior to this, the cover of Placebo's haughtily titled compilation LP *This Is Phoenix Not The Circle Jerks* featured Mighty Sphincter raising hell on the mat. (They feature on the disc alongside JFA, Sun City Girls, Soylent Greene, Zany Guys and Conflict—not the UK anarchist band, and actually from Tucson, AZ.)

The list of Mad Garden guests includes practically the entire early 80s USHC canon; the venue's efforts in making Phoenix a common-sense DIY tour destination was invaluable, albeit helped by bands in general picking up on Black Flag's 'get in the van' ethos. "Pretty much every band that was anyone at the time would play there", beams Brian Brannon, "and we got to see them all and play with most of them because they all loved the idea of playing in a wrestling ring."

"I enjoyed much of it", Tony Victor says, in retrospect. "The unpredictability was a real buzz for me and others too, I suspect. In the beginning, covering costs was hit and miss. I got better at it as I went along but there was never a great deal of money involved. The Mad Garden visits from both the Dead Kennedys and [Residents associate] Snakefinger were memorable shows; the first appearance of The Feederz with JFA was a great culture clash at the time. There was a great nervous energy in the Garden that night." (Dan Clark's memory of this show: "The JFA punks were afraid of Frank. He rounded up at least 20 of them like cattle, swinging his Danelectro over his head as they ran up the grandstand.")

Two of Victor's shows ended in literal riots with multiple police cars and helicopters deployed. The first, at the Garden in February 1982, was headlined by iconic Californian punks The Adolescents, whose singer Tony Cadena drunkenly smashed a bottle on the dancefloor. Security sprang to accost him and a few minutes later the scene was akin to a saloon brawl in a Western. Later that year,

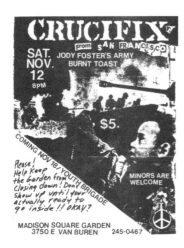

Above top and bottom

Mad Garden flyers.

TSOL and The Vandals stopped by to play the Salty Dog, a tiny and quasi-legal venue; the reasons for the disorder have been lost to the mists of time, but history repeated itself. The Meat Puppets played there the following week—during which, recalls Victor, "I was arrested for contributing to the delinquency of minors. The police came bursting in—'Who's in charge here?' The Meat Puppets didn't stop playing. I believe Cris Kirkwood responded, 'You are. You've got the gun.'"

"There were, in fact, many cops that harassed us unfairly at the Garden—but overall, it was the behaviour of our own crowds that kept us in trouble. We were easy targets: little money, no insurance, lack of proper permits. It was hard for me not to feel resentful of people who were causing damage to property just for fun."

Although Phoenix was far from unique in this respect, this naive boneheadery was tied up with a shift in the tastes and aesthetics of the scene—from arty outrage and unfettered experimentalism to the 'loud fast rules' of hardcore. By the mid-80s, it had planted its flag as a genre and a culture, and (as often happens in these instances) become increasingly beholden to orthodoxy. This dismayed some of the more exploratory Phoenix figures and made 'the scene' far less inclusive, at least from their point of view.

Don Redondo muses: "Punk used to be whatever—there were really different bands in LA and Texas as well. Somewhere along the way, somebody picked a generic sound and determined you needed to sound like this to be hardcore. Luckily we were before all of that. We sound nothing like the Phoenix bands, just like we sound nothing like the Dead Kennedys or the Big Boys. Later, a lot of Phoenix bands did start to sound alike, which is why nobody has ever heard of them."

Richard Bishop—not, as a rule, the greatest fan of what gets tagged as punk rock—has an interesting, personalised take on this period, and how Sun City Girls made lemonade from lemons.

"There were so many bands that would play the same exact thing every show and because of that they never progressed. We did the opposite by never playing the same show twice. And because we experimented all the time and did things that most people didn't understand, let alone like, we were hated by a majority of the people who went to the shows. They came to see whatever other punk bands were on the bill—but we made sure that by the end of the night, there was one band that stood out from the rest. After a few years, people started coming just to see us play because they didn't know what was going to happen."

Alan Bishop: "Early on, shows would be diverse; after a while the hardcore scene began to dominate, and groups within the scene would form and fights would happen. Skinhead gangs, straight-edge, Nazi skins, there were many cliques that created more tension and division—then by 1984 or 1985 the original idea of many different styles of music and people co-existing together was a memory. We were always on the edge of the scene artistically so it didn't affect us much at all. We always did whatever the fuck we wanted to do."

David Oliphant also considers the bond between punk and the avant-garde in Phoenix to have dissolved by around 1985:

"The more popular something is, the lower the common denominator. Hardcore punk quickly became much more popular than the experimental side of things. Over a very short period of time, the younger kids first arriving to the scene became exposed to less and less of the underground side and most often saw just punk and hardcore."

Maybe Mental and acts of their ilk were best supported by CRASHarts, an industrial artspace which opened in '85.

David Oliphant of Maybe Mental/Dali's Daughter
c. 1981–1982. By Neal "Doc" Holliday.

Dan Clark, too, takes the c'est-la-vie stance. "That stuff is always going to be more popular. It's more like football than music. But big deal, who cares, there's a place for it. It was cool for The Feederz as we played to both audiences."

The growing schism between 'hardcore' and 'everything else' was exemplified when JFA and Sun City Girls toured North America for two months in the summer of '84. The former group had a solid profile with punks nationwide by this point—helped by Don Redondo's connections back in Huntington Beach, his hometown, and their skateboarding lifestyle resonating with fellow skaters—whereas SCG had barely played outside Phoenix. The reasons for such a chalk-and-cheese bill were chiefly practical: JFA bassist Mike Cornelius didn't want to tour and a replacement was needed. Tony Victor asked Alan Bishop if he fancied it, with a bonus dangled carrot: "If I agreed, he'd book Sun City Girls as the opening band on every show of that tour. I had zero interest in playing with JFA but with the possibility of getting SCG on the road, I couldn't refuse."

"'Fondly' is probably not the word I would use", muses Richard Bishop, regarding his memories of the jaunt. "It was our first tour so going into it I was sort of excited, but after a while it became increasingly frustrating for me, mainly because we weren't making any money at all and we were broke enough as it was. We travelled in a big old green school bus and the conditions weren't exactly hygienic. I remember that a couple of people got ringworm."

Even considering JFA's own broadening horizons at the time (their eponymous LP from that year features Bowie, Funkadelic and Ventures covers, and only brief recourse to straight-ahead HC), Sun City Girls proved way too much for the headliner's audience to deal with. "We had a decent idea that reaction would be hostile at times, but that's what we loved and hoped for because otherwise the whole experience would have been lame", Alan says.

"There were usually four or five bands playing every night and they were always punk bands. We stuck out like a bad dress", adds his brother. "It's funny to watch some of that old footage and see how the audiences really did hate us. Some wanted us dead! But we lasted another 23 years while most of the other bands lasted 23 weeks."

Brian from JFA: "I always enjoyed watching Sun City Girls get folks worked up. Some people just take themselves too seriously and those that do would get really mad, while those that didn't just thought the whole scenario was funny as heck. Again, if you have to cling to some rigid definition of punk, you're missing what it's all about."

Considering that punk rock had such a huge role in giving the bands in this story a platform, it's hard to find one who earnestly endorse the development of the scene. Take the lurid gothic whirlwind Mighty Sphincter, who date back to 1980, the brainchild of Hate House resident Doug Clark (his brother Dan, a biology student at the time, came up with the name); they became a serious proposition a couple of years on when Ron 'Reckless' Grotjan joined on vocals. According to Doug, "we wanted to make fun of all the incredibly annoying hardcore bands that started touring all over the country. Actually, Mighty Sphincter was started to make fun of the entire punk scene in general." Placebo aided them in their mission, releasing their debut 45 in 1984: four songs of brain-itchy post-punk that sounds addled by speed, but demonstrates the chops of the musicians involved.

Later Sphincter releases revel in a tattered-ballgown kind of grandeur and triumphalism, all the more impressive for being made in a state of chemical chaos. Ron Reckless was turfed out of the band prior to *Ghost Walking*, their '85 full-length bow, for heroin abuse; Doug assumed vocal duties and the band informed concerned parties, wholly untruthfully, that Ron had died. For *The New Manson Family*, its 1986 followup, Phoenix's exalted shock-rock son Alice Cooper was credited as producer—

Mighty Sphincter at the Mason Jar, 1984.
By Joe Cultice.

again, a bald-faced lie, but one which scored them precious attention. (According to Doug, Alice later professed to be a huge fan of Sphincter's music.) The album happens to be a grotesque gem, cruelly lost amidst hundreds of seminal 80s goth releases. Possessing as much unhinged squall as The Birthday Party, manly brood equal to Bauhaus, if it came out in the 2010s it would probably be greeted with rapture by noise rock sorts.

After another EP, *In The Kingdom Of Heaven*, Mighty Sphincter fell apart, sporadically returning in the 90s and 00s with fluctuating lineups. Their most recent release was a 2011 seven-inch, on which Dwid Hellion of apocalyptic metalcore band Integrity guests, and was the primary force behind its issue. In recent years, including the time of writing this chapter, Doug Clark's fragile mental health has rendered him a social recluse, but his band's cult appeal continues to thrive. "You don't get much more freaky than Dougie, he is the real deal fuckin' freakazoid. And a sweetheart", affirms Cris Kirkwood, by way of a tribute.

By the time of Mighty Sphincter's late-80s implosion, the Phoenix underground scene as a whole was beginning to unravel. Despite the efforts of Tony Victor and Greg Hynes to keep things fresh, Placebo Records closed its doors in 1988. It had been moving away from the local focus that got it started for a while, releasing LPs by out-of-state weirdos like Artless, a bawdy project led by *Maximum Rocknroll* columnist Mykel Board, prolific Zappa-esque prankster Eugene Chadbourne, and *Dry Lungs*—a three-part series of heavyweight noise compilations which featured Merzbow and Jarboe to name but two.

Joe Albanese of Mighty Sphincter, from a show
at the Party Gardens opening for Dead Kennedys.
Greg Hynes: "I believe it was 1986. Could have
been late 1985."

(Placebo also performed a fine public service by releasing a split LP between
Victory Acres and Joke Flower, some years after both bands had ended. Both projects
of Dan Clark and his wife Mary, who sings, VA were augmented by Cris and Derrick
from the Meat Puppets, while Sun City Girls' Charlie Gocher contributes to JF. Flipping
from Teenage Jesus-style no wave to eccentric Canterbury prog and electric folk,
it's an utter crime that this LP is barely known.)

There was still an enthusiastic DIY punk scene in the region, although most of
the bands seemed to hail from Mesa, a small city in the Phoenix metropolitan area.
Desecration played generic breakneck thrash but ticked enough HC boxes (Reagan-
bashing lyrics, mushroom cloud artwork, self-published 'zines) to gain a decent rep
between '85 and '88. Wind of Change and Youth Under Control were both fuelled
by the growing straight-edge movement, and seemed to revel in their clean-cut
image. WOC guitarist Alex Dunham moved to Washington DC and played in emotional
hardcore band Hoover during their brief but thrilling lifetime. The pick of the Mesa
bunch was Last Option, whose all-but-forgotten LP *Burning* is a punchy yet thoughtful
slab of HC that compares positively to contemporaries like Turning Point and Four
Walls Falling.

Of the old guard, the Meat Puppets, who Cris Kirkwood says "were never that
fuckin' big" in their home town, were touring the States pretty much constantly,
growing into legitimate alt-rock crowdpullers, and looking to sign to a major—which
they eventually did in 1991. JFA released *Nowhere Blossoms* in 1988, a highly odd
confection of post-punk and keyboard-heavy pop, then kept a low profile during
the 90s (to the extent that many wrongly assumed them to have broken up).

"By '88", says Don Redondo, "I was living back in Huntington Beach and when I would come to town the vibe from some of the other Phoenix bands was that they were better than us, we were old news, they were going to get signed, etc.. Well, none of them ever did and a lot of them never really played out of town. "

Richard Bishop: "Most of the punk bands were long dead and forgotten and there really wasn't much going on musically that was interesting at all. All of the older venues closed up or were torn down and the only places to play were in dive bars and art galleries. Sun City Girls played CRASHarts often, and a bar in Tempe called the Sun Club. Our last Phoenix show was there in 1989 and opening up for us was a band that nobody had yet heard of called Nirvana." As it happened, the guitarist moved to Seattle shortly after, with Alan Bishop and Charlie Gocher joining him a couple of years later. True to form, they paid as little attention as possible to the ongoing grunge frenzy centred around the city.

Music scenes come and go, but their finest participants tend to transcend them, and survive without their oxygen. Both Alan and Richard Bishop tour regularly and consistently add to their expansive discographies; Richard in fact released a collaborative LP with David Oliphant, *Beyond All Defects*, last year. JFA also brought out a new album in 2012, *Speed of Sound*, while Meat Puppets—laid low for some years by Cris Kirkwood's drug addictions—reformed in the mid-00s and unveiled their fourteenth album *Rat Farm* in April 2013.

The survivors are nevertheless tempered by the list of those who were taken too soon. Prior to Rick Bertoni's OD in 1991, John E Precious of The Feederz and Killer Pussy, International Language frontman George Dillon, plus two Consumers personnel—David Wiley and Doug Gauss—all didn't see the end of the 1980s. Sun City Girls' Charles Gocher died in 2007, having been stricken with cancer for some time; the Bishops retired the band name thereafter, but have toured as The Brothers Unconnected by way of a tribute to the drummer. Joe Albanese of The Brainz and Mighty Sphincter was one of five people fatally shot during a seemingly motiveless attack on a Seattle coffeehouse in May 2012. And in December of that year, during the initial stages of research for this essay, Bob Cox—one of JFA's many drummers, and also of Phoenix skatepunks Our Neighbors Suck—passed away aged 49.

Lucy Lamode: "After John E Precious died, it was very sad and it devastated me. Eventually we brought in Vanya [Houatomaki] on drums and continued to play sporadic gigs up until about 1993. In the second half of the 80s, the whole punk/ new wave thing tapered down but there were still a lot of good local bands like The Strand, Gentlemen Afterdark, and the Gin Blossoms who attained national success."

Cris Kirkwood: "There were a few places around the country like Phoenix, where cool things sprang up: Minneapolis, eventually Seattle, Austin—neat little pockets of places that made you go, 'what in the living fuck is that?' Humans and their little cultural ripples, they do the darndest things."

Tony Victor concludes: "I wanted to promote original shows with original bands; run a record label and to expose some of those bands to larger audiences; get out of Phoenix and tour. I was able to do those things. After, things changed. It wasn't so much fun anymore. Timing has a lot to do with it. Time was up."

An interview with Brian Brannon
and Don Redondo (JFA)

JFA formed partly out of two bands, The Deez and Jr Chemists. I know both played shows, and Jr Chemists had songs on a split seven-inch. How "serious" were they as projects?
Don: I thought we were serious with The Deez, but the singer, an Andy Warhol type that kinda ran the Hate House, got bored easily and we only did a few shows.

When The Breakers started [shortly changing their name to JFA], was there an immediate wish to establish the band in the scene, play shows out of town, do an EP, whatever?
Don: We almost immediately wanted to play out of town—an excuse to go skate and to get to the West Coast to surf. We formed in May [1981] and by July we already had the .22 Caliber (small) Tour, consisting of Mad Gardens in Phoenix with The Alley Cats, a show in Tucson and then opening for The Crowd at the Cuckoo's Nest in Orange County, California. Tony Victor [Placebo Records] saw the growing following we were developing and offered us the EP.

When JFA was just getting started in 1981, how aware were you of other local bands around playing fast punk music? The Meat Puppets were about as new as you were and The Feederz would move out of state not long afterwards.
Don: There was nobody else except the Meat Puppets and, like you said, they were new too—their early shows were *gnarly*! The Deez were really slow and heavy. The Feederz were mid-speed at best and The Nervous and Killer Pussy were more new wave.

Was the Phoenix scene cliquey at that time?
Don: I would not call it cliquey, but there was definitely the Hate House crew—The Deez, The Roll Ons, the Extremes, Killer Pussy, Meat Puppets initially, and The Feederz—who were friends with the Tempe guys and then the rockabilly guys. All of those folks were basically friends though and part of the bigger scene—it is not like today—there were lots of different eclectic bands in the same scene [as opposed to] all grouping around different genres of music.

Did you have any problems getting accepted by the older participants, especially considering how young you were?
Don: I wasn't young like Brian—I was 19 when I moved to Phoenix—but there was definitely a culture clash when we started playing and drawing lots of younger skater kids. First off, we were playing two times faster than anybody had heard before and then there was the slam dancing that got exported from the West Coast—a lot of our friends would go to

California for skate contests and go see bands like the Circle Jerks afterwards so they kinda brought "the pit" back with them. Phoenix had no idea what hit them—especially the fall-down-drunk leather jacket guys who could not deal with high-energy skaters on the dancefloor.

Do you have any specific examples of this?
Brian: There were definitely issues with the 'pogo harshly' crowd when we started slam dancing. They took it as an attack and actually started fighting us when we were slamming at an Industrial Dance at the Knights Of Pythias hall in Tempe. And those were people who were in the scene. No-one had any idea what it meant, they just saw us getting rowdy, punching and kicking each other in an anarchic fashion. When we played, the local dive bars only ever had cover bands doing Journey and Styx songs and then all of a sudden JFA gets up there with short hair, ripped jeans, playing loud, fast, screaming tunes and all our friends start a rumble on the dancefloor. We ended up being banned for life from quite a few local bars before some punk clubs were established.

Apart from yourselves, were there any other Phoenix bands that skated?
Don: Todd Joseph of Junior Achievement was an awesome skater sponsored by Sims—they still say he had the best layback airs in the business.

Brian: Jon Yousko and Todd Joseph of Junior Achievement definitely skated. They were both High Roller locals, which is the skatepark where a lot of the early hardcore Phoenix punks came from. It was at 7th Street and Dunlap and had two pools, two pipes, two snake runs, a clover bowl and a big reservoir. A lot of us miss it terribly. Even after it closed, we were able to sneak in for a few months and skate before it got bulldozed. The influence of the High Roller crew on what would become the Phoenix hardcore scene is rarely talked about, but it definitely had a big impact.

It is not something I can turn off… I have been like that since 1972 when I got my first set of (open bearing) urethane wheels and the whole world opened up with possibilities as to what was ride-able. Most of these other self-professed "skate rock" clowns are not even from the same planet as me in that they are not really skaters—they just say they are. There are some real skate bands out there though (Frontside 5 comes to mind) and I look forward to playing and skating with the real deal skaters like them.

What was the relationship like between 'skateboard culture' and 'punk culture' in the area?
Don: I'm not sure anymore—there were so many fakes because skating went from not cool, pulled up jock-sock hippies, to being a prerequisite to being in a punk band.

Also, I would like to make something clear: just owning a skateboard sometime in your life and then forming a band does not make you skaterock—everybody has had one at one point. I may not skate as much as I used to, but I will be a skater until I die! Something is wrong with me in that I still look at schoolyards, drainage ditches or pipes—even when I have no board and am on vacation with my family.

I think it's fair to say that most Phoenix bands never really sounded much like each other, would you agree?
Don: Punk used to be whatever—there were really different bands in LA and Texas as well. Somewhere along the way, somebody picked a generic sound and determined you needed to sound like this to be hardcore. Luckily we were before all of that. We sound nothing like the Phoenix bands, just like we sound nothing like the Dead Kennedys or the Big Boys.

Brian: The early 80s were kind of a golden age for Phoenix punk—everyone was going in so many different directions and no one thought twice about going to a gig with George Dillon's International Language playing some weird industrial music type of stuff, and then having Grant And The Geezers go on afterwards and throw down some tight rockabilly jams.

However most of the bands who really made a name for themselves mixed it up a bit in their own music.

Don: Later, a lot of the Phoenix bands did start to kind of sound alike, which is why nobody has ever heard of them. It comes down to writing songs that are worth remembering too—not just how you look and how fast you can play.

Is this something you felt you had in common with these bands—like, "Hey, we're not outcasts in Phoenix, these guys have attitudes like us!"

Don: It goes deeper than that: most of these other bands, at least from the old scene, were really good friends of mine. They just sounded way different when they picked up a guitar because they had different influences. At one point I wanted Cris Kirkwood on bass—he played for The Feederz as well—and we worked at the same restaurant—parking cars out front and talking about music.

Brian: The other thing at the time was the jocks, hippies, shit kickers, preppies and various authority figures lumped you into punk no matter what type of subgenre you were into. And being a punk was an ass-kicking offense: you were going to get hassled simply for standing out from everyone else. These things tended to weed out the poseurs because there was nothing to gain from pretending that you were a punk, so we naturally gravitated to other punks we saw on the street and knew that while they might not be into exactly what we were into, at least they weren't afraid to be themselves. So there was that, and all the other Phoenix bands at that time pretty much ruled!

Alan Bishop of the Sun City Girls was JFA's bass player for a while. How did this come about exactly—why him over any number of bassists from more, uh, straight-ahead bands? Was it a successful partnership, and did you stay in touch when SCG moved to Seattle in the late 80s/early 90s?

Don: He joined because Mike [Cornelius] did not want to do the nine-week summer tour in 1984. Alan liked our music and learned all of the songs on his own before I ever even practiced with him. He fit in so well, we never even thought of trying anybody else out. He also brought a new song to that first practice, "Rushing Bull" on the *Mad Gardens* EP, and played a smashed trumpet on the song "I Want". Brian still stays in touch—he went up there when Charlie Gocher [Sun City Girls' drummer] died—that was a big loss—Charlie was really cool. Another factor is if you are going to spend nine weeks in a bus with somebody they better be pretty easy going—Alan was all that in spades.

Alan's stint on bass also included a JFA/Sun City Girls tour—going on interviews it sounded like he really got off on pissing off the punk audience. Were you enjoying it equally, thinking back?

Don: I think Alan got off on pissing folks off where we did not care enough to try. It's not like we added paisley shirts and keyboards [on later LP, *Nowhere Blossoms*] just to piss people off—it's just who we are/were, but looking back I'm sure the hardcore 'establishment' might have taken offense to it.

Brian: I always enjoyed watching the Sun City Girls get folks worked up. Some people just take themselves too seriously and those that do would get really mad, while those that didn't just thought the whole scenario was funny as heck. Again, if you have to cling to some rigid definition of punk, you're missing what it's all about.

I've always figured JFA shows were more about blowing off steam rather than 'confrontation' or whatever...
Don: For me it's not about blowing off steam—playing fast is really fun. Brian saw Henry Rollins work himself into a lather pre-show one time and it was just so stupid, like an act. We just get up there and let the music rip.

Both of these bands, plus several more, were regulars on bills at the Mad Gardens. Can you tell me a bit about those times?
Don: The Mad Gardens was a special time in that it put Phoenix on the map. Thanks to Tony [Victor], all of my friends' bands would come out—Vandals, TSOL—but also bands we would have never seen or only seen on the road like Bad Brains, Butthole Surfers, Agression.

Brian: It was a place for all the desert outcasts to come together and listen to music from all over. Big respect to Tony Victor for making that happen despite all the hassles with the Phoenix police at the time and everything that went into bringing bands to town and dealing with all the different types of us weirdoes who would come to the shows.

For a while it was just the ring and you could climb up on the ropes and launch yourself into the crowd, but that started getting out of hand so they put up a big chain-link fence in front of the stage (kind of like in the first *Blues Brothers* movie when they're at Bob's Country Bunker) and people would just start climbing up the fence and hanging off it and fling themselves back into the pit. When Mad Gardens finally closed, it was a very sad day but luckily other clubs like the Salty Dog came along to pick up the slack.

What Phoenix band or bands from those times do you think have been unjustly forgotten by history, and why?
Don: There were some from the old [pre-JFA] scene that I liked a lot. The Nervous were good, Grant And The Geezers were good. I never saw them, but there was a band called The Consumers that were supposed to be good—I think they included Don Bolles, later of Germs and 45 Grave, and Paul Cutler of 45 Grave. Don Bolles took his name from a Phoenix reporter that was allegedly blown up in his car by the mob.

Brian: International Language was a great experimental/industrial type of band. Killer Pussy were greatly entertaining. NRA (No Real Attitude) were amazing. They later became Kludged and were pretty much punk on wheels—you never knew what you were going to get when they played.

If we fast-forward to, say, 1988, can you describe what Phoenix was like at that point, and how JFA fitted in? You guys were still releasing records, but a lot of the bands from the early 80s scene had broke up, moved away, or had a tenuous relationship with punk.
Don: After Mad Gardens, anybody with a couple of friends had the ability to start a band and get a show thanks to Tony Victor. They took it for granted and had no idea how hard it was in the old days to actually put shows together—that is why the Hate House and the guys from The Nervous, who would rent halls and put on industrial dances, were so important in the old scene.

By '88, I was living back in Huntington Beach and when I would come to town the vibe from some of the other Phoenix bands was that (in their minds) they were better than us, we were old news, they were going to get signed, etc.. Well, none of them ever did and a lot of them never really played out of town.

Brian: And you know what, they were right, we were never going to 'get signed'. But that wasn't why we formed a band in the first place. We just did it to have fun and we didn't think that anyone owed us anything so we never had to be disappointed when our dreams of becoming big rockstars never materialised because we never had them in the first place. The secret to our longevity is that we only cared about seeing our friends, making new ones and having fun. And now, 30-something years later, we're having more fun than ever while so many of these other bands that were legends in their own minds have fizzled and died.

An interview with Richard Bishop
(Sun City Girls)

If I have this right, you and Alan grew up in Michigan and moved to Arizona in your teens.
Alan [Bishop] and I left Michigan in 1979. I was 19 years old and my brother had just turned 20.

Did Phoenix and the surrounding area strike you as a place with an especially vibrant culture?
We weren't really looking for culture when we arrived. We just wanted a different environment to that which Michigan offered.

How did you get involved with the local music/art scene?
There was an active punk scene in Phoenix long before we arrived. It took us a few months before we started to notice what was going on underneath the surface. Upon arrival we settled into the local open mic venues that dotted Phoenix. Within a year or so, we started hosting an open mic night in a lounge in the back of a pizza joint. It was here where we grew tired of the run-of-the-mill folk crap that seemed to dominate all open mic venues. By then we had met a few musicians and artists who seemed more interested in pushing boundaries by doing things that were a little more challenging to the average lounge hopper.

Sun City Girls began life as The Next. Was there any significant difference between The Next and Sun City Girls, aside from the name?
Musically they were two separate entities. For The Next we had a drummer named Joe Musico. He was a great drummer and he came from the John Bonham school of pounding the skins. We played mostly original songs with Alan responsible for the majority of writing. They were straight up pop/rock songs with many of the lyrics being political. Eventually Alan and I grew tired of what we were doing so we began to improvise and experiment, moving away from regular song structure. We started creating musical pieces and utilising ideas that bore no resemblance to our previous work. Our drummer Joe didn't feel comfortable working in this new direction so he decided to leave the band. Charles Gocher replaced him shortly thereafter. Gocher had many ideas of his own and they fit in well with the directions Alan and I were moving in.

The band's early performances took place in the open mic 'scene' rather than at punk rock shows or whatever. What advantages, or disadvantages, did this have for the development of your music?
I'm not sure if there were any advantages other than these were the only places we could play at that time. We did play a little with Charlie at the open mics before he joined SCG. We called ourselves the Free Form Orchestra and there was a rotating cast of additional

players each week. It wasn't popular with the usual patrons in these places but that encouraged us to keep thinking in terms of collective improvisation and things continued to take off from there. So I guess that worked to our advantage in the long run.

After a while, however, you did fall in somewhat with the punk scene in Phoenix, through playing at the Mad Gardens etc., being on the *This Is Phoenix...* compilation, and so forth. How do you look back on those days, with up to 30 years' hindsight?
I just remember that for the most part I enjoyed those early days because of the people I was hanging out with and how different the music we were making was compared to other local groups. It's cool to think about how things developed in my tastes in music as well. I was turned on to so many things that I now take for granted. When I left Michigan I was mainly listening to classic rock. Meeting Jesse [Srogoncik, SCG associate], Charlie [Gocher, SCG drummer] and others led me into Captain Beefheart, free jazz, and all kinds of other things. That all came at the perfect time and my guitar playing began to reflect some of those ideas. So that was a very important time for me.

How did a band like SCG fit in with other bands of the time, and to what extent were you 'accepted' (or not)?
We didn't fit in and we weren't accepted. It was as simple as that. But that was the best thing that could have happened to us. If we played the game and tried to fit in, we would have lasted about two years. There were so many bands that would always play the same exact thing every show and because of that they never progressed. They were limited in what they could do. That was our worst nightmare. We did the opposite by never playing the same show twice. And because we experimented all the time and did things that most people didn't understand, let alone like, we were hated by a majority of the people who went to the shows. Remember, they didn't come to see us. They came to see whatever other punk bands were on the bill. But we made sure that by the end of the night, there was one band that stood out from the rest, and we used this to our advantage. After a few years people started coming just to see us play because they didn't know what was going to happen.

You've said before that, then as now, you're not much of a punk fan—partly because of how identikit punk bands tend to be. In your view, was Phoenix an example of this, or an exception?
Phoenix had quite a few punk bands and even though I knew a lot of the musicians, and even liked many of them personally, I never got into their music. I went to the punk shows mainly to hang out with my friends. All the major punk bands from across the country would come through town often so there certainly was an audience for it. There were also a lot of 'new wave' bands that grew out of that punk scene but these didn't hold my attention either.

It seems to me, listening after the fact, that most of the bands from the city sounded pretty different to each other at least.
There were bands that I did like such as Destruction, Maybe Mental, Meat Puppets, Knebnagauje, Mighty Sphincter, Victory Acres, Eddy Detroit, Killer Pussy, and a few others. Many people considered some of these groups to be punk bands but I never did. They were way more interesting musically than any punk band ever could be.

The first three Sun City Girls LPs were released by Placebo. Did you have a good working relationship with the label, and Tony Victor in his other musical ventures (booking shows, etc.)?

We had a great working relationship with Placebo. No other label would have had any interest in Sun City Girls. We were not a money making band. So without Tony's help who knows what would have happened to us? It is my opinion that if Tony Victor wasn't around in Phoenix there would have been no scene whatsoever after 1982. He made everything work. If you wanted a gig, even if you were from out of town, you pretty much had to deal with Tony. It would have been totally different if somebody else played that role.

Do you look back fondly on the JFA/SCG tour in 1984?
Fondly is probably not the word I would use. Alan was asked to play bass for JFA and the deal was that he would if SCG could be the opening band for the tour. It was our first tour so going into it I was sort of excited about it. But after a while it became increasingly frustrating for me mainly because we weren't making any money at all and we were broke enough as it was. We travelled in a big old green school bus and the conditions on the bus weren't exactly hygienic. I remember that a couple of people got ringworm.

Did you guys find it as easy to enrage JFA's audience as descriptions suggest?
There were some memorable shows during the tour and we have a lot of it on video. It's funny to watch some of that old footage and it's great to see how the audiences really did hate us. Some wanted us dead! But we lasted another 23 years while most of the other bands lasted 23 weeks.

By the late 80s the SCG trio started to move away from Phoenix to relocate in Seattle. What were the reasons for this? What was your impression of the scene in Phoenix in, say, 1988 compared to 1982?
I believe it was in 1990 when I left Phoenix and moved to Seattle. I just needed to get away to a new environment. Alan and Charlie followed about a year later. By the late 80s in Phoenix, things had really changed within the music scene. Most of the punk bands were long dead and forgotten and there really wasn't as much going on musically that was interesting at all. Tony Victor had stopped booking shows long before the end of the decade and nobody could really fill his shoes. The only places to play were in dive bars and art galleries. One exception was a place called Crash (later known as The Ice House). This place still managed to get some interesting musical acts and performance art and installations happening. We also played a lot at a bar in Tempe called the Sun Club. Our last Phoenix show was there in 1989 and opening up for us was a band that nobody had yet heard of called Nirvana.

After moving, did you feel a similar kinship to Seattle as to Phoenix?
It wouldn't have mattered where we moved to. I still wouldn't have liked the local scene. We avoided scenes.

Did you integrate into the local scene?
Grunge was just starting to happen in Seattle when I moved there and like the punk scene in Phoenix, it was nothing special to me. It was just rock music dressed up in a different set of clothes. At 30 years old I felt I had already outgrown it. So we made sure that we were never associated with grunge. It wasn't our audience. We carved out our own local niche by not trying to be a part of anything.

I don't know if this is a really corny question or what, but what influence does the landscape of Arizona have on the outlook of bands from the state? The big open spaces between metropolitan areas, as well as how hot it is in summer.
I never associated the desert landscape with any particular outlook or anything like

that. Of course when other people try to describe us from that era the first thing they all mention is how sun-damaged we were.

What Phoenix band or artist from those times do you think has been unjustly forgotten by history, and why?
The only person that comes to mind is David Oliphant who was the driving force behind the groups Destruction, Dali's Daughter, Maybe Mental and Life Garden. I don't know if history has forgotten him or whether David would care either way. I just think that more people should be familiar with his work. In my opinion, everything he's created musically has been way ahead of its time and his earliest work still holds up well against everything that today's so-called noise artists are doing.

Was Arizona a tough place to live for young, non-conservative people at the time, and what influence would you say this had on the music and culture produced in Phoenix?
It was easy and pretty laidback. But Arizona did have a crazy governor at the time named Evan Mecham who was a hardcore Republican and an easy target for any artist that cared to pay any attention to him. And of course Ronald Reagan was president for most of the 1980s so that also provided some material to work with if anybody needed it. Sun City Girls' 1987 release *Horse Cock Phepner* sort of captured a lot of what was going on politically at the time, even though that wasn't the intention. It was probably the most political album to ever come out of Phoenix.

An interview with Tony Victor (Placebo Records)

The only other Phoenix-area label I know of which existed circa 1980/81 and leaned towards punk rock was Anxiety, but it seems to have only lasted for three releases. Do you know much about them? (I assume you had contact with them when you licensed The Feederz seven-inch at least.) Did Placebo take over from the work they started doing in any sense?
I definitely never thought of taking over from them. I had heard about The Feederz as they and their shows were infamous in Phoenix by then [1981]. Dave Albert came to me with the idea of Placebo buying the rights to the seven-inch that included "Jesus Entering From The Rear". It was so controversial at the time, that there were people who refused to even touch the record in the stores thinking that just putting their fingers on it might hurt their eternal souls! There were other one-off records back then [by bands] like Blue Shoes, Billy Clone And The Same, The Spiffs, The Brainz, etc.. The only other label that had a long run through the eighties in Phoenix was an American Indian label.

Probably the highest profile band from Phoenix you didn't do a record with was the Meat Puppets. Cris Kirkwood said that this was due to World Imitation, and later SST, offering to put out stuff by them so quickly—from your point of view, did you have ambitions to make them a 'Placebo band' at all?
Of course—you would have had to be deaf in 1981 not to hear how special they were. I did many shows with them and recorded them for the Placebo compilation LP *Amuck*. My time was always stretched thin but Cris and I spent hours on the phone just talking about anything and everything except business usually. I was not socially adept and probably a hard person to be friends with at the time. I'm not sure if I ever discussed a record or management

with the Meat Puppets or not. I guess it just wasn't on the cards, so to speak. I would have loved it, though.

In general, how did releases on the label come about—was it more common for bands to approach you and ask if Placebo could release something, or would you seek them out?
Most of the early releases were with friends of mine like The Teds, JFA, Sun City Girls, Mighty Sphincter, Pemulis and Poet's Corner. Later I got more comfortable working with others. I was approached a lot to put out records. I did not listen to people's demo tapes, which was kind of a mistake that came from my concert promoter hat. With the shows, I really didn't want my personal tastes in music to determine who got booked to play so I would just toss the tapes in a box and give the band a date to play, as long as they claimed to have 30 minutes or so of original music. It was my way of trying to keep the shows fresh and especially unpredictable. It probably caused me to overlook some tapes that might have been worthy of recording for the label.

Looking at the Placebo discography, the period 1986-88 is notable for being much less Phoenix-centric in what was released than the years before that. What were the reasons for this? Had you had a wish from the start to release music from a variety of places, rather than just the locale?
I think the original thought was to stick with the local bands. There was plenty of talent and variety in Phoenix in those early years as you can hear on *Amuck*. The money was always scarce and that was a factor with everything. I think by 1986 the real "time" for Placebo and my participation in the live scene was starting to get late. By 1988, I knew I wanted to move on to something else. The youthful magic in it was about over for me by then. I remember speaking to other participants at the time and many could see themselves still in the business for years to come but I didn't feel that way by then.

In regard to punk and hardcore, the trend [by the late 80s] seemed to be for bands to be fast and metal-influenced.
I looked at it as more people and money at the shows but at the same time, the end of the really special time for me which was roughly 1979 thru 1986.

You've said before that you don't really think of the 80s scene in Phoenix as a 'punk' scene per se, due to all the different types of music that got absorbed into that scene. Was this one of the things that kept it interesting, would you say?
Phoenix was not a punk scene from 78-84 in my mind. It was an eclectic mix of oddballs and misfit artists/musicians that just sort of started to find each other. There were small groups of people doing things independently of one another and mostly without knowledge of each other. There were some early dances/shows then Mad Gardens and finally the label. People found out about each other, which took some time. We called that process a scene I guess.

Regarding your stint as a gig promoter at the Mad Gardens (and other venues), what were a few of the most memorable lineups you booked there and why?
The Mad Garden visits from both the Dead Kennedys and Snakefinger were memorable shows with great local bands. Both did two shows there. The first appearance of The Feederz with JFA was a great culture clash at the time. There was a great nervous energy in the Garden that night. Great fun! There was at least one show at each of Mad Garden and the Salty Dog that ended in riots with lots of fighting, police, etc.. Those are memorable for different reasons but again, the idea was not knowing what you were going to see, hear and feel on any given night.

Did you cover costs with it?

In the beginning, covering costs was hit and miss. I got better at it as I went along but there was never a great deal of Money involved. Many early shows were $3 to $5 and had three to five bands.

The venue closed in 1984 due to neighbour/police complaints—were these justified? Did Phoenix have an overly zealous police force at the time?

It closed as a result of my uncle, who ran the wrestling on Friday nights, getting tired of battling with the police, the neighbourhood and the city to keep it open. There were, in fact, many cops that harassed us unfairly at the Garden. But overall, it was the behaviour of our own crowds, especially outside, that kept us in trouble. We were easy targets. Little money, no insurance, lack of proper permits at most of the venues.

Did you resent the fact that kids would come to shows and get rowdy without thinking of who might have to take the rap for it?

It was hard for me not to feel resentful of people who were causing damage to property just for fun. I would get an earful from venue owners, have to pay and eventually get sent packing. I went through a couple dozen venues over those eight or nine years.

Can you recall the stories of the shows that ended in riots?

In the second half of 1981 or early 1982, the Adolescents from LA came to play at Mad Gardens. Towards the end of their show, the lead singer threw an empty liquor bottle onto the dance floor. He had been nursing the bottle during their performance so he was, no doubt, feeling good. The bottle smashed into pieces which caught the attention of my uncle Barry and his wrestler/security people. With vandalism being routine at the venue at the time, my uncle had security after him. He jumped the ropes and headed up the black wooden bleachers that were on the opposite wall facing the wrestling ring that the bands performed in. Two security guys went up the bleachers, grabbed him and carried him down. One had his feet and the other his arms as they marched down the bleachers holding him like a human stretcher. When they reached the concrete floor at the bottom, the guy holding his arms dropped him. His head hit the green concrete floor, hard, and split open. There he was, in a pool of blood. The whole place just erupted into a chaotic, mass brawl. Police, ambulances and eventually even helicopters were brought in to clear the scene. I know the singer went to the hospital and several were arrested. He did an interview somewhere about this incident. Other members of the band may have accounts of their own.

In late 1982, TSOL and the Vandals came to Phoenix to play the Salty Dog. The Salty Dog was a very tiny club that had closed and was waiting to be torn down. The late David Wiley had bribed the keys to it from its Chinese owner who ran the nearby Szechuan Inn restaurant. I took over the club from David. It was way over packed that night and a fight broke out. I don't remember why. Others might. The fight flowed out to the parking lot and progressed into a riot of sorts. Again, police cars and helicopters came to disperse the crowd. Maybe a couple hundred people were there. A week later, with the Meat Puppets on stage, I was arrested at the Salty Dog for contributing to the delinquency of minors. There were no more than a few dozen people there that night. The police came bursting in: "Who's in charge here?" The Meat Puppets didn't stop playing. I believe Cris Kirkwood responded to the question: "You are. You've got the gun." No charges were filed against me after I agreed to close the Salty Dog.

There were a few other situations in those years including the Anti-Them Rally at Squaw Peak Park and a few other police raids at various venues.

Did being the main guy in town, when it came to releasing punk/underground music and booking similar shows, present its own problems (eg pressure from workload, or resentment from people who considered you to have a 'monopoly')?

Yes it did. All of the above. I loved the workload part of it but I took the criticism very hard. I was young and, mistakenly, I always thought people had a point. I was wrong about that. Most did not have a point to make. I was doing my thing and they were doing their thing, which was complaining. They should have spent that energy putting together their own shows and/or records. Some did just that. Some local bands found plenty of shows and put out records without my involvement while still playing for me when I called on them. Of course, those weren't the ones doing the complaining.

To what extent would you agree with something that gets said often in punk rock/DIY culture—that once you make a career out of what was a hobby, you lose focus of why you started it in the first place?

I don't think that applies that often. I had a vision and was determined to make that happen. Sometimes as you achieve goals, you start to get bored, lose interest or start to feel the negatives more. I wanted to promote original shows with original bands. I wanted to run a record label and to expose some of those bands to larger audiences. I wanted to get out of Phoenix and tour. I was able to do those things. It was fun getting there. After, things changed. It wasn't so much fun anymore. Timing has a lot to do with it. Time was up.

With hindsight, would you say this subculture actually caused much change in the 1980s— musically, politically, in regard to the music industry?

It definitely brought independent labels into the light. Major labels had to all start paying attention. College radio became important. Records and then CDs became cheaper and easier to make as there became a market for the smaller pressings. Of course, all music influences future music so I think that's a given. I'm not sure it had much of a real impact on culture in general. Cosmetically, maybe yes.

IMAGE CREDITS

cover
Photography Jason Leatherman.

pp. 4, 16–17, 20–21
Photography Steve Zimmerman.

p. 10 (left and right)
Courtesy Ben DeSoto and Dave Ensminger.

pp. 11 (top and bottom), 12, 14, 15 (top and bottom), 18, 24, 25
Photography Ben DeSoto. Courtesy Ben DeSoto and Dave Ensminger.

pp. 13 (top and bottom), 19 (all), 39, 43 (left and right), 48 (left and right), 49, 54 (top and bottom), 69 (bottom), 121 (top and bottom), 125 (middle and bottom), 161 (right), 162 (middle and bottom), 169
Personal collection.

p. 23
Courtesy Dave Ensminger.

pp. 26 (left and right), 27
Courtesy Bliss Blood.

pp. 40–41
Photography Jeremy Gilbert.

pp. 44, 47
© Laura Levine.

pp. 50–51, 52, 53
Photography © Paul Wright.

pp. 60–79 (Chapel Hill)
All photography © Jason Summers.

pp. 90–106 (Drag City)
All images courtesy Drag City Records.

pp. 112, 114, 115, 116, 118
Courtesy Tom Niemeyer.

p. 117
Photography © Tom Street. Courtesy Tom Niemeyer.

p. 120 (left and right)
Courtesy Daniel House.

pp. 122, 123, 124, 125 (top), 126
Courtesy Daniel House/Skin Yard.

p. 128 (top and bottom)
Photography John Leach. Courtesy Tom Niemeyer.

pp. 135, 136–137, 146 (left and right)
Photography © Lucy Hanna.

pp. 141, 142 (left and right)
Courtesy Steve Moriarty.

p. 152
Photography David Sine.

p. 161 (left), 169 (bottom), 172 (top and bottom), 174
Photography Neal "Doc" Holliday. Courtesy Aaron Rand and Tony Victor.

p. 162 (top)
Photography © Robert Steinhilber.

pp. 163, 173 (top and bottom)
Courtesy Bill Cuevas.

pp. 164–165, 166–167, 168 (top and bottom)
Photography Edwin Arnaud.

p. 170
Photography Neal "Doc" Holliday. Courtesy Alan Bishop.

pp. 175, 176
Photography Joe Cultice. Courtesy Greg Hynes.

Unless otherwise stated, photography also indicates provenance.

WRITER BIOS

Noel Gardner was raised in Cornwall and has spent his whole adult life in south Wales, hence his interest in things taking place several thousand miles away from either of them. He has spent the last 13 years writing about music for publications and/or websites including *NME*, *BBC Music*, *The Quietus* and *Terrorizer*. From time to time he also puts gigs of marginal appeal on in Cardiff, under the promotional name Lesson No.1.

Pavel Godfrey writes about extreme music and contemporary culture for publications like *The Quietus* and *Lurker's Path*. He grew up in the Midwest and moved to New York, where he went to college and a lot of punk shows. He's back in his hometown, Ann Arbor, doing a PhD in English. He still goes to a lot of punk shows.

Brian Howe is an arts, entertainment and culture journalist living in Chapel Hill, covering the Triangle and abroad. He writes about music for *Pitchfork*, *eMusic*, and North Carolina's *INDY Week*, among others. He is a columnist and editorial contributor at the UK's *Edge* Magazine, and is a former contributing editor at *Paste*. In 2013, he completed a year-long series of interviews, with dozens of world-class performing artists, for Duke Performances at *The Thread*. // waxwroth.blogspot.com

Jimmy Martin is a London-based writer and musician, who has contributed to *Terrorizer*, *The Quietus*, *Iron Fist*, *Plan B* and *BBC Music* amongst others. He has lectured at the ICA, curated for Supernormal Festival and currently plays in the band Teeth Of The Sea, whose third album on Rocket Recordings, *MASTER*, is released in 2013.

Kevin McCaighy is a music writer based in York. For the past decade he has published *SALT*, an underground music and culture fanzine—an eleventh and final issue is due out before the end of 2013. He is also a longtime contributor to *ROCK-A-ROLLA* magazine and more recently, *The Quietus*. // kevinmccaighy.wordpress.com

Louis Pattison is a London-based writer and journalist. He has contributed to *NME*, *Plan B*, *Uncut*, *The Guardian*, *The Wire*, *Zero Tolerance* and Black Dog Publishing's *Black Metal: Beyond The Darkness*.

ACKNOWLEDGEMENTS

Thanks to Pavel Godfrey, Kevin McCaighy, Brian Howe, Jimmy Martin, Louis Pattison, Noel Gardner, John Doran, Brandon Stosuy, Byron Coley, Delight Hanover, Frances Morgan, Everett True, Jason Ferguson, Marc Masters, Philip Sherburne, Shawn Rogers Nolan, Edwin Arnaud, Bill Daniel, Edward Colver, Alternative Tentacles, Merge Records, Ben DeSoto, Ben Ensminger, Lucy Hanna, Ron Liberti, Jason Summers, John Leach, David Sine, Laura Ballance, Matt Gentling, Bill Cody, Brian Bannon, Don Redondo, Steve Zimmerman, Tom Niemeyer, Bliss Blood, Bill Cuevas, Patrick Tilley, Nayoung Hyun, Oliver Cussen, Robert Steinhilber, Alan Bishop, Jeremy Gilbert, Jason Summers, Steve Moriarty, Marc Cornelius Nuckballs, Duncan Stubbs, Tim Kerr, Jeff Nelson, Tony Victor, Greg Hynes, Valerie Agnew, Elizabeth Davis, Ryan Moore, Aaron Rand, Neal " Doc" Holliday, Franz Kunst, Ric Wallace, Steve D Hammond, Paul Wright, Ross Grady, Jackie Ransier, Daniel House, Joe Cultice, Drag City Records, Laura Levine, Jason Leatherman, Tom Street. A special thanks here to those individuals who so readily and generously donated images of friends and bandmates now departed.

At Black Dog Publishing, many thanks to Albino Tavares for his sterling design work on the book—not least for arduously hand-drawing every title and page number—and Alex Wright for the cover design and initial treatments; to Leanne Hayman for initial research; and a colossal thanks to Richard Duffy for his tireless image research and consistently cheery demeanour in the face of looming deadlines.

COLOPHON

Copyright 2013 Black Dog Publishing Limited, London, UK, the artists and authors.
All rights reserved.

Edited by Thomas Howells and designed by Albino Tavares at Black Dog Publishing Limited.
Cover design by Alex Wright.
Cover photography by Jim Leatherman.

Black Dog Publishing Limited
10a Acton Street, London WC1X 9NG
United Kingdom

Tel: +44 (0)20 7713 5097
Fax: +44 (0)20 7713 8682
info@blackdogonline.com
www.blackdogonline.com

British Library Cataloguing-in-Publication Data.
A CIP record for this book is available from the British Library.

ISBN 978 1 907317 97 2

Black Dog Publishing Limited, London, UK, is an environmentally responsible company. *Late Century Dream—Movements in the US indie music underground* is printed on an FSC certified paper.

art design fashion
history photography
theory and things

www.blackdogonline.com